FOREIGN POLICY ON LATIN AMERICA 1970–1980

Edited by the staff of

FOREIGN POLICY

I0896586

Routledge
Taylor & Francis Group
LONDON AND NEW YORK

First published 1983 by Westview Press, Inc.

Published 2018 by Routledge
52 Vanderbilt Avenue, New York, NY 10017
2 Park Square, Milton Park, Abingdon, Oxon OX14 4RN

Routledge is an imprint of the Taylor & Francis Group, an informa business

Library of Congress Catalog Card number: 83-50492
ISBN 13: 978-0-367-01551-0 (hbk)

ISBN 13: 978-0-367-16538-3 (pbk)

CONTENTS

ACKNOWLEDGMENTS

FOREIGN POLICY EDITORIAL STAFF 1970-1980

FOUNDING EDITORS

Samuel P. Huntington	1970-1977
Warren Demian Manshel	1970-1978

EDITORS

Richard H. Ullman	1978-1979
Charles William Maynes	1980-

MANAGING/ASSOCIATE EDITORS

John Franklin Campbell	1970-1972
Richard Holbrooke	1972-1976
Sanford J. Ungar	1977-1980
Leigh H. Bruce	1978-1983

FOREWORD

The attitude of the United States toward Latin America is paradoxical. For long stretches of U.S. history, the Western Hemisphere has been among Washington policy makers' lowest world priorities. As recently as the 1970s, both the Ford and the Carter administrations paid more attention to black Africa than to Central America.

At the same time, few foreign events evoke such panic-stricken reactions in the United States as unfavorable developments in "America's own backyard." When the United States suffers a major political setback in this hemisphere, the country tends to plunge into paroxysms of anger or fear. The policies of even such a tiny country as Grenada can suddenly be accorded international importance. The consequences of foreign-policy failure are portrayed as ominous in the extreme for the United States. Reflecting the national neurosis regarding this hemisphere, President Reagan recently warned that if the American effort in El Salvador failed, U.S. prestige would decline and U.S. alliances would crumble. The president, in effect, suggested that the fate of a small country in Central America could shift the entire balance of world power.

Further complicating the present U.S. approach to Latin America is the so-called Vietnam syndrome, the popular fear that the United States will be dragged into a misguided military adventure in a previously little-known part of the Third World. At first glance, the comparison would seem completely misplaced. The countries of concern this time are small, close, and traditionally susceptible to U.S. influence and control. The North Vietnamese had China as a friendly neighbor and a secure source of supplies, whereas the guerrillas in El Salvador have only tiny Nicaragua as a sanctuary. U.S. interest in Vietnam developed suddenly, while U.S. involvement in Central America is long-standing and expected by the rest of the world. Thus the problems of El Salvador and/or Central America seem manageable in a way that events demonstrated the conflict in Vietnam was not.

Yet time is not on the side of the United States in Central America. The pro-U.S. governments in power there seem increasingly on the defensive. The U.S. position does not even enjoy the support of major powers such as Mexico or Venezuela.

Nor is the overall U.S. position in Latin America much brighter. The Reagan administration moved early to improve relations with the right-wing dictatorships of Argentina and Chile, both of which are now in serious political difficulty. U.S.-Cuban relations have reached their lowest point since the early 1960s. Many of the regional giants—Brazil, Mexico, Venezuela—are experiencing the kind of grave economic trouble that in almost any political system leads to popular unrest. Few Latin American governments are comfortable with the key international policies pressed by Washington.

To help explain how U.S.-Latin American relations came to this unhappy pass is the purpose of this volume, which brings together articles on Latin America that appeared in FOREIGN POLICY in the 1970s. One virtue of the volume is that the issues that have surfaced prominently in the early 1980s were repeatedly adumbrated in the pages of the magazine during the previous decade.

The disastrous misreading of national character that took place in both Washington and Buenos Aires during the British-Argentine war over the Falkland Islands, or Malvinas, should have been no surprise to the readers of Mariano Grondona in FOREIGN POLICY.

In the middle of the Carter presidency, FOREIGN POLICY contributor Abraham F. Lowenthal warned that nowhere was the gap between announced policy and actual decisions more notable than in U.S.-Caribbean relations. Articles on Mexico warned of the looming problem of external debt.

A persistent theme runs throughout these essays as does a recurring controversy. The theme is the steady decline in U.S. control over the politics and economies of Latin America. The controversy is whether the explanation for this decline is to be found in poor policies in Washington or in trends in Latin America that no U.S. administration can expect to control.

The decrease in U.S. influence, of course, is a worldwide phenomenon; the causes are many. In this volume, Norman Gall points out in his important essay on the Brazilian-West German nuclear agreement in 1975 that U.S. international domination after World War II rested on three pillars: U.S. command of strategic nuclear weaponry; the role of the dollar in assuring monetary stability; and U.S. control through U.S. firms of the world's fuel supplies of oil and uranium. In the 1970s all three pillars were shattered with consequences for the U.S. position in the world far more serious than those resulting from the American misadventure in Vietnam.

In Latin America itself, however, there seemed to be another dimension to America's problems, and the first article on Latin America published in FOREIGN POLICY—Lawrence E. Harrison's "Waking from the Pan-American Dream"—expressed it cogently. Harrison warned in late 1971 that power in the region was passing from the oligarchy into new hands—"if not the hands of the masses, at least hands increasingly influenced by or catering to the masses." Harrison also noted that "anti-Americanism," heretofore largely confined to far-left-wing circles, was spreading to the "moderate left, to businessmen, to the military, and to the church."

The 10 years since the publication of that article have confirmed this observation about Latin American public opinion to the great distress of policy makers in Washington. Washington's response to the challenges of Latin America has not been very effective, however, both because of powerful political currents in Latin America itself and because the traditional tools of U.S. policy toward its hemispheric neighbors have been blunted. A congressional mandate to concentrate U.S. foreign aid in programs designed to help the poorest of the poor has had some unintended consequences. U.S. foreign aid to Latin America, overall the richest area of the Third World, has declined sharply. Denied this tool, many U.S. leaders, particularly in the executive branch, were also distressed to recognize that the vigorous nationalism of Latin American countries effectively raised the cost to the United States of using force to impose its will. Then, rising protectionist pressures began to limit the ability of administrations in Washington to use trade as a positive instrument of policy.

Despite vigorous efforts by the Reagan administration to refurbish some of these policy tools, the likelihood is that the United States will have to live in the future with a Latin America much less subject to its will than in the past. For the 1980s, therefore, the key problem for U.S. foreign policy in Latin America will be to manage and even to accommodate this change. Specifically, the United States will have to decide what kind of radical regimes it can tolerate in the Western Hemisphere. The effort to prevent their rise altogether will almost assuredly fail. The United States will have to find ways to meld its diplomatic efforts with those of the regional powers such as Mexico and Brazil, which now demand a much larger voice in hemispheric affairs than they sought in the past. Finally, the United States will have to accept that its overwhelming dominance in the postwar period was unique. Because the European powers were so weak after World War II, their influence in Latin America was temporarily but sharply diminished. Now they have regained their prewar strength and have returned to the hemisphere in a major way. Never again will the United States be able to formulate its policy toward Latin America without taking into account several new actors on the scene—West European friends, who again have extensive interests in the region, as well as the Soviet Union.

Sometime in the 1970s, in other words, the underpinnings of the Monroe Doctrine eroded badly without anyone calling attention to the damage. These essays plot the consequences of that fundamental change in America's hemispheric fortunes.

June 1983

Charles William Maynes
Editor, FOREIGN POLICY

WAKING FROM THE PAN-AMERICAN DREAM

by Lawrence E. Harrison

Pan-Americanism, at least under U.S. leadership as it was understood by Presidents from Franklin Roosevelt to Lyndon Johnson, is in its death throes, if, indeed, it ever lived. The ties that bind together the nations of North and South America become fewer and weaker; the policies and actions of the countries south of the Rio Grande become increasingly independent of U.S. influence. The vision of two great continents, joined by common liberal values and aspirations as well as by geography, marching hand-in-hand into a better future for all is distorted almost beyond recognition by the events of the last several years. Many idealists and pragmatists alike among U.S. observers are alarmed, feel frustrated, and are searching for explanations.

In the short run, only the most optimistic can foresee any strengthening of hemispheric solidarity. A large majority expects further deterioration. In the longer run, many think that the attitude of Latin America toward the United States will range from Third World indifference to Communist hostility. For this state of affairs, scapegoats abound: the Eisenhower Administration's lack of concern, the Kennedy Administration's lack of realism, the Johnson Administration's lack of restraint, the Nixon Administration's lack of commitment. Very rarely does one hear, however, what may be a far more accurate explanation of the disintegration of Pan-Americanism: that its basic concept is so flawed as to have assured the failure of virtually any U.S. policy in its pursuit. An appreciation of these flaws will not only help to explain the disintegration. It may also help illuminate some foundations for a new, more promising and durable inter-American relationship, but one which cannot be expected to materialize for many years yet.

Two Different Worlds

The differences between North America and Latin America are enormous, covering virtually all aspects of human life. They go deeper than geography and language. The North American and the Latin American have differing concepts of the individual, society, and the relationship between the two; of justice and law; of life and death; of government; of the family; of relations between the sexes; of organization; of time; of enterprise; of religion; of morality. These differences have contributed to the evolution of societies which are more unlike one another than our past policy-makers appear to have appreciated. In fact, it can be argued that there are some Asian societies (Japan is an obvious candidate) which have more in common with the societies of North America than do most of the societies of Latin America.

One crucial result of the disparate value structures of the two Americas has been a dramatic difference in the pace of modernization. Differing economic and population growth during the past few decades may mean that the average Latin American today is less well off compared to the average North American than he was when Franklin Roosevelt announced the Good Neighbor Policy in 1933. North America even in the Great Depression was so much more "modern" that the definition of "Neighbor" inevitably had to be a limited one. The chief significance of the Good Neighbor Policy was its rejection of the Big Stick in hemispheric relations. One cannot expect a truly neighborly relationship to develop between poverty and affluence, between traditional and modern societies. In fact, what should have at least in part been expected—and what probably in part materialized—was a new dimension of Latin-American bitterness, self-doubt, and self-reproach to add to the psychic problems precipitated by the era of intervention. Where Latin America had earlier been intimidated by the might of the United States, it now was being intimidated by North American virtue and accomplishment.

Few Americans appreciate how intimidating our culture can be for all but the most vigorous and integrated Latin-American societies. Many Latin Americans see the Colossus of the North not only in terms of physical greatness but also in terms of a super-society inhabited by supermen. And although the recently increased Latin-American awareness that the United States has its own serious problems may have attenuated the impact somewhat, the Latin American's ego is still likely to be jolted when he objectively compares conditions in his own country with those in the United States. Or, as has happened with the extreme left in Latin America, he may simply refuse to look objectively at the United States at all.

The facts are that the average North American is something like 10 times better off economically than the average Latin American; he has twelve grades of education as compared to three; and he regularly gets a chance to pursue his interests within a political system which, although at a less than ideal pace, has nonetheless demonstrated irrefutably its capacity for change. The contrast was not significantly different in 1933. Yet, the success of the Good Neighbor Policy had inevitably to depend on common values, goals, and interests.

World War II added a further artificiality to the myth of inter-American solidarity. The hand-in-hand image was transformed into a locked-arm defense of the hemisphere against Axis totalitarianism. While there was a considerable Latin-American identification with the Allied cause, there was also a twofold irony: the economic backwardness of Latin America rendered it militarily impotent, and dictatorship—in various forms and degrees, to be sure—was at the same time flourishing in Latin America, where it had found fertile ground ever since the first Latin-American countries achieved independence. The irony was intensified by the existence of at least some Latin-American sympathy for the Axis cause. While this sympathy was principally rooted in Latin Americans of German and Italian extraction, there may also have been a more generalized secret hope for the satisfaction of seeing Uncle Sam get his nose bloodied.

It is difficult for us today to comprehend how our Latin-American policy of the 1930's and 1940's, at least in its long-term projection, could have been so out of touch with reality, so obviously based on an imagined mutuality of aspirations and interest. To some extent, the myth was probably explainable by the special romantic qualities of that period of U.S. history, qualities in some ways similar to those that appeared in the early 1960's. Perhaps the pragmatists of those years saw the reality but advocated the myth as a means of protecting our interests as they saw them. Also relevant may have been the kind of view of Latin America we were getting: through the eyes of diplomats who had never heard of Mao Tse-tung, rising expectations, or racial violence, and whose contacts were often confined to the educated, frequently English-speaking oligarchies, the military, and the clergy, all of whom had something to gain from American favors and who were prepared to pay lip service to democracy if that were the price; through the eyes of U.S. businessmen who were sometimes not above buying their way to influence and profits; through the eyes of tourists who looked at extreme poverty and injustice and saw something picturesque. Whatever the explanation, Pan-Americanism moved into the 1950's with its Northern component growing increasingly conservative, its Southern component increasingly restive, and much of the glue being supplied by alleged Soviet threats to hemispheric security, the Panama Canal, and "our way of life."

The First Taste of Reality

When anti-American demonstrations surged around Governor Nelson Rockefeller's 1969 fact-finding mission, few informed Americans were surprised. Many expected worse. Yet, when Vice President Richard Nixon made a similar trip 11 years earlier and encountered hostility and violence, the United States was shocked and incredulous. Even informed Americans were taken aback by the intensity of the hostility in an area of the world that had always been considered "safe" and "friendly."

It was alleged following the Nixon trip, and, especially, as events in Cuba grew more ominous, that "Latin America had been neglected." The United States, in attending first to the enormous problems of European reconstruction and then to an Asian land war, had forgotten its good neighbors and was paying the price—or at least so the deterioration in hemispheric relations was frequently explained.

In many ways, the deterioration had little to do with the United States. Above all else, anti-Americanism was a side-effect of a social ferment so intense and widespread that the late 1940's and the 1950's will probably be viewed as an historical watershed in Latin America: the years when, throughout the region, power started shifting leftward, at least in the sense of moving out of the hands of the oligarchy, the traditional military, and the traditional church, toward new hands—if not the hands of the masses, at least hands increasingly influenced by or catering to the masses. While the modernization process had started before, and while it was relatively advanced in a few countries, it was the post-World War II period when the process really began to take hold.

At the root of the unrest, the willingness to look for new solutions and new relationships, was the same internal malaise which had made a true good neighbor policy unattainable: extremes of injustice, poverty, ignorance, and national indignity, and the indifference of the ruling classes. The relationship of the United States to the ferment has been indirect. We provide a standard against which, consciously or otherwise, shortcomings are measured (which does not necessarily make us any more popular); our diplomacy and overseas business interests have on occasion identified us with the national power elites, who have for the most part shied away from social responsibilities in their pursuit of personal interest. And, for those who would prefer to look for the explanation of Latin America's social problems outside of Latin America, we are handy. The role of scapegoat was more justified in the case of the few countries which had suffered the humilating trauma of U.S. military intervention. But even in these countries, the goads to revolutionary action existed before—and after—the interventions.

Because so much of the Latin-American problem is internally rooted, there is real doubt that, even if begun in the 1930's, any reasonably conceivable U.S. trade and aid programs could have deterred the ferment or channeled it into significantly less violent, less anti-American manifestations. The credibility of this assertion gathers strength when one considers how difficult it would have been to develop a constituency in the United States for a major effort in Latin America during the Depression, the Second World War, European reconstruction, or the Korean war. Some might argue that, by the time the United States had both the will and resources to mount an effort of the proportions of the Alliance for Progress, it was too late. What is indisputable is that the Alliance for Progress has failed to make Pan-Americanism a reality.

The Alliance That Stumbled

The Alliance for Progress was the expression of the first broad U.S. awareness that there was something fundamentally amiss in Latin America, something which threatened our vision of a secure, progressive hemisphere. The Alliance was one of the most idealistic and at the same time arrogant undertakings in the history of U.S. foreign policy. The Charter of Punta del Este, signed on August 17, 1961, is the complete liberal democratic, free enterprise prescription for modernization: "This

Alliance is established on the basic principle that free men working through the institution of representative democracy can best satisfy man's aspirations, including those for work, home and land, health and schools. No system can guarantee true progress unless it affirms the dignity of the individual which is the foundation of our civilization." It is a compelling, even moving declaration which Americans would do well to reread from time to time for its relevance to our own society.

However, it had limited relevance to most Latin-American societies in 1961. Parts of it may have more relevance today, and, hopefully, all of it will have more relevance tomorrow. But while the Charter of Punta del Este may have meant a great deal to the New Frontier United States, it was fashioned not for our benefit but for the benefit of Latin America. It is now clear that, for many Latin-American governments, Punta del Este was important not for its explicit liberal philosophy but for the implicit promise of major new resource flows from the United States.

It is currently fashionable to criticize the Alliance for Progress for its overambitious goals, its general lack of realism. When it comes to economic development and some aspects of social development (e.g., education, health, population growth), this criticism may be little more than carping: what was scheduled to take 10 years may take 15 or 20. But even over the longer period, the progress is still likely to be impressive and significant. What was truly naive—and arrogant—was the belief that Latin-American societies should and could be transformed into mirror images of modernized Anglo-Saxon societies *at all*, to say nothing of doing it in a period of a decade or two.

What was even more arrogant was the belief that the United States government knew so much about Latin-American societies, not to mention the development process, that it could play a major role, through carrot and stick paternalism, in bringing about the modernization of Latin America. United States government activism and interventionism—well-intentioned to be sure—often influenced decisions involving basic questions of national policy and sovereignty for several years after Punta del Este. It is true that progress occurred during this period in Latin America, and it is also true that some of the progress was attributable to the activism of representatives of the United States government. But in many instances, the progress might well have occurred without the intervention; in some cases, the intervention backfired; and without exception, two costs had to be paid: (1) further loss of Latin America's confidence in its own capacity to solve its problems, the kind of confidence which is so closely linked to better hemispheric relations in the future; and (2) annoyance and, at worst, alienation of Latin-American officials who couldn't help but ask themselves, "Where does this representative of a foreign government get off telling my government—and me—what to do?" On occasion, the simple fact of the United States government's promoting a policy has resulted in its rejection by officials and interest groups who might otherwise be sympathetic to it.

In the Alliance for Progress, then, the United States government created (it was done largely on a unilateral basis) a mechanism which responded to our first real appreciation of Latin America's problems, but a mechanism, nonetheless, which, in its simplification of the problems and its overestimate of U.S. power to precipitate change, inevitably fell far short of what it set out to achieve.

The first U.S. Coordinator of the Alliance for Progress, Teodoro Moscoso, a person who saw the Alliance in its early years as a noble crusade and communicated that sense of purpose to his colleagues, had the following to say less than seven years after Punta del Este: "The Latin-American case is so complex, so difficult to solve, and so fraught with human and global danger and distress that the use of the word 'anguish' is not an exaggeration.

"The longer I live, the more I believe that,

just as no human being can save another who does not have the will to save himself, no country can save others no matter how good its intentions or how hard it tries. The Latin-American countries have been too dependent on the United States, while the United States has been too nosey and eager to force down the throats of its southern neighbors its way of doing things."

And, as part of his prescription for how the United States can "assist as much as it can its southern neighbors in helping them to solve their own problems," Moscoso suggests, "Extend all economic and technical aid only through multilateral agencies . . . . Dismantle the United States aid apparatus in Latin America."

To the extent, then, that the Alliance for Progress was designed to restore hemispheric harmony by modernizing Latin America along North American lines with the United States government leading the way, it has failed and will continue to fail. Nonetheless, the Alliance must be viewed as an important step forward. For the first time, U.S. policy reflected an appreciation of the need for change in Latin America if satisfactory hemispheric relationships were to be achieved. It has provided major new resources to help accelerate the process of change. It has given the United States government its first real opportunity to perceive the depth and breadth of the Latin-American "anguish" and at the same time develop some humility about our capacity to influence the process of change.

For all that, 10 years after Punta del Este, Pan-Americanism seems farther out of reach than at any other time in the history of inter-American relations.

Down the Drain

In the past, we have tended to judge relationships between Latin America and the United States on the basis of Latin America's responsiveness to or acceptance of our policies. The inter-American community we have sought has been one in which the U.S. voice would be dominant on such matters as relations with the Communist world, hemispheric trade policy, even hemispheric development policy. This is the kind of hemispheric order, so often identified as Pan-Americanism, which is in the process of going down the drain.

There is compelling evidence that the disintegration is occurring. Perhaps the most significant indicator of the past few years has been the emergence of CECLA (a Spanish acronym for the Latin American Special Coordinating Commission), a body whose principal reason for existence is to develop positions reflecting purely Latin-American interests with which to confront the developed world, and particularly the United States. CECLA came into being without the least encouragement from the United States; in fact, for those Americans clinging to the vision of Pan-Americanism, CECLA was viewed, quite rightly, as a serious threat to "hemispheric solidarity." Notwithstanding the lack of U.S. enthusiasm, CECLA has acquired a special vitality, evidenced by Latin-American enthusiasm for it and its impact on U.S. policies and programs, which suggests that CECLA is likely to be with us for quite some time.

Other inter-American institutions, in which the U.S. voice is loud—and which, in fact, were created largely at U.S. initiative—do not seem to possess CECLA's vitality and responsiveness to what Latin America sees as important in hemispheric relations. While the Organization of American States has acquired new vigor under Galo Plaza, its genesis, its role in the 1965 Dominican intervention, and the fact that it has virtually become a symbol of a U.S.-dominated hemispheric community, have tarnished its respectability in many Latin-American countries. In part because of increasing resource infusions by the United States, the Inter-American Development Bank has grown both in developmental impact and prestige over the past decade. But Chilean Felipe Herrera, its president for 10 years, was not welcome on the campuses of some Latin-American universities, in large part because of the Bank's identification with the United States.

The foreign policy of Latin-American countries is increasingly independent of ours, particularly when it comes to their relations with Communist countries. The number of Communist diplomatic and trade missions has grown rapidly over the past few years, as have trade relations. Finally, the tone of our bilateral relations has become unprecedentedly strained in the cases of Chile, Peru and, until the recent overthrow of the Torres government, Bolivia. There are few observers who expect that the trend towards increasingly difficult bilateral relationships will be stemmed, at least during the next several years.

This is not to say that U.S. relationships are uniformly bad. At least for the time being, Brazil, Argentina, Mexico, and Colombia, which together dominate Latin America in terms of population and area—and are all relatively self-assured—are more or less favorably disposed toward the United States. But even in the case of these countries, to say nothing of Chile and Peru, there is a new willingness to carry issues to a confrontation, to run greater risks of giving offense, to pursue independent foreign policies. Expropriation of U.S. investments and the seizure of fishing boats are clear manifestations of this new wave of nationalism. While the pattern of nationalism is far from uniform, the trend is apparent in most countries. The burden of proof rests upon those who foresee developments which move toward rather than away from Pan-Americanism.

Four Future Trends

The disintegration of our vision of hemispheric solidarity is viewed by some with alarm. It is argued that forces hostile to the United States will exploit the resulting vacuum, as has happened in the case of Cuba; that we will be cut off from important raw materials, markets, and investment opportunities; that we will no longer be masters in our own house.

There can be little doubt that the disintegration will carry with it—and indeed already has carried with it—costs to the United States. But there is also a chance, at least in the long run, that there will be some benefits for us, too. In fact, it is possible that from the ashes of Pan-Americanism will emerge a more rational, durable set of hemispheric relationships, one which is more consistent with our own tradition, or at least vision, of how relationships should be ordered within a community. While the parallel has to be stretched somewhat, it is not irrelevant to cite the case of our relations with Western Europe. Twenty years ago, our influence there was much greater than it is today. That does not mean, however, that the relationship today is either unhealthy or unstable, or that the old relationship is to be preferred to the new.

While only the rash would attempt to forecast developments in Latin America over the next two or three decades with any real specificity, there are certain trends for which the antecedents are sufficiently apparent as to warrant their use at least as working hypotheses:

1. *It is unlikely that the internal political changes that occur will follow a uniform pattern beyond a continuation of the general shift to the left.* Diversity is the current norm for Latin-American politics. While military governments predominate, there is considerable difference between what is happening in, for example, Peru and Paraguay. Some countries, e.g. Costa Rica, Colombia, Venezuela, may be in the process of finding durable solutions through representative democracy. The Mexican one-party experiment has proven thus far to be both lasting and capable of bringing about change. Chile searches for its solutions in the direction of a socialism which may or may not remain within Chile's democratic tradition.

Aside from the wide variety of political forms, economic and cultural factors also point toward diversity. On the basis of per capita GNP, Venezuela and Argentina are approaching the ranks of the developed countries. Haiti is as poor as some of the poorest Asian countries. The different mixes of European, Indian, and African cultures have had much to do with past diversity among Latin-American countries and are likely to influence the Latin America of the future toward diversity. Size will also contribute to diversity in national evolution: we must remember that Brazil is larger than the United States without Alaska; Argentina is almost the size of India; and El Salvador is just slightly larger than Massachusetts. It is indeed difficult to foresee any single pattern crystallizing out of this mélange beyond the continuation of the movement leftward which started after World War II. And even this general movement is likely to be manifested in diverse ways and at widely varying speeds.

2. *There are likely to be frequent political changes.* With a few exceptions, Latin America is an area of political instability. Mexico, Chile, Uruguay, and Costa Rica are the only countries that have known continuity within a constitutional framework for 20 years or more. In almost every other country there has been at least one violent change; in several countries, political violence has been commonplace. When one considers, against the backdrop of political volatility of recent years, that the process of power transfer which started in the late 1940's is, in several countries, in its incipient stage; when one reflects on the length of the road the process has to travel in many countries; and when one ponders the implications of the apparently growing gap between expectation and realization, it is difficult not to conclude that instability is going to continue to be widespread during the next few decades. The internal instability is likely to be accompanied by instability in international relations, particularly relations with the United States.

3. *Economic and social development are likely to proceed at least at the pace of the last 10 years, quite possibly faster.* Latin America is an area of ample resource endowment. The principal obstacle to development has been a shortage, at all levels of the public and private sectors, of people with the attitudes and preparation demanded by the development process. Education made important strides in the 1960's, both in terms of preparing people as well as in terms of building institutions. The institutions will be producing more and more better-prepared people in the future, and it is from these people that a more effective development process can be expected to emerge. Reinforcing this hopeful expectation are three other factors of importance: (1) Although population pressures are currently acute, family planning programs are likely to reduce perceptibly the population growth rate in several —perhaps most—countries, thereby improving chances for greater degrees of individual well-being and at the same time reducing some of the pressures for investment in social services; (2) Major technological improvements are likely to make development easier to achieve in the 1970's and 1980's than it was in the 1960's; and (3) There is at least a fair chance that regional economic integration schemes will reach levels of sophistication and efficacy which will add a major impulse to economic development as markets broaden to permit production at optimal scale.

In addition to Venezuela, whose per capita GNP already approximates $1,000, Argentina, Chile, Costa Rica, Mexico, Panama, and Uruguay could all have reached—or at least be close to—the $1,000 per capita GNP level by 1990. And most other countries could be approximately where Mexico is today (about $600 per capita). What is more, as politics drift leftward, income distribution is likely to become more equitable.

4. *Nationalism will continue to be a dominant political theme, often at U.S. expense; Latin America will look increasingly outside the hemisphere; but there is also likely to be an increasing feeling of community among Latin-American nations.* While unrest in Latin America in the past 25 years has been importantly related to social injustice, the failure of several Latin-

American countries to develop a broad national integration, and the consequent feebleness of the idea of nationhood, has also played a role. Both kinds of shortcomings have shaken the Latin American's confidence in himself, and this lack of confidence has contributed to some of the manifestations of the new Latin-American politics of the past several years: the search for new ways of organizing societies; the persistence and shrillness of calls to national unity; and anti-Americanism.

As suggested before, Latin-American anti-Americanism is probably more reasonably explained by problems internal to Latin America than by the inadequacies or provocations of U.S. policies and actions. This does not make anti-Americanism less real or less in the ascendancy. While it was confined largely to far left-wing circles in the mid-1950's, it has since spread to the moderate left, to businessmen, to the military, and to the church—surely not all elements of these sectors, but to unprecedented numbers within them.

The quest for national identity and purpose which is likely to occur over the next decades will probably sustain, if not broaden, anti-American sentiment. But there is some reason to expect that the fulfillment of this quest, with its resultant boost to Latin-American self-confidence, may reverse the tide, just as Latin America's lack of self-confidence has largely caused it to flow. Several of the countries where anti-Americanism is relatively muted are countries that have found, or are finding, a place in the sun, e.g. Argentina, Brazil, Costa Rica, Colombia, Mexico, and Venezuela. While the pattern is not sufficiently uniform to justify the axiom that national confidence is inversely proportional to anti-Americanism, there is at least some evidence that this is true.

Strengthened relations, particularly trade relations, with other areas of the world are likely to evolve, motivated in part by the psychological impediments to relationships with the United States but particularly by a wholly legitimate economic self-interest. Yet geographic and economic realities will place important limits on Latin America's ability to turn away from the United States; trade will be expanded not only with Communist countries but also with Western Europe and Japan; and it is unlikely that any of the new trading partners will develop a dominant position, except in special cases such as Cuba.

The quest for national identity and purpose is likely to be paralleled, although probably not as vigorously, by a quest for regional—Latin American—identity. The sense of regionalism, which in a way has been reborn with CECLA, and the sense of nationalism are likely to be mutually reinforcing. And while, in the short run, the emergence of subregional groupings (e.g. Central America, the Andean Group) may impede broader identification, experience with subregional groupings may make the formation of a regional grouping easier in the longer run.

If it is true that Latin America in 1990 will know less poverty, more social justice, less economic dependence on the United States, better national integration, and better regional integration, it will be an area both less troubled and more confident, an area with which a more truly neighborly relationship—a relationship more nearly of equals—should be possible.

It would be fatuous to expect that the millennium in hemisphere relations will arrive 20 years hence. The problems of Latin America will not have vanished, although they should be less acute. There may well be one or more countries which are intransigently hostile to the United States because of ideological incompatibility. There will still be great inequality between North America and Latin America. Latin America will doubtlessly still be sensitive to any suggestion of U.S. dominance or intervention. And we may still have our own problems of national integration, to say nothing of difficulties with other parts of the world. But for all that, both Latin America and the United States should be finding it easier to live with ourselves, both at home and in the hemisphere.

The Difficult Decades

At best, the relationships of the United States with Latin America over the next decade or two are going to be difficult. If it is true that significant trends are largely beyond our control, then U.S. policy-makers are going to be operating within a narrow margin of options and a wide margin of frustrations. The choices that we make can, however, influence the pace of maturation of hemispheric relationships and the extent to which additional stresses appear.

Our goal is something comparable to our relationship with Western Europe, one in which Latin America is no longer our "responsibility," one guided by enlightened self-interest. Latin America's ability to participate in this kind of community with us depends on its self-confidence, and this in turn depends importantly on its success at modernization.

The kind of U.S. policy which is likely to be most helpful will combine restraint, disengagement, and expanded assistance. The tide of nationalism is flowing in Latin America, and history and proximity dictate that its force will often be directed against the United States. Provocations are likely to increase; a failure on our part to exercise restraint will usually aggravate matters.

The United States government and its officials should give wide berth to the policy and decision-making apparatus of Latin-American governments; the recent downtrend in U.S. representation in Latin America is encouraging on this score. Disengagement is also preordained in the private sector, and U.S. investors and entrepreneurs have to reconcile themselves to a new ball game in Latin America, one which will remain open to them only if they are able to adapt to an increasingly nationalistic psychology on the part of their public sector hosts and private sector competitors. (Hopefully, both of the latter will recognize the inability of their countries to save enough to achieve adequate investment levels and will not make the adaptation impossible.)

The style of our relationships with Latin America will be particularly important. Paternalism is not going to be tolerated, nor is a language of diplomacy which communicates overtones of U.S. national power. It will be more important than ever that care be taken in the selection of our representatives in Latin America.

These are not propitious moments in the United States for liberalization of trade and expansion of foreign aid. Yet the need is no less great, and there is substantially more capacity to make good use of additional resources. While we cannot live comfortably in a poor neighborhood, we at least stand a chance in a middle-class one. We would, however, be deceiving ourselves if we concluded that, even with the end of the war in Southeast Asia and headline-gathering changes in the structure of our aid program, we are going to be able to achieve substantially more liberal trade and aid policies. Until the link between these policies and U.S. self-interest is more demonstrable—and widely appreciated in the United States—we shall have to live with more restrictive trade policies and smaller aid budgets than we might like and with the inevitable Latin-American criticism that we are not doing enough.

To some extent, trade and aid are substitutable. Because aid is always somewhat demeaning, it is preferable to find trade solutions. We would do well to press for policies which will promote Latin-American exports, in the best of circumstances within a world-wide scheme of preferences for all less-developed countries.

There will, nonetheless, be an important role for foreign aid, particularly when technology as well as physical resources must be transferred. The style of our aid-giving is highly important, and we would do well to move in the direction suggested by Teodoro

Moscoso: phase down our bilateral aid programs and increasingly channel aid resources (hopefully in greater overall amounts) through international institutions. By so doing we will attenuate a friction-inducing reminder of U.S. dominance and "superiority." We will also mitigate the problems which attend the inevitable proximity of bilateral programs to short-term U.S. foreign policy considerations, prominent among them the dilemmas which flow from our direct identification with authoritarian governments. It will then be easier for us to stand more firmly on the Charter of Punta del Este, which is, after all, where we must stand if we are to avoid the schizophrenia which comes from domestic and foreign policy values that are not harmonious. We need not and should not preach the ideological principles of the Alliance for Progress; but it must be made unmistakably clear to all that we are committed to the democratic process and to the pluralism enshrined in the Charter of Punta del Este, and that our relationships abroad as well as at home will be governed by these principles.

The "mature partnership" policy of the Nixon Administration has been frequently criticized by those who allege that the United States is turning its back on its Latin-American "responsibilities," its economic interests, and the vision of a U.S.-dominated, "safe" hemisphere. These critics do not perceive the reality of Latin America today. They cling to an illusory vision that has guided our thinking for almost two generations; and their proposals would perpetuate the errors of the last decade. Restraint and realism born of the often painful lessons of the past are being confused with inaction and apathy. It would be most unfortunate if this misunderstanding, partisan politics, or anything else detoured us from the admittedly difficult route staked out by the new policy: toward hemispheric relationships more consistent both with reality and our national commitment to pluralism.

Can We Do Business With Radical Nationalists?

CHILE: NO

by James F. Petras & Robert LaPorte, Jr.

The I.T.T. documents and memoranda which Jack Anderson has published raise a number of critical issues in assessing the true nature of U.S. policy toward economic nationalists. In the Chilean case covert political action was an element of U.S. foreign policy—although there were substantial tactical differences between the C.I.A., the State Department, and the White House over the measures to be adopted and over the timing of events. Nixon's position and the measures, speeches, and behavior of the lame-duck Frei administration were intended to create economic collapse over a *protracted* period of time—while the C.I.A. and I.T.T. seemed to see that as their *immediate* goal. The political assessment in Washington of the relationship of forces in Chile appears to have been more realistic than the C.I.A.'s. The prudent course chosen—limited to economic pressure—was based on a long term strategy of political and economic attrition. Key U.S. policy-makers were and are firmly opposed to the Allende government. However they firmly rejected the "adventurist" proposals to upend Allende because they felt that a coup was premature and its failure would trigger a move to the left. This assessment was essentially correct: the abortive rightist coup leading to the assassination of the Commander in Chief of the Chilean army, General Schneider, contributed to the increase of leftist support from 36 percent in September 1970, to 50 percent in April 1971.

While the extreme "military" measures proposed by the C.I.A. and I.T.T. to policymakers were rejected, many of the economic proposals were put into practice by private businessmen and public policy-makers. Banks have not renewed credits and/or are delaying any new decisions. Companies are not making new investments. Delays of deliveries and shipping of spare parts have occurred. Technical assistance has been withdrawn. In a word the Anderson Papers provide us with further evidence to substantiate the thesis of this paper (written before the I.T.T. memos were released) that U.S. policy was and is trying to do everything possible short of military intervention to keep Allende from succeeding.

The Chilean decision to nationalize U.S. property is the most recent direct confrontation with U.S. business interests and the most significant challenge to U.S. policy since the Cuban revolution. What happens to U.S.-Chilean relations as a result of the struggle over the Chilean copper industry will have repercussions for U.S.-Latin American relations during the rest of the decade. The Chilean situation can be viewed as a "test" of U.S. commitment to defending U.S. investors or as an "opportunity" to develop a new set of relationships with nations in Latin America as well as the rest of the world.

The recent measures taken by the government of Chile in nationalizing the Anaconda and Kennecott mining properties emerge from and are a logical extension of a pattern followed throughout the region by regimes with significant social, political, and economic differences. Rather than viewing the Chilean government's actions as sinister ideological moves engineered by Marxists, their actions should be seen as part of the regional response to deep-seated national needs to direct and control their own resources. What we are seeing in Chile is much more than the action of a single government; it is a Latin-American phenomenon with both long and short range implications for the industrialized nations of both East and West.

A great variety of regimes, with differing approaches to internal problems, have adopted nationalist measures in recent years. The modernizing Peruvian junta nationalized the International Petroleum Corporation (IPC) in 1968. The conservative Ecuadorian government seized U.S. fishing boats which violated its 200 mile limit (an action to exert control over maritime resources). The rightist as well as populist Bolivian juntas (under Ovando and later Torres) nationalized Gulf Corporation assets (1969) and a number of other U.S. owned mining enterprises. In Colombia rightist President Pastrana signed the Andean pact restricting foreign investment. In Argentina the Peronist labor unions have pressured the military to adopt a nationalist posture (buy Argentine campaigns, takeover of the Swift packing house, abstention on the China question in the U.N., friendship agreements with the Allende government, etc.). In addition, the Andean countries have signed an investment code which purports to restrict areas and terms of foreign investment. The pro-business Social Christian COPEI government of Venezuela has passed a law leading to the gradual expropriation of all major oil resources and has forced the major oil companies operating in Venezuela to accept more government control.

Meanwhile, Back in Chile . . .

When Dr. Salvador Allende Gossens was elected President of Chile in September 1970, U.S.-Chile relations entered a new phase. The Nixon Administration proclaimed that it would adopt a "low-profile," wait-and-see policy towards the Chilean "experiment" with democratic socialism, but it was not long before President Nixon announced a tough stand on expropriations, aid, credits, and other financial agreements which, while not explicitly aimed at Chile, were widely understood to be a clear warning to the new government in Santiago.

It was clear, even during the election campaign, that the United States was hostile to Allende. The American Ambassador preferred the rightist Alessandri but could have lived with the Christian Democratic Tomic.

After the election, hostility towards Allende was evident not only in the behavior of U.S. officials but also in the liberal American press, including the *New York Times*, which contended editorially on September 6, 1970, that the election was "a heavy blow at liberal democracy."

During the administration of Allende's predecessor, Eduardo Frei, the United States had presented Chile to the world as a "showcase" country—an example of what the Latin countries could do with U.S. technical and economic assistance. Chile had received the highest per capita U.S. aid of any country in the hemisphere. Chile was going to be the liberal alternative to "Castro-Communism." Now, in 1970, the situation was to change drastically.

The result, despite some internal debate in the U.S. government and the business community, seems in retrospect to have been foreordained—in favor of the hard-line conservatives. Their victory, and the implications of the anti-nationalist U.S. foreign policy, are far-reaching: an increasingly close and vastly expanded relationship with the pro-U.S. military junta in Brazil, tacit support of rightist military coups such as occurred in Bolivia, and economic isolation and pressure on nationalist governments such as the one in Chile.

Despite the appearance of a pluralistic decision-making structure with competing viewpoints, the over-all thrust of U.S. foreign policy is largely in the direction of supporting U.S. business interests abroad. Policy tends to follow the line favored by a single interest—the U.S. investor community. U.S. economic interests appear to be the only concrete, specific, and visible reference point to which policy-makers refer. U.S. corporation images of political reality have become the point from which policy-makers begin to define their positions.

Congress has increased its efforts to influence policy, but with limited success. Congressmen continue to press for specific interests—individual firms or lines of industry which have had problems with Latin governments. Congress serves as a forum for airing dissident and critical opinions, but has been of little importance except where the position of Congress coincides with that of the executive branch and the business community—in which case congressional opinion is perceived by the executive branch as a "pressure" to get things done quickly. Thus Mr. Nixon's announcement of a "hard line" on expropriations; his aides revealed that it was intended to "head off congressional action." But, as we shall soon see, Nixon's top appointees had already adopted harsh policies opposed to expropriations long before Congress had taken a poll of its own members.

Rhetorical and Symbolic Response

U.S. policy toward the democratically elected Socialist president is in stark contrast to its policy to the authoritarian military dictatorship in Brazil—toward the former unmitigated hostility, to the latter lavish praise and aid. The strategy of U.S. opposition to Allende operates on three levels of policy making: (a) an "outsider" strategy; (b) an "insider" strategy; (c) a regional strategy.

The "outsider" strategy includes basically three types of policy moves: (a) symbolic hostility; (b) veiled threats; (c) overt hostility. Symbolic hostility has taken the form of not extending to the Allende government the usual courtesies on ceremonial occasions: for example Nixon snubbed Allende after his electoral victory.

The speeches of Rogers, Laird, and Connally regarding Chile's nationalization policies have been full of threats of U.S. economic reprisals. The purpose of these speeches is to make other countries aware of possible negative reactions from the United States if they follow the Chilean route.

President Nixon and other policy-makers have repeatedly stated that the U.S. objective was to "have the kind of relationship with the Chilean government that it is prepared to have with us." Charles Meyers, Assistant Secretary of State for Inter-American Affairs, has emphatically insisted that the U.S. government has taken a neutral position, refraining from any hostile acts. More direct and serious actions have been taken to underscore U.S. displeasure toward Chile's President. Short of economic blockade a number of economic measures designed to pressure the government have been adopted; thus far, U.S. policy-makers have avoided the more extreme policies adopted vis-à-vis Cuba, such as freezing of assets and other massive global pressures.

Economic pressure on Chile has taken the form of cutting U.S. and "international" lines of credit to the Allende government. Two examples of this response present themselves. Chile's application for a small loan from the Export-Import Bank for the purchase of commercial passenger aircraft from Boeing (a U.S. firm) for the Chilean National Airlines was denied. As a result the United States has forced Chile to consider alternative European producers, perhaps a minor inconvenience. U.S. representatives within the Inter-American Development Bank reacting to threats to reduce or withhold U.S. funds to IDB because of its willingness to listen to Chilean requests for development loan funding have "delayed" Chilean requests (which has the same effect as an overt denial). U.S. AID funds have not been either requested or suggested in the case of Chile since the end of the Frei regime.

A third form of U.S. pressure on the Allende regime has been in the area of diplomatic relations between the United States and other Latin nations. This can be seen in U.S. relations with Chile's two neighbors, Peru and Bolivia. United States relations with Peru have improved considerably during the past year with State Department officials attributing the "change" to a shift in Peruvian politics from a nationalist to a more "open" position regarding foreign investment. According to one State Department official, Peru was a "dirty word" two years ago; now that has changed. In Bolivia, the United States now has a new rightist regime which in part owes its existence to U.S. Air Force personnel who "advised" Colonel Hugo Banzer and his associates. This regime can be counted upon to facilitate U.S. policy toward Chile. With Brazil the United States enjoys close to a "model" relationship, according to State Department officials we interviewed. Brazil considers Chile's experiment with Democratic Socialism to be a "threat" to its own aspirations for regional hegemony. Thus, the Brazilian government is actively supporting U.S. efforts to diplomatically "isolate" Chile in Latin America. Given Chile's dependence on meat and grain imports from Argentina, a successful blockade in Latin America can have economic as well as political consequences over the short and long run.

The regional strategy that U.S. policy-makers are developing has two basic ingredients: (1) strengthening Brazil as a counter-revolutionary center and possible source of military intervention—if not directly in Chile at this time, at least on bordering countries (Uruguay) if they should decide to go the Chilean route; (2) isolating Chile on its borders—especially with regard to Peru, Argentina, and Bolivia. In part this strategy has already brought about some immediate payoffs: two days before Chile and Bolivia were to open relations, the U.S. military and embassy (along with Brazil and Argentina) provided logistical support, intelligence reports, and medical supplies to aid the Bolivian army in its overthrow of the nationalist-populist Torres government. The United States now has a loyal government in Bolivia led by Hugo Banzer which can increase border pressures on Chile as well as provide a passageway from Brazil through Bolivia to Chile. Regarding Peru, the United States has moved in the direction of closer relations—there are agreements on most issues which have been pending, especially since the "nationalist" Peruvian military has come around to seeing the "need" of foreign investment for economic development. If U.S.-Peruvian differences narrow, the United States may be able to push the Peruvians into a more distant relationship with Chile.

The over-all purpose of U.S. policy is to create economic dislocation and provoke a domestic social crisis that could lead to either the overthrow of the Allende government by a civil-military coalition made up of the Army, the Christian Democrats, and the extreme right-wing National Party, or the discrediting of the government and its defeat in the 1973 congressional elections, thus undercutting the basis for future changes.

The Copper Issue

The U.S. dispute with Chile over the copper issue must be viewed within this hostile atmosphere of U.S.-Chilean relations. The copper issue itself is not new—the Frei government felt compelled to begin to "Chileanize" copper—and the idea of nationalization of copper was no surprise to U.S. policymakers. Furthermore, the notion of uncompensated expropriation has precedent in other Latin contexts. The reaction of the U.S. government toward Chile can best be understood through a discussion and analysis of the attitudes of congressmen, State Department and other Administration officials, as well as policy advisers.

These include two executive agencies (Treasury and State), the Congress (Senate and House Committees and Subcommittees and individual members), the "international" banks. Also, the actions of the Chilean government trigger, in turn, further U.S. actions. Finally, the policy inputs of U.S. business—the individual firms (commercial/financial as well as extractive and manufacturing) who do business and/or have financial investment or other economic ties with Chile and other Latin American countries—have very important consequences for U.S. policy.

The Department of State

On October 13, 1971, Secretary of State William P. Rogers stated:

> "The Controller General of Chile announced his findings on October 11 that no compensation would be paid for the U.S. copper mining investments expropriated on July 16 except for modest amounts in the cases of two smaller properties.
>
> The U.S. government is deeply disappointed and disturbed at this serious departure from accepted standards of international law. Under established principles of international law, the expropriation must be accompanied by reasonable provision for payment of just compensation. The United States had made clear to the government of Chile its hope that a solution could be found on a reasonable and pragmatic basis consistent with inetrnational law. . . .
>
> Should Chile fail to meet its international obligations, it could jeopardize flows of private funds and erode the base of support for foreign assistance, with possible adverse effects on other developing countries. . . ."

This statement, the official policy of the Department of State, is an explicit endorsement of the position of the U.S. copper companies. The State Department's claim that it holds a "position of moderation" is hardly convincing. This policy statement also obliquely refers to and warns against other countries following the Chilean example. This was the first officially stated concern not so much about Chilean actions *per se* but concerning action that might be taken against all U.S. business holdings in Latin America. Thus, the statement is clearly directed not only at Chile's ability to garner U.S. public and private loans and investment but is also directed toward other Third World countries. By wielding the weapon of economic sanctions and exhibiting the capacity to manipulate international financial funds the U.S. can, in the Secretary's words, produce an "adverse effect on the international development process."

Despite the blunt language and obvious threats explicitly stated, officials continued to argue that the State Department is the voice of reason and moderation between both Chile and U.S. decision-makers.

The State Department's influence over Administration decisions affecting Latin-American affairs appears to have been greater prior to the rise of Secretary John Connally in the Nixon Administration. Latin America was a low priority area in the eyes of most officials in the Nixon Administration. Apparently the Nixon Administration was fairly satisfied with the configuration of regimes in Latin America, in part the product of the Johnson Administration. The nationalization of U.S.-owned copper interests in Chile coincided with a shift in the Nixon Administration decision-making structure. A major part of the responsibility for Latin-American policy shifted from the State Department to the Treasury Department and Secretary Connally. To the outsider it appeared that State and Treasury were making independent policy contributions; nevertheless, it appears that even statements by Rogers were agreed upon by Connally and the Treasury officials.

While legal forms of opposition existed and while the United States can effectively apply "diplomatic pressures," U.S. officials did not feel that irreversible changes would be brought about. Not all officials interviewed agree in their evaluations of present and future prospects for Chile, Allende, or U.S.-Chilean relations. Privately, officials express a range of attitudes toward all three subjects. The negative appraisal of some State Department officials is not shared by others. Some reject the idea that the United States should "write off" Chile as a result of the nationalization of copper.

However, the "hands-off" viewpoint carries little weight in policy-making circles. The input of the State Department to the making of U.S. policy toward Chile under Allende has not been great. By their own admission, other executive department officials have "the ear of the President" and the State Department has not been frequently consulted since the copper nationalization crisis.

The Department of Treasury

It appears that the decisions as well as the decision-makers in the U.S. Department of Treasury are more closely linked to U.S. corporate and business interests than is the Department of State. In any case Treasury is more likely to articulate and defend U.S. private economic interests than other agencies within the executive branch. This is all the more significant in light of the above observations that in critical moments involving conflicts between U.S. private interests and Latin nationalist governments it is Treasury that emerges as the spokesman of U.S. policy.

According to a *Business Week* writer who interviewed Secretary Connally (July 10, 1971):

> "The Secretary is especially miffed when foreign nations expropriate U.S. assets. Under his orders, U.S. representatives have taken to abstaining from votes on World Bank and other loans to expropriating countries, and Connally is forcing the reopening of debate at top levels on what U.S. policy should be. He is particularly bitter about Latin-American hostility toward U.S. investment. . . ."

What has emerged publicly is a business-oriented Secretary of the Treasury who has not been reticent about expressing opposition toward Latin-American nationalist leadership and the Chilean leadership in particular. Once policy has been defined through Connally's initiative, the State Department has moved toward the more extreme position, shedding its reservations and "flexibility."

The input of the Treasury Department to executive policy-making regarding U.S.-Chilean relations does not end with Connally's access to the President. Treasury Department officials claimed Treasury control over other public institutions (Export-Import

Bank, the World Bank, the International Monetary Fund, and the Inter-American Development Bank) in carrying out their anti-Chilean position. According to one high Treasury official we interviewed:

> ". . . Treasury is having an input (to U.S. foreign policy) that it hasn't had in the past. The National Advisory Council passes [on] credit programs, Export-Import Bank loans, [the] whole range of Federal Government financial activities abroad. Connally [has an] increasing input in financial aspects which other agencies sometimes tend to play down. Executive Directors of the IMF and the World Bank are both under the Secretary of the Treasury so we have a considerable punch in both of those. . . ."

Treasury control over the international public lending agencies was claimed by Treasury officials interviewed and substantiated by State Department officials.

In short, the Treasury position and input to policy regarding Chile has been to exert as much pressure on Allende as possible. The strategy of outside influence (the denial of direct loans, credits, and aid) has been directed to force a favorable settlement for U.S. business interests. Equally important has been the action taken to isolate Chile by increasing the "external" costs, thus discouraging other Latin nations from following the example.

The Congress

The range of congressional opinions concerning U.S.-Chilean relations and the copper issue appears to parallel the diversity of opinions and attitudes in the State and Treasury Departments. Congressional "hard-liners," "moderates," and a few "liberals" are present in the hearings and congressional activities concerning U.S.-Chilean relations. Up through the early part of 1972 no House position existed. Individual congressional members presented their positions and indicated their pleasure or displeasure over U.S. policy on an individual basis. Neither House nor Senate leadership has enunciated a specific policy toward Chile. Congressional activity has taken shape through committee hearings and reports and through the efforts of individual congressmen. The differences between the Senate and House membership on this issue are sufficient to warrant a separate discussion.

The Senate

An interesting facet of the Chilean copper crisis has been the extent to which some Senate liberals have responded in a very unliberal fashion. Senator Javits of New York has been especially hostile to economic nationalism not only in Chile but in other Latin American countries as well. At the same time he has been one of the most outspoken defenders of foreign investors. On May 10, 1971, Javits defended foreign investment:

> "The role of private foreign investment in Latin America is one of the most pressing questions of the day, and one that must move toward resolution. . . .The lack of a logical coherent policy works to the detriment of Latin-American growth objectives. This 'no policy' approach or 'highly restrictive policy' approach—such as the one just developed by the countries of the Andean group—not only impedes foreign capital flows, but also *threatens to exacerbate the economic and political relationships between the United States and Latin America.*"

As a senator who has outspokenly supported the multinational, U.S.-based corporations, Javits represents the view that American capital should not be infringed upon even when foreign political leadership has a democratically-based consensus to limit exploitation of national resources by these corporations. The Javits' position exposes the marginal differences that exist between conservative and liberal U.S. political leadership on a key foreign policy issue. Javits' stand is indicative of the inflexible congressional posture—a position corresponding closely to that advocated by the major copper corporations. Not surprisingly, the Javits-corporate position was the one adopted by the Nixon Administration.

Other, more identifiably conservative senators chose different means of expressing their hostility toward Chilean and Latin-American economic nationalism. Their positions and attitudes, and the techniques that they advocate to intimidate the Chileans, are illustrated in the Senate debate over the U.S. contributions to the Inter-American Development Bank Fund in October 1971. Senator Byrd (I-Virginia) opened the debate by arguing that American taxpayers should no longer support the "giveaway programs that the Federal Government has engaged in over the last 25 years." Senator Dominick (R-Colorado) wanted to be assured that the U.S. control of the Bank would prevent loans going to Chile.

It was clear from this debate, however, that conservative and liberal opinion was united in the desire to take all actions necessary in support of U.S. business interests. The key question was not whether a pro-business policy was to be adopted but to select the measures which would be most *effective.*

The left-liberals in the Senate approached the Chilean situation from a different standpoint. Senators Church and Kennedy have expressed opinions and attitudes quite different from the bipartisan liberal-moderate-conservative coalition which dominated the Senate on this issue. Both Senators agree that the current government of Chile was "a decision of the Chilean people" and that the copper issue is "a matter between the companies (Anaconda and Kennecott) and the Chilean government" and not an issue in which the U.S. government should interject itself.

Kennedy has publicly gone on record in support of the present Chilean Government:

> "A wise Administration policy would have recognized that the Chilean experiment in socialism had been decided by the people of Chile in an election far more democratic than the charade we saw last week in Vietnam. But the Administration response was brusque and frigid, colored by its attachment to the ideology of the Cold War. We can never know whether a more sensitive policy toward Chile might have helped to avoid the expropriation decision, which we learned of today. . . .We should halt the tendency to identify U.S. Government interests with the interests of U.S. private investment." (Oct. 12, 1971.)

The "hands off Chile" position of both Church and Kennedy, however, represents a small minority in the Senate and, for that matter, in Congress as a whole. Most senators of both parties who have spoken on this issue take the position that the Chilean expropriation of U.S. copper corporations is a "threat" to U.S. public interests and that the U.S. government must undertake all steps to ensure that these actions do not become habit-forming in other Latin-American or Third World nations.

The House

House attitudes and opinions, as a body and individually, reflect a high degree of unanimity regarding the policy the U.S. should adopt toward Latin-American governments (such as in Chile) which challenge private U.S. business interests in their countries. Given the importance of the committee structure of the House, the attitudes and opinions of members of the two House committees most involved in Latin-American policy determination—the Committee on Foreign Affairs and the Committee on Banking and Currency—demand the greatest attention. The most important hearings in the House to date have been organized by the Inter-American Affairs Subcommittee of the Committee on Foreign Affairs, chaired by Dante Fascell (D-Florida).

According to one staff member, the position of the majority of members of the Inter-American Affairs Subcommittee is "moderate"—a position and role which has "counseled moderation" to both the Treasury and State Departments as well as to other members of Congress. It has attempted, also, to preach "moderation" to the government of Chile so that Chile would not become a victim of economic "repercussions" that would certainly occur if Chile does not change its compensation policy. The difficulty with this description lies in what is, indeed, "moderate" as opposed to "immoderate." An examination of the recent Hearing on U.S.-Chilean relations, reveals that Representative Fascell is "hopeful" as well as "disturbed" by the nationalization of copper.

The Hearing included testimony and memoranda from leading executive branch officials involved in U.S.-Latin American relations, including Charles A. Meyers, Assistant Secretary of State for Inter-American Affairs, Marshall T. Mays, General Counsel for the Overseas Private Investment Corporation (OPIC), Walter C. Sauer, Vice-Chairman and First Vice President of the Export-Import Bank of the United States, and John W. Fisher, Director of the Office of Bolivian-Chilean Affairs, Bureau of Inter-American Affairs, Department of State. For the most part, the testimony of Administration officials was directed toward defending the hostile Nixon position toward economic nationalism in Latin America and Chile with terse and/or ambiguous responses to congressional queries.

The general drift of the House Subcommittee was that harsher measures should be adopted to pressure for a favorable compensation settlement. The congressmen, far from being concerned with parochial economic interests, were concerned with all U.S. private investments and the possible impact of Chilean policy.

Perhaps the final measure of House attitude toward Chile and Latin-American nationalism can be seen in the House version of the bills to fund the international lending agencies for 1972-74. The total authorization was for $1.96 billion for the World Bank, the Inter-American Development Bank, and the Asian Development Bank. The Senate approved the same dollar total; however, House amendments have forced a House-Senate conference to resolve the differences. The House amendments to the three bills require U.S. representatives to the banks to vote against loans to any nation that expropriated American property without just compensation. These amendments were very similar to the defeated Brock-sponsored amendment to the Senate bill.

The role and nature of the international lending agencies had been discussed during the Senate debate over additional funding for both the World Bank and IDB; likewise, the House discussed similar issues in its debate over similar funding proposals. What emerged was an assessment of the World Bank and the Inter-American Development Bank as transmission belts of U.S. policy. Congressional control through appropriations coupled with U.S. representation in sufficient numbers on the Boards of Directors of both institutions (40 percent in the case of the World Bank) insures that loans to countries out of favor with the United States will not be granted. The U.S. representatives on the Inter-American Development Bank, the Executive Director of the World Bank, and the U.S. representative on IDA are directly responsible to the Secretary of the Treasury.

Several recent incidents further illustrate the role of the international lending agencies (World Bank and IDB in particular) as implementers of U.S. policy. The case of Peru best illustrates this. After the Velasco government nationalized the International Petroleum Company, U.S. aid dropped from $60 million to $9 million in 1969, causing the Peruvian President to accuse the Inter-American Development Bank "of being used as a weapon of political pressure."

In terms of formal decision-making structure of the International Banks overt U.S. control is not always manifested because, as the historian Mark Chadwin has pointed out, "to date the U.S. never has voted formally against a loan request either in the World

Bank or the IDB but that is partly because the bank boards operate by consensus; issues on which there is disagreement are not brought to formal vote."

Protestations to the contrary, the public and private statements of Administration officials illustrate the degree of control that the Secretary of the Treasury has over the Export-Import Bank. His willingness to *use* this control to retaliate against countries such as Chile merely underscores the fact that political values have first priority over banking criteria in shaping loan decisions.

It is clear from the record that the "international" lending agencies are mere appendages of the U.S. government. Contrary to the preoccupation of some conservative congressmen, there is no danger that these institutions will deviate from the official, articulated, hard-line position taken by the Nixon Administration.

U.S. Business Interests

In many ways the most important input to U.S. policy-making in Latin America is that of U.S. business interests—a collage of private sector operations, major and minor, which have direct investments of between \$10.4 billion and \$11.7 billion in Latin America. U.S. private investments are distributed in a variety of sectors roughly corresponding to overlapping historical periods. Investment and direct ownership in extractive industries (mining and petroleum) and related service industries (utilities such as electric, other power, and telephone) was characteristic of the period up through the 1950's. In the last 20 years U.S. investors have shifted toward manufacturing, trade, and banking.

The pattern of U.S. investment for Latin America as a whole is maintained in Chile. Table I indicates the date of initial investment and the type of U.S. investment and activity in selected major industries prior to copper nationalization. It is clearly discernible from this table that pre-World War II investments were basically those in extraction of raw materials or in basic utilities. With the end of World War II, the growth of a large internal consumer market and high tariff walls, U.S. private investment began to "diversify." The

TABLE I

Selected U.S. Firms with Majority Investment in Chile Prior to Copper Nationalization: Ranked by Date of Operation

Firm	Date of Operation in Chile	Principal Activity
W. R. Grace	1881	Transportation
Bethlehem Steel	1913	Iron Mining
Anaconda	Circa 1916	Copper Mining
First National City Bank (N.Y.)	1916	Banking & Finance
Kennecott	Circa 1920's	Copper Mining
Dupont	1920	Explosives
I.T.T.	1927	Telephone
R.C.A.	1942	Radio & Television
I.T.T.	1942	Radio & Television
Kaiser (Argentina)	1946	Iron & Steel Products
Oscar Kohorn & Co.	1948	Textiles & Fibers
Englehard Minerals & Chemicals	1955	Iron Mining
American Cyanamid	1955	Pharmaceuticals
Standard Oil (N.J.)	1959	Oil Distribution
Parke, Davis & Co.	Pre 1960	Pharmaceuticals
Chas Pfizer	Pre 1960	Pharmaceuticals
Sterling Drugs	1960	Pharmaceuticals
Armco Steel	1960	Iron & Steel Products
Mobil Oil	1961	Oil Distribution
International Basic Economy Corp.	1961	Banking & Finance
W. R. Grace	1961	Food Manufacturing
CPC International	1961	Food Manufacturing
General Motors	Pre 1962	Auto Assembly
Simpson Timber Co.	1965	Pulp & Paper
Sperry Rand Corp.	1966	Office Equipment
Singer Sewing Machine	1966	Iron & Steel Products
General Mills	1967	Food Manufacturing
Ralston Purina	1967	Food Manufacturing
Dow Chemical	1967	Petro Chemicals
Firestone Tire & Rubber	1967	Rubber Tires
Northern Indiana Brass	1967	Copper Fabricating
Bank of America	1967	Banking & Finance
Ford Motor Co.	1968	Auto Assembly
Monsanto Co.	1969	Petro Chemicals
General Tire	1969	Rubber Tires
IRECO Chemicals	1969	Explosives
Cerro	Late 1960's	Copper Mining
General Telephone & Electronics	1970	Radio & Television
Chemtex Inc.	1971	Textiles & Fibers

Source: North American Congress on Latin America, *New Chile* (California: NACLA, 1972), pp. 150-168; "Recent Developments in Chile, October 1971," *op. cit.*, p. 18; and D. Lynne Kaltreider, "A Tale of Two Interventions and Other Related Actions," unpublished paper, November, 1971.

1960's witnessed a rather wide variety of investments designed to tap and exploit the potential Chilean consumer market which had developed as a result of the boom in the copper industry during the Korean conflict. The "appetite" of the Chilean middle class for U.S.-type consumer goods is well known; investments in the 1960's reflect the attempt of U.S. firms to cash in on this Chilean tendency to use precious foreign exchange to produce middle class consumer items.

Despite the diversification of investment, the bulk of U.S. direct investment in Chile remained in the mining and smelting category (53.4 percent—see Table II). The balance of U.S. investment was in consumer-type industries (34 percent). The critical area of manufacturing accounted for only 7.7 percent with trade making up the remaining 4.8 percent.

TABLE II

U.S. Direct Foreign Investment in Latin American Republics and Other Western Hemisphere (Excluding Canada)

(book value at end of 1969 in millions U.S. dollars)

		Percentage Breakdown by Sector					
Country	Total	Mining & Smelting	Petroleum	Manu-facturing	Trans. & Utilities	Trade	Other
Latin America	11,667	11.5	26.4	34.9	5.3	11.2	10.6
Mexico	1,631	8.3	2.1	67.9	1.7	11.7	8.2
Panama	1,071	1.8	22.3	8.4	5.2	32.2	30.1
Other Central America[1]	630	1.3	24.4	17.9	20.5	6.8	28.9
Argentina	1,244	*	*	63.4	*	5.5	31.1
Brazil	1,633	6.1	6.1	68.1	1.5	11.5	6.6
Chile	846	53.4	*	7.7	*	4.8	34.0
Colombia	684	*	50.0	23.2	4.2	9.2	4.4
Peru	704	62.9	*	13.8	*	8.4	15.1
Venezuela	2,668	*	66.4	15.6	.7	10.3	7.0
Other[2]	554	9.0	34.3	12.1	9.9	5.9	28.7
Other Western Hemisphere[3]	2,144	26.9	30.0	12.6	3.5	4.6	22.6
Total	13,811	13.9	26.9	31.5	5.0	10.2	12.5
Latin American Republics & Other Western Hemisphere							

*Combined in other industries.

[1]Includes Costa Rica, El Salvador, Guatemala, Honduras and Nicaragua.

[2]Includes Bolivia, Dominican Republic, Ecuador, Haiti, Paraguay and Uruguay.

[3]Includes all of the Western Hemisphere, except Canada and the 19 Latin American Republics.

Source: U.S. Department of Commerce, *Survey of Current Business*, October 1970.

Only Peru has a higher proportion of foreign investment concentrated in the mining sector, and Chile has the lowest percentage of foreign investment in manufacturing of any Latin-American country. A nation-by-nation examination suggests that in each country foreign investment is concentrated in one sector rather than diversified throughout the economy. Taking Latin America as a whole there appears to be a greater dispersion. This sectoral specialization, while perhaps the result of the profit-maximizing behavior of investors, leaves their investors *isolated* and vulnerable to nationalist coalitions which embrace or cross socio-economic sectors—as was the case in Chile.

Table III reveals that U.S. investments spread throughout the industrial sector remain after the nationalization drive and disinvestment that occurred since the election of Allende. These firms represent, perhaps, the type of foreign investment that the Chilean government desires, will permit, and possibly even encourage in the future. From the political standpoint, these firms are enmeshed in the sector of the economy most closely linked to the middle class and to the political opposition.

TABLE III

Remaining U.S. Investments in Chile, Not Nationalized, Bought Out, or in Process of Buyout

Firm	Principal Activity
Continental Copper & Steel	Steel Products
Crown Zellerbach	Manufacturing
Dow Chemical	Petro Chemicals
Ensign Bickford	Manufacturing
Firestone Tire & Rubber	Rubber Tires
General Cable	Copper Fabricating
General Electric	Electrical Equipment Manufacturing
General Motors	Auto Assembly
I.T.T.	Hotels & Electrical Equipment Manufacturing
RBCO	Chemicals
Xerox	Photo Reproduction Equipment

Source: "Recent Developments in Chile, October 1971," *op. cit.* p. 18. These firms own either a part or all of their Chilean operation—they account for $75 million direct, U.S. private investment in Chile.

As a result of the long private investment ties to Chile, U.S. business groups, particularly the large copper concerns (Anaconda and Kennecott), have staged rearguard legal action in Chile attempting to receive compensation for their investments. The copper companies even will seek compensation from the U.S. government and taxpayers.

More important, U.S. copper companies may be acting to seize Chilean markets by increasing their sales from the U.S., thus driving the Chileans out of established markets.

In addition, AID loans have been extended to Yugoslavia to develop copper mines to be jointly owned with foreign investors. It is clear that the U.S. corporations will concentrate their struggle in the international commercial arena—an area where the Chileans may be at a disadvantage.

The principal lobbyist for U.S. business interests in Latin America has been the Council of the Americas—an interest group with a membership of some 210 firms representing 90 percent of all U.S. investments in Latin America. Originally, this organization was more descriptively called the Business Group for Latin America. Through formal and informal meetings at regular intervals the Council and key U.S. government officials work closely in shaping U.S. policy. The Council's activities and the ability of its members to secure sensitive decision-making positions within the executive branch of the U.S. government assures corporate representation and decisive influence over major governmental decisions in areas which affect them.

The Nixon Administration's hostile policy toward economic nationalism in Chile and Latin America is substantially shaped by officials in government who are or were the representatives of U.S. firms in Latin America.

The Council on Foreign Relations

The range of policy options open and under consideration to U.S. policy-makers was discussed at a series of meetings held by the Council on Foreign Relations (CFR) during 1971. Corporation executives, international functionaries, State Department officials as well as academics and others with an interest in Latin America attended. The free and uninhibited discussion which occurred presents an unusual opportunity to examine the position of opinion leaders from influential segments of "public opinion."

The general impression left after a reading of the CFR "confidential" minutes (which were published in the *Newsletter* of the North American Congress on Latin America) is the lack of any innovative thinking and of any coherent proposals to meet the key problems discussed but hardly explored in any depth. The participants did not pose any specific alternative policies to confront the problems of mass marginality, dictatorship, the growing gap between the United States and Latin America, and the failure of the Alliance for Progress, nor did most of the participants seem to understand the dynamic forces underlying the growth of the nationalist challenge. The best that some of the participants could come up with was either a return to a revised version of dollar diplomacy or a policy of "disengagement." The few participants with a relatively clear set of ideas around which to focus U.S. policy were mostly the executives from private corporations—they defined U.S. policy and interests in terms of promotion and protection of U.S. business and more specifically corporate investments in Latin America.

A spokesman for Standard Oil called for overt direct action: "The U.S. should frankly acknowledge the role of senior partner and should take some initiatives." He then went on to suggest the establishment of "international" machinery to defend private investments as well as a unilateral policy which would not tolerate "economic aggression." More specifically, he urged that "U.S. policy should aim at protecting and promoting U.S. interests (investments) in the region but within an international context." Underlying the corporate viewpoint was a general malaise and growing discontent with the behavior of Nixon's foreign-policy-makers: U.S. policy was attacked as being the "antithesis of protector and promoter of U.S. interests"; the government was accused of being "passive" toward Chile and Peru, Nixon was attacked for not encouraging U.S. investment where it was not welcome (presumably the implication is that Nixon should make the proper political arrangements in Latin America *to make* investment welcome). Rather than using the inter-American councils as active instruments to promote and protect U.S. interests, the U.S. representatives are perceived as "passive." Projecting current problems in Latin America into a global context, the corporate spokesman warned that failure to act against nationalization in Latin America could generate a "ripple effect" in other areas—a point of view taken up and supported by others during the discussion. A spokesman for the State Department suggested sanctions against uncompensated expropriation, fearing the "demonstration effect of Peruvian and Chilean actions on the rest of Latin America." Most government advisors—public and private—felt that the Latin Americans perceived the United States as "wavering as to whether it will take up the cause of private investors." An executive from Standard Oil called for the U.S. government to "make its position clear before incidents arise."

On January 19, 1972, Nixon announced the tough U.S. stand on expropriations, backing the strong position advocated by the overseas investors and their supporters in the Treasury and State Departments. The Nixon announcement terminated loans and aid to countries nationalizing U.S. property. The proviso calling for "prompt, adequate and effective compensation" is a euphemism for opposition to nationalization since few, if any, underdeveloped countries have large sums of hard currency available to divert from socio-economic development to U.S. corporations. The key passage of Nixon's speech reads:

> "When a country expropriates a significant United States interest without making reasonable provision for such compensation to United States citizens, we will presume that the United States will not extend new bilateral economic benefits to the expropriating country unless and until it is determined that the country is taking reasonable steps to provide adequate compensation or that there are major factors affecting United States interests which require continuance of all or part of these benefits."

The gradual escalation of U.S. pressures against economic nationalism in Chile took a new turn when a U.S. court in New York blocked the bank accounts of 14 Chilean agencies. Despite Chile's agreement to pay over 90 percent of the Kennecott debt which had purportedly caused the attachments, the Federal judge refused to lift attachments against nine Chilean enterprises. Chile's agreement to pay the enormous debts incurred by past regimes has led to efforts to renegotiate the payments schedule. Once agreeing to renegotiation, Chile has become increasingly vulnerable to external pressure which may have adverse internal social, economic, and political effects on the Allende government. For example, part of the price Chile has to pay to obtain refinancing of her debt is the agreement to allow the International Monetary Fund to periodically "review" Chile's monetary, credit, and trade performance. Part of an IMF "review" are "recommendations" that usually include credit and wage freezes, which if not heeded by the host country can result in an unfavorable "review" and new credit restrictions. If past experiences are any indication, Chile's acceptance of IMF recommendations could lead to undermining the Allende government's social basis of support. The involvement of the IMF in Chilean politics along with the blocking of the Chilean accounts in the U.S. reinforce the notion that the Chilean government is being economically encircled in order to create the necessary and sufficient conditions for the internal opposition to take power.

What Low Profile?

Dominican-style "gunboat diplomacy" has been replaced by "credit-diplomacy"—for now. The low profile approach suggests that U.S. policy-makers will give increasing importance to indigenous military elites and oppositionists in dumping the economic nationalists; this has already occurred in Bolivia and more recently in Ecuador. By confining themselves to maintaining credit pressure from the outside, U.S. policy-makers allow their national allies inside the country to mobilize on internal issues—a strategy which appears to be paying off in Chile.

The more immediate experiences concerning U.S. policy and overseas investment suggest that when a crisis situation emerges—when a major U.S. investor group in a Latin country is endangered—there is an increasing convergence of U.S. government and business responses. Once the crisis passes the two major interests may diverge. The overlap in policy is largely a result of the career patterns and prior socialization of many of the leading policy-makers; individuals who have come from corporate or corporate-related careers and/or who may be headed for such a career, but who in any case share many of the key beliefs associated with business enterprise ("foreign private investment is essential for the development of underdeveloped countries"—and similar beliefs).

Whatever the value of any particular enterprise affected by economic nationalism, it has been shown how U.S. policy-makers have a tendency to view the particular problem from the standpoint of the impact on the whole overseas investment community. Hence, the constant preoccupation not only of high Administration officials but of seemingly "parochial" congressmen with the so-called "ripple effect."

U.S. policy-makers perceive the real challenge to be neither the Soviet Union nor China but economic nationalism and social revolution in these Third World areas under U.S. hegemony. Thus, while the U.S. policy-makers propose an opening to China they heighten pressures on Chile and the rest of Latin America. While the U.S. "opening" toward China is a major new development in U.S. foreign policy, the objectives are not very different: recognition of a Great Power is the first step toward mutual agreement in defining traditional spheres of influence. It is within this framework that we can understand why the United States can open relations with the major Asian Communist power, China, but not with revolutionary Cuba. We can also understand why the United States plans to increase trade with an authoritarian Communist regime in Asia while limiting credits and eliminating loans to a parliamentary, Democratic Socialist government such as governs Chile.

Despite the hostility of U.S. policy-makers and private investors toward economic nationalism, there are important factors which should encourage some restraint on U.S. public activities. The large foreign debt which Latin nations (including Chile) owe to U.S. financial institutions is a double-edged sword; while it provides the creditor nation leverage to pressure for favorable policies, it also provides the debtor nation with a bargaining weapon which can be expressed in the form of a threat to repudiate the debt and thus influence important financial interest groups in the creditor country. Conservative but prudent bankers who still have hopes of recuperating their loans may wish to moderate the extremist demands of U.S. private investors whose properties have been nationalized. While the non-nationalized U.S. economic groups continue to have an economic stake in Chile and feel that there is some hope for partial or total recovery, it is to be expected that bargaining, negotiation, and some agreements can be reached regarding specific areas. More specifically, it is likely that Chile will be allowed to refinance the debt in exchange for guarantees that the Allende government will make prompt, complete payment. Thus, within a framework which locks U.S. private interests and government in combat with Latin-American economic nationalists, the possibility of short-term arrangements are possible and probable, given the loss of U.S. omnipotence in this hemisphere and the emergence of somewhat "durable" nationalist regimes in Latin America.

THE CHALLENGE OF VENEZUELAN OIL

by Norman Gall

> Each year we, the countries which produce coffee, meat, tin, copper, iron or petroleum, have been handing over a larger amount of our products in order to obtain imports of machinery and other manufactured goods, and this has resulted in a constant and growing outflow of capital and an impoverishment of our countries. . . . To cite the particular case of Venezuela, petroleum prices showed a steady decline for many years, while our country was obliged to purchase goods from the United States at ever-higher prices, which, day after day, restricted even further the possibilities of development and well-being for Venezuelans. The establishment of the Organization of Petroleum Exporting Countries (OPEC) was a direct consequence of the developed countries' use of a policy of outrageously low prices for our raw materials as a weapon of economic oppression.
> —President Carlos Andrés Pérez of Venezuela, September 24, 1974.

With these words in an open letter to President Ford, published as a full-page advertisement in *The New York Times* last fall, the new President of America's leading foreign supplier of oil hurled a now familiar challenge to the United States. But the nation was not in the Middle East; the Israeli question was not remotely a consideration; and the nation in question, Venezuela, has traditionally been regarded by the U.S. and Latin-American Left as a strategically vital province of U.S. imperialism.

Within a few months, Venezuelans are expected to nationalize their oil industry. How successfully they do it—the exact details and the nature of the relationships which come into being after nationalization—may help decide the degree of future U.S. dependence on Middle East oil, the structure of the international petroleum industry, and the prospects for democracy in Latin America.

For years, Venezuela has played an important role in the formation and growth of the oil cartel, OPEC. As an outsider, Venezuela was to play a leading role in unifying the squabbling states of the Middle East. Despite her backwardness in other respects, Venezuela had a far more sophisticated and progressive political leadership that the other states that formed OPEC.

A "Devilishly Difficult" Problem

It is one of the many ironies of the present oil panic that OPEC might never have come into being if the United States had protected Venezuela from the economic hardship resulting from the oil import quotas imposed by the Eisenhower Administration in 1959 to protect domestic producers and the oil majors against the flood of low-cost Middle East crude then glutting the world market. Venezuela was then emerging from a decade of military dictatorship in an economic slump that grew out of the U.S. recession of the late 1950's, aggravated by a loss of oil revenues due to the price-cutting in the Middle East. In this atmosphere Venezuela spent much of the 1960's pleading with Washington for "hemispheric preferences" for access to the U.S. market along lines similar to those given Canada. Indeed, at one point, President Rómulo Betancourt (1959-1964) thought that he and John F. Kennedy had worked things out. Kennedy "promised me that this Venezuelan aspiration for preferred entry to the U.S. market would be satisfied before the end of his mandate and mine," Betancourt recalled. "He told me the problem was 'devilishly difficult' because of the special interests involved. But he assured me that justice would be done to Venezuela."[1] The gunshots of Dallas left this explicit promise unfulfilled.

To the credit of Venezuela's young democracy, never has the public debate over nationalization of a great extractive indus-

[1] *Rómulo Betancourt, "Un recurso energético que no tiene igual,"* Visión, *February 12 & 26, 1972.*

try taken place in a more open and peaceful political climate. The possibility of nationalization, distantly contemplated for about 1984 when most of the concessions were due to expire, became an imminent reality with the October 1973 war. The discussion intensified greatly after the war and the landslide election, two months later, of Carlos Andrés Pérez as President of Venezuela. Since then, Venezuela has moved to nationalize its oil and iron industries and take a leading role in hemispheric politics.

The main question is no longer whether Venezuela will nationalize, but what the future modus operandi of the oil industry will be. The central issue of the nationalization debate is whether at least some of the 16 foreign companies—Exxon and Shell subsidiaries alone account for more than 80 per cent of Venezuelan production—will be allowed to remain in Venezuela as operating or marketing contractors to the new state holding company, Petroleos de Venezuela, in return for some share of future production, or whether the government will try to run the industry itself. Some companies have been quietly trying to play upon the percolating fears of mismanagement and to promote jobs for their employees in the future state marketing organization. This would give the present concessionaries more leverage in the future production of a nationalized industry. Expecting some kind of amicable dissolution of the old concessions, companies seem less interested in indemnification for installations already heavily amortized and depreciated than in some role in the Venezuelan industry's future.

At stake is the most important source of non-Arab oil for the United States, a source that becomes all the more critical during periods of threatened or actual embargo. And, as in the past, developments in Venezuela may affect events elsewhere.

Democratic Solidarity

Venezuela became the world's leading oil exporter in 1929, and held this position for the next four decades. Since the end of the long dictatorship of Juan Vicente Gómez (1908-1935), oil and democracy have been closely linked in their development.[2] The flow of oil money into the cities has generated such enormous urban-rural income differentials that the countryside has been depopulated in one of the most intense internal migrations of this century, transforming Venezuela from a nation that was nearly 80 per cent rural in 1920 to one 80 per cent urban today. Meanwhile, Venezuela has moved fitfully toward creation of a complex and broadly based social democracy, with the economic leavening of oil revenues.

Venezuela received especially gentle and considerate attention in Washington after Mexico kicked out the foreign oil companies in 1938. Venezuela became a primary target for the Good Neighbor policy, and the State Department put heavy pressure on the oil companies to make their policies and personnel less offensive to Venezuelans, as well as to give in to Venezuela's demands for more oil money in order to avoid a repetition of the Mexican nationalization. By the 1960's, democratic solidarity had developed to the point where the Kennedy Administration viewed Venezuela as a test of its own hopes for the Alliance for Progress, and, later, as its only clear success in promoting reform, counterinsurgency, and private investment in Latin America.[3]

When Betancourt became the first popularly-elected ruler in Venezuela's 150-year republican history to finish his constitutional term of office, it was a triumph of his own

[2] *For a view of this relationship and of the structural weaknesses in Venezuelan society that have impaired the rational use of oil revenues, see my* Oil and Democracy in Venezuela, *American Universities Field Staff Reports, East Coast South America Series, Vol. XVII, Nos. 1 & 2, 1973.*

[3] *The Roosevelt and Kennedy policies toward Venezuela contrasted strongly to the official decoration given dictator Marcos Pérez Jiménez by Secretary of State John Foster Dulles in 1954 at the Caracas conference of the Organization of American States. However, the medal was awarded to the dictator over the objections of high State Department officials and only at the insistence of the U.S. military that anti-Communist rulers in Latin America must be given visible support.*

tenacity and of the people's awakening democratic vocation. To do this, Betancourt had to survive armed insurrections from the Left and the Right. He put down an outbreak of guerrilla warfare far more sustained and bitterly fought than Fidel Castro's Cuban insurrection. Two of his aides were killed and his own hand mangled in a 1960 assassination attempt by henchmen of Dominican dictator Rafael Trujillo, who rolled a car full of explosives into Betancourt's motorcade. This attempt was one of the considerations that led Washington to allow the CIA to supply arms to the men who killed Trujillo in May 1961.[4]

Venezuela Forms OPEC

As Venezuela's internal violence escalated, Betancourt's Minister of Mines and Hydrocarbons, Juan Pablo Pérez Alfonzo, was traveling in 1960 among the capitals of the Middle East to persuade the rulers of the oil-producing nations to form OPEC to defend their economies against the price-slashing being carried on by the companies and to find markets for the low-cost crude that was flooding the international oil trade in ever-increasing quantities. Pérez Alfonzo knew that only control of supply would enable Venezuela to influence price levels. If the oil-producing countries could unite, then the power of the integrated majors could be curbed. Later, a bargain could be struck with the United States and Canada to parcel out the hemispheric oil trade, giving Venezuela more security of access to its main markets.[5]

When Betancourt and his Acción Democrática (AD) party first ruled Venezuela in a reformist regime in the 1945-1948 period, the imaginative Pérez Alfonzo already had achieved much toward reversing the tendency of the oil companies to enrich rulers rather than governments. Under his leadership, Venezuela in 1947 pioneered establishment of the 50-50 principle of profit sharing between companies and governments. AD governments in the 1940's and again in 1959 were the first among the oil-producing countries to formulate a policy of "no more concessions" to foreign companies. Trying to prevent her higher tax-paid costs from making her oil uncompetitive in world markets, Venezuela, in the late 1940's, began explaining to Middle East governments the terms of her new 50-50 deal with the companies, which led to the establishment of the 50-50 principle there as well.[6] By then, Venezuela had become so important to Jersey Standard (now Exxon) that half of its worldwide profits in 1948 were generated by Creole Petroleum, its Venezuelan subsidiary and the world's largest producing company, which supplied the crude for half of its worldwide refining capacity.[7]

The financial concessions that were wrung from the major companies by the host governments in the 1940's and 1950's, under Venezuela's leadership, did not disrupt the majors' cartel-like marketing arrangements, but only began a continuing escalation of the producing countries' share of the companies' profits. The next major mutation in the system came in 1960 with the formation of OPEC in response to the price erosion of the late 1950's. The U.S. import restrictions had created such an oil glut on the world market that British Petroleum (BP), with an oversupply of crude and rela-

[4] *See my "How Trujillo Died,"* The New Republic, *April 13, 1963.*

[5] *See Franklin Tugwell,* The Politics of Oil in Venezuela *(Stanford: Stanford University Press, 1975).*

[6] *The Iranian Ambassador to Caracas, Manoucher Farmanfarmaian, who was Iran's Director-General of Mines in 1949, recently told a meeting of the Inter-American Press Association that the 1949 Venezuelan mission to Teheran "opened our eyes, showing us and discussing the contracts between Venezuela and the oil companies that were based on the 50-50 principle. This was the first time Iran got to know about these contracts. This shows how much influence the companies had. . . . In the following years, the Venezuelan system became our goal. The 50-50 was our objective but the resistance was so tenacious that finally there was no other solution but to nationalize."*

[7] *See "Creole Petroleum: Business Embassy,"* Fortune, *February 1939, p. 180. The 87 cents per barrel earned by Creole in Venezuela compares with the return for the seven majors of 78 cents for lower-cost Middle East oil in 1957, during the post-Suez oil emergency.*

tively few marketing outlets of its own, unilaterally cut prices in 1959 for Iran, Kuwait, and Qatar production. Since the British government was then the majority shareholder in BP, the Venezuelan government addressed a memorandum on the price cuts to the British Embassy in Caracas, arguing:

> BP, the largest producer in the Middle East, has by this action brought prices below the 1953 level. Since that year, all the factors affecting production cost have increased substantially and the general level of prices in international trade has also risen. In the United States, the largest world producer, not only did costs rise, but the country also failed to discover sufficient oil in the past two years to replace the production of that period. The United States appears to have reached the depletion curve within a relatively short time, and other important producing centers of this irreplaceable natural resource will also reach a similar situation. In general, the costs of exploration and drilling are increasing throughout the world and the more widely dispersed the search to find new reserves for human needs, the more each new barrel will cost . . . the additional lowering of prices, by encouraging consumption, could very soon bring oil to the historic cycle of scarcity. This would force consumers to pay much higher prices to finance the exploration and discovery of new areas. It is evident that for the good of mankind, a stable situation would much better guarantee the interests of all concerned.[8]

Pérez and Oil

Since then, despite recurrent political crises, Venezuela has gone far toward consolidating her constitutional democracy. Today, flush with oil money and votes, President Carlos Andrés Pérez has embarked on a series of popular domestic reforms, including general wage increases, under special powers given him by his AD majority in Congress. A tough Andean politician who, as Betancourt's Interior Minister, had taken the lead in crushing the Castroite guerrilla insurrection of the 1960's, Pérez became a prime mover behind the efforts to end the Organization of American States' diplomatic sanctions against Cuba last November. Failing to marshal the two-thirds majority needed to lift the sanctions, Venezuela then established diplomatic relations with Cuba, and, in other actions, championed higher prices for Latin-American primary products.

Venezuela is also trying to use her excess oil income to finance more rapid economic development in Latin America. After the tripling of her oil revenues between 1973 and 1974, Venezuela is recycling abroad more than one-third of her trade surplus, or about one-tenth of her whole GNP, in $500 million loans to both the World Bank and the Inter-American Development Bank, and in another $125 million distributed among the Andean, Central-American, and Caribbean development banks. Another $500 million was lent to the International Monetary Fund's oil recycling facility. Discussions are being held for lesser projects like financing a paper factory in Honduras, and an oil refinery in Costa Rica. This is more public money than the United States ever committed to the Alliance for Progress. In December, President Pérez met with the six Central-American presidents in the Venezuelan iron and steel center of Puerto Ordaz to announce that Venezuela would pay up to $80 million to Central-American coffee producers to enable them to withhold part of their crops from the market in an effort to support declining prices. Pérez announced that the six republics would only have to pay $6 of the $12 selling price of Venezuelan oil in dollars. The rest could be paid in local currencies into counterpart funds for soft loans such as those the United States made for decades to countries like India and Bolivia in the Food for Peace program.

In this way, Venezuela was able to advance her long-cherished ambitions for influence in Central America, and project her image throughout the Caribbean. A leading Dominican economist wrote recently that

[8] *The memorandum was reproduced in* Venezuela and OPEC *(Caracas: Imprenta Nacional, 1961), p. 99.*

"1974 probably represents the close of a period that began in 1961, of great dependence of our country on the United States, and unfortunately the beginning of another period of economic dependence on Venezuela and other nearby oil producers." [9]

Venezuela's oil power gave President Pérez center stage in Lima, at the December celebration of the 150th anniversary of the Battle of Ayacucho that won independence from Spain, where he urged the assembled military dictators of Bolivia, Panama, and Peru, and envoys of other Andean nations, to stop squabbling in ideological and border disputes. It also helped him in seeking to transform Venezuela into a democratic counterpoise to the influence of Brazil's military regime in Latin America and into a champion of economic justice for all underdeveloped countries.

Crisis of Democracy

But Pérez's trendy Third World rhetoric and some policy initiatives of his first year disguise much Venezuelan discomfort about how the oil revenues of the past two decades were wasted. How can they now absorb the much greater flood of oil money into what is essentially a rentier economy—some $10 billion in 1974, which is triple normal budgetary needs? Venezuela entered the 1973 election campaign in a mood of crisis due to the erosion of public faith in the parties that have run the country since the overthrow of dictator Marcos Pérez Jiménez (1948-1958).[10] The two big parties, AD and the Social Christian COPEI party of President Rafael Caldera (1969-1974), were able to dominate the election only through lavish advertising and by changing the constitution a few months before the balloting to rule out a possible presidential candidacy of the ex-dictator, who had made a sensational political comeback in the five years since his release from jail for stealing public funds. The Yom Kippur war and the overthrow of Chilean democracy occurred within three weeks of each other at the height of Venezuela's election campaign, providing at once the economic impetus for oil nationalization and concern among Venezuelan leaders for the consequences of mismanagement of nationalized industries as under Allende. Many responsible Venezuelan politicians realize that their democracy could be washed overboard by incompetent handling of the nationalized oil industry or the tidal wave of oil money now pouring into the country. As Pérez himself said in a speech in Maracaibo three weeks after sending his public message to Ford:

> We have immense economic resources that the economy cannot absorb. We have the traditional and insatiable voracity of public spending, and the negligence with which the public and private sectors have used oil income. We are either at the beginning of an ascent toward consolidation of our nationality, or at a precipice that could leave us, not in catastrophe, but at a point back where we would have to start our development all over again.

In the same speech, Pérez attacked mismanagement of the state petrochemical industry, in which Venezuelan governments over the past two decades have invested roughly $2 billion, much of which has been squandered because of corruption and political interference. The new President said that, in its first six months of operation, the huge El Tablazo petrochemical complex near Maracaibo had some 50 breakdowns "from deficiencies in diligence and supervision." Previously, audits of the costs of building the $92 million El Tablazo complex found suppliers' and contractors' overcharges variously estimated at $20 million and $35 million. A few days after Pérez's speech, the head of the state petrochemical industry was fired amid

[9] *Bernardo Vega, "1974: Año del Cambio en Nuestra Dependencia Económica Externa," in* Listín Diario, *November 22, 1974.*

[10] *The Kennedy Administration extradited Pérez Jiménez from his Miami exile in 1963 at the request of the Betancourt regime. He was finally released from jail in August 1968 and went to live in Madrid. Four months later, he ran, in absentia, for a Senate seat in Caracas, sweeping all but one of the city's 16 parishes. He gained the most votes in the poor workers' districts, where people had poured into the streets to overthrow him a decade earlier.*

charges of price-rigging that allegedly cost the Venezuelan government $3 million in a deal with a U.S. firm.

Venezuela's difficulties in developing her state petrochemical industry, and in managing other state enterprises, have led to considerable self-doubt as she develops plans to nationalize oil, which before 1973 produced 90 per cent of her foreign exchange earnings and two-thirds of her government income, and today produces much more of both. While Venezuelan politicians have been talking for nearly four decades now about "sowing the petroleum" to diversify the economy, and despite widely publicized investments in modern infrastructure, heavy industry, agricultural development, and social programs, Venezuela has become more rather than less dependent on her oil revenues. The decision to immediately nationalize the oil and iron industries came in the weeks before and after the December 1973 elections, when the Arab oil boycott stimulated leaps in the posted price of Venezuelan crude to $14.08 per barrel, compared with the January 1973 price of $3.10. Although Venezuela's two big parties, AD and COPEI, had quietly agreed not to debate oil issues in the election, all but one of the 14 presidential candidates in the race had vaguely backed an "early reversion" of the industry to the state before the scheduled expiration of the concessions.

Doubts about Nationalization

Pérez began fulfilling this promise in May by appointing a 36-man Presidential Commission on Oil Reversion, representing the full range of political parties, professional associations, universities, and business and labor groups concerned with nationalization. As it was working on a draft nationalization bill last November, one member, Carlos Alberto Piñerua, president of the oil workers' union FEDEPETROL, expressed the growing nervousness of both politicians and the public over nationalization when he told me: "This is a kind of forced nationalization because of what is happening in the Middle East. Without the rise in oil prices, Venezuela would not have moved so swiftly. The oil companies have started a campaign to frighten workers about the future. There is much more fear among the engineers and white-collar people than the workers, who want to conserve their social benefits, as well as technology and markets for Venezuelan oil production."

Pérez will be under great pressure to articulate policies in line with the conservative nature of his electoral mandate, with the feeling that Venezuela's rentier economy depends on one commodity that Venezuelans, lacking sufficient organizational and technological capacity, know they cannot produce and market alone. Many politicians privately say that the movement to nationalize comes not from any public clamor, but from pressures from within the smaller community of politicians, and from recent dramatic changes in the oil industry outside Venezuela.

Alternative to Middle East Oil?

One of the stakes is the degree of future U.S. dependence on Middle East oil. While Venezuela was overtaken in the ranking of oil exports by Iran in 1970 and Saudi Arabia in 1971, she remains the leading oil supplier to the United States. In 1973, Venezuela produced 35 per cent of net U.S. imports, mainly as heavy fuels for heating and electric utilities along the Eastern Seaboard.[11] However, Venezuelan production peaked at 3.7 million barrels daily (MBD) in 1971 and, according to both government and company projections, is expected to decline to below 2.0 MBD by 1984 from presently existing fields, mainly around Lake Maracaibo, many of which have been operating continuously for more than 50 years. This process of natural decline of the traditional producing areas has been temporarily obscured in 1974 by the conservationist production cutbacks of about 11 per cent of a government swim-

[11] *This includes the heavy oil exported by Venezuela to Canada's maritime provinces, offset by oil exported by Canada to the U.S. north central states.*

ming in oil revenues it cannot use. These cuts were made at the suggestion of the companies, which told the government that world demand had declined at the 1974 price.

If current predictions of rapid decline in Venezuelan oil production come true, then the United States will have to search elsewhere for supplies of heavy oil for her largest energy market, the Eastern Seaboard, or revert to greater use of coal. If the controversial conversion to coal is not made immediately, and the United States continues to rely on oil imports for its needs, then the international rivalries for access to Middle East oil may intensify. While world oil consumption continued its rapid rise over the past decade at an annual rate of 7.7 per cent, the volume of oil moving in world trade during the 1963-1973 period rose even faster, at 10.8 per cent annually. Because of steep rises in domestic demand, the role of U.S. oil imports since 1970 in world oil trade expanded even more dramatically, at more than twice the rate of international oil sales in the rest of the world. Between 1972 and 1973, U.S. imports rose by nearly one-third—to 6.2 MBD—while the volume of imports from Arab countries nearly doubled.

The relative immunity of the United States from the economic consequences of political convulsions in the Middle East has been based largely on U.S. domestic production and Venezuelan oil, both of which were taken for granted. Just as in the U.S. domestic oil industry, supplies from Venezuela are imperiled by the exhaustion of the reservoirs that have been producing now for several decades. Moreover, the anticipated production declines in Venezuela could be greatly accelerated by mismanagement of politicization of the nationalized industry. On the other hand, productivity could remain high if certain conditions are created. These are efficient management of the industry, and effective short-term investments in secondary recovery—gas and water reinjection systems to maintain underground pressure in the older wells. These investments in high-cost recovery techniques have become more attractive after the tripling of Venezuela's oil prices during 1973. Moreover, any major exploration program probably could enable Venezuela to remain an important exporter at least for the rest of this century. To develop these new production possibilities soon, new tradeoffs will have to be devised to provide incentives for Venezuela, already overflowing with oil revenues, to at least maintain present production levels.

The strategic value of Venezuelan oil to the United States was again illustrated during the 1973 Arab oil boycott. Exxon's worldwide production of 6.3 MBD was cut by 20 per cent between the third and fourth quarters, but her 48 per cent share of Venezuela's 3.5 MBD production flowed normally to the United States. According to Exxon's 1973 annual report: "Supplies of heavy fuel oil . . . were not affected as seriously by the Arab embargo. Virtually all of Exxon USA's heavy fuel oil supplies are imported from refineries in Venezuela and the Netherlands Antilles operated by Exxon's affiliates. . . . Venezuelan crude supplies utilized in these refineries were maintained at normal levels." On the other hand, the tripling of the price of Venezuelan heavy fuel oil has had a major economic impact on the Eastern Seaboard.

Geologically speaking, there are promising prospects offshore in the Caribbean, in the 150-mile-wide delta of the Orinoco River, and in the Gulf of Venezuela, which is practically contiguous—separated only by a strait and some sandbars—to the great oil-producing basin of Lake Maracaibo. Apart from these conventional oil prospects, Venezuela contains one of the world's largest petroleum reserves in the Orinoco Tar Belt, estimated by geologists to contain 700 billion barrels of heavy oil. If only 10 per cent of the volume were recoverable, Venezuela could produce, from this basin alone, five times her present reserves. Because this heavy Orinoco oil contains large amounts of nickel and vanadium, new technologies will have to be developed for large-scale lifting and refining operations by the 1990's. However, though the problems may be formidable, they may be less costly than producing oil from Colorado shale or Canada's Athabasca tar sands—the other major prospective sources of nonconventional oil in the Western Hemisphere.

The Future of the Majors

Beyond its role in determining the degree of future U.S. dependence on Middle East oil, the Venezuelan oil nationalization also may help shape the way the major oil companies will operate over the next few decades. Last November I talked with the government's chief economic negotiator, Manuel Pérez Guerrero, a soft-spoken, fragile-looking former Minister of Mines, who was one of OPEC's leaders in the mid-1960's. He said:

> We want this nationalization to be acceptable as an act of sovereignty within the law. Our greatest political problem is management capacity. We will need help from foreign technologies, but the reins of the business must be in our hands. We are not nationalizing buns and cakes, but important strategic commodities that cannot be left entirely in the baker's hands. We will be the owners and must make the basic decisions ourselves. We feel an obligation not to bring about any upheavals, nationally or internationally. . . . Under these new conditions, the major companies will be reduced to the role of traders, intermediaries, refiners, and providers of technical services. This is no small thing, but much less than before, when they had what seemed unlimited supplies of crude under their exclusive control. We must force the majors to be more aboveboard than secretive, and this will be good for the industry and the world.

In the worldwide wave of oil nationalizations that began in 1971 and is expected to reach its climax this year, two-thirds of the production of the seven major oil companies outside North America, or an amount roughly equivalent to more than half of the 34.1 MBD that moved in world trade in 1973, will be taken from the proprietary control of these companies with the end of the old concession system. Although much of this oil will continue to move through the majors' marketing network as a result of new production and purchase agreements with the exporting countries, the security of abundant and low-cost supply that was the basis of an integrated industry now may be a thing of the past. Saudi Arabia, Venezuela, and the Persian Gulf sheikdoms, with a combined 1973 production of 15.8 MBD, are expected to announce the terms of their state takeovers this year. With the old structure of the international industry badly shaken, today's high prices and the insecurity of future supplies have made the oil contingencies less of a question of entrepreneurship and more of a question of state. The stresses caused by oil payments and supplies have led the governments of consuming as well as producing countries to consider taking a stronger hand in the management of the industry, just as the British government did on the eve of World War I, when Winston Churchill, First Lord of the Admiralty, told the House of Commons in 1914:

> Nobody cares in wartime how much they pay for a vital commodity, but in peace . . . price is rather an important matter. . . . I cannot feel that we are not justified . . . in considering how in years of peace, and in a long period of peace, we may acquire proper bargaining power and facilities with regard to the purchase of oil. The price of oil does not depend wholly, or even mainly, on the ordinary workings of supply and demand.

The occasion was the British government's purchase of a 51 per cent share of the Anglo-Persian Oil Company (now British Petroleum) as her navy's warships were converting from coal to liquid fuel. Today, consuming governments are pressed more urgently to reconcile the dual character of oil as both a strategic resource and a commodity traded throughout the world.

Through tax policies, Washington favored the oil companies with depletion allowances and credits for taxes paid governments of producing countries, and indirectly stimulated consumption by using a gasoline tax to finance the building of an interstate superhighway system. Now other tax policies are being discussed to limit oil imports. Going beyond this kind of fiscal improvisation, Walter J. Levy observed recently that "the problems of oil have become matters that in many key respects can only by handled directly between governments," adding that oil prices must remain high so as not to endanger the economic viability of expensive alternatives, such as development of tar sands, shale, and coal gasification as energy sources. Levy wrote that "avoiding dependence on foreign oil dictates public support and a substantial measure of price guarantees by individual countries, notably the United States . . . acting . . . in coordination." [12] During the Arab boycott another leading oil analyst, Edith Penrose, saw the possibility of the companies becoming "public utilities with appropriate public regulation," arguing that "it will no longer be possible for the governments of the oil-importing countries to leave the international companies as free a hand in the industry as they have had in the past in view of the fact that the governments of the exporting countries will be deciding the major issues affecting the terms on which oil is sold." [13]

A U.S. Government Share in Big Oil?

These arguments seem to provide strong reasons for U.S. government purchase of large minority stockholdings in one or more of the major American oil companies. First, the capital accumulation and reduced levels of consumption that will soon be needed in the energy field to lower oil imports and develop alternative sources of energy will require a strong public guarantee that the oil industry's "obscene profits" will actually fulfill the stated purpose of energy investment and not be diverted into unrelated activities (such as Mobil's attempted purchase last year of Montgomery Ward, as part of its efforts at corporate diversification, to relieve its dependence on an increasingly regulated yet unstable industry). Second, with the oil companies losing their control of foreign supplies of crude, their self-advertised role as buffers and intermediaries between producing and consuming governments has become less meaningful. What do remain important are their managerial and technological skills. Third, such direct government leverage in the industry would facilitate long-term government-to-government arrangements on price and supply that repeatedly have been urged by producing countries, especially Venezuela.

In the coming months, Venezuela will be faced with a choice between two kinds of nationalization: the Latin-American tradition of the operating state oil company, such as PEMEX of Mexico and PETROBRAS of Brazil, or the developing Middle East pattern, now working in Iran, by which the state owns the industry but foreign companies continue to operate under varying degrees of government control. The Iran formula may soon be applied, with modifications, in Saudi Arabia and the Persian Gulf sheikdoms, and the major concessionairies in Venezuela have expressed hope that they will be able to remain on similar terms. The Middle East formula is a variant of the "service contract" concept first formulated in Venezuela in 1959 but not applied there until 1970. In its 1973 annual report, Exxon said it was "optimistic that whatever changes may take place and whatever relationships may evolve, there will be a basis for continuing operations" in Venezuela.

While the state oil company has been the dominant operating entity in Chile, Argen-

[12] *See Walter J. Levy, "World Oil Cooperation or International Chaos,"* Foreign Affairs, *July 1974, p. 699.*

[13] *From Edith Penrose, "Origins and Development of the International Oil Crisis,"* Millenium, *Vol. III, No. 1, 1974.*

tina, Uruguay, Bolivia, Peru, and Colombia as well as Mexico and Brazil, none of these countries has a major export industry like Venezuela's. Moreover, some repeatedly have called in foreign companies to find oil that their state enterprises have lacked the financial and technical resources to discover. While the producing countries agree that the technical and organizational services of the majors and large contractors will be needed for at least the near future, the Middle East formula remains an anathema to many Venezuelan nationalists.

In Venezuela, the draft law approved by the nationalization commission prohibits "creating mixed enterprises or participation in profits for activities reserved to the State." However, toward the end of 1974, the AD government showed many signs of moving away from this restricted definition of nationalization to allow itself much more flexibility in running the industry. In the final months of the commission's deliberations, the AD party and government representatives pointedly stayed away from the sessions to allow President Pérez and his advisers more room for maneuvering before presenting the final version of the nationalization bill to Congress. Pérez's attack on the management of the petrochemical industry has been seen as an effort to reinforce the public's fears that the government cannot directly manage the oil industry and that some deal with the companies should be made. Moreover, in December, when he announced the negotiated nationalization of the iron mining operations of U.S. Steel and Bethlehem Steel, Pérez called it "a magnificent solution that opens very favorable prospects for the more difficult and complex situation that will arise with the expiration of the oil concessions that will occur by Venezuela's sovereign decision in coming months."

The iron nationalization arrangement calls for the companies to run the mines during a transition period of one year, in exchange for a continuing supply of ore to U.S. steel mills, and leaves the way open for future technical assistance in mining and joint ventures in intermediate stages of processing. Significantly, all the opposition parties refused to support the iron nationalization deal in Congress, arguing that it was too generous to the companies, and only AD's parliamentary majority and a small party sympathetic to ex-dictator Pérez Jiménez voted for approval. Since there were persistent rumors of oil company support for AD in the election campaign, the debate over oil nationalization may prove to be even more bitter if a formula is presented that would enable the companies to continue operating the industry.

Once nationalization is approved, difficulties are anticipated by conservatives and Jacobins alike. For one thing, automation and a sharp decline in exploratory drilling since Venezuela's "no more concessions" policy was announced in 1959 have resulted in a halving of the industry's work force over the past 15 years to 21,000, or less than 1 per cent of all persons employed in the country. The fact that so small a proportion of the labor force is employed in the capital-intensive industry on which the country is so dependent has permitted a pervasive ignorance of the oil business among even educated Venezuelans.

Scared Workers and Scarce Technicians

Automation and attrition have left the oil industry with a work force composed largely of middle-aged men (averaging 45 years old and 19 years on the job) who are economically privileged, politically conservative, and, on the whole, deeply worried about their future. Said a Marxist union leader, "both the iron and oil workers are against nationalization. They're afraid of what will happen to social benefits like company medical care and their retirement plans. The iron workers want all of their retirement payoff now, but if they were to get it they'd all leave the iron mines and never come back." The government has promised to place the retirement money of the oil and iron workers in a special fund in the Central Bank. But unrest in the industry is likely to continue until the government provides strong proof that the nationalized industry will be effectively managed in the interests of both the workers and the country. Otherwise, both the iron and oil work forces will become hosts to agitation by opposition political parties that will make the transition to state ownership much more difficult.

While Venezuela proportionately has more of her own professionals in the oil industry than any other OPEC nation, she is still short of technicians to run the nationalized industry without outside help. Although the companies have made an effort in recent decades to put Venezuelans in high-level jobs, there are still 635 foreigners in key technical and executive positions. While many of these foreigners, if encouraged, would stay on after nationalization, many middle-level Venezuelans already have taken early retirement from the companies with the approach of a state take-over.

High Venezuelan officials have said many times that, after nationalization, they will maintain intact the organizations of the four largest concessionaires—Exxon, Shell, Gulf, and Mobil—and will gradually consolidate the operations of the smaller companies into larger production units. But there will be a continuing need for something like the logistical and technical support that always has been provided by the majors to their overseas subsidiaries. Moreover, most of Venezuela's oil has been sold abroad by the majors' marketing organizations outside Venezuela. While some of these limitations can be overcome with time, any attempt by Venezuelans to overreach these limitations now could prejudice their nationalized industry.

Curiously, some of the most important nationalizations since World War II[14]—Iranian oil in 1951, Bolivian tin in 1952, and Chilean copper in 1969-1971—seem to have occurred when world prices for the commodity have peaked and begun to decline. Instabilities in the supply of oil can be anticipated from the wave of nationalizations now taking place throughout the world and from possible political conflict in the producing areas. Because of new oil from non-OPEC countries that probably will be available for marketing in the late 1970's, just as consumption restraints in the industrialized nations begin to take hold, it may be reasonable to expect dramatic fluctuations in the price and supply of oil for the rest of this decade. Despite their recent success in driving up oil prices, the OPEC countries have a long history of bickering among themselves, and, until 1974, have been especially unsuccessful in limiting production, as any cartel must, to protect prices. With most big producers now operating below capacity because of consumer response to high oil prices and the spreading world recession, coordinated production cuts by OPEC may be needed in the near future. Mexico's recent decision against joining OPEC indicates that new oil-producing areas may not be easily absorbed into the cartel.

Not that OPEC, of itself, is a bad thing. One of the most ardent advocates for primacy of the majors has argued persuasively that, in an inherently unstable industry given to boom and bust cycles and to gluts and scarcities of supply, "the oil industry, to exist at all, calls for concerted effort and, however often a cooperative structure may have been disturbed or broken up, it will soon begin to form again." [15] The problem is that OPEC has attempted to justify its 1974 price levels as being below competing sources of energy. This is a fallacious argument because, in the short term, there are no competing sources of energy, and OPEC could just as well charge $40 or $50 per barrel as $10 or $12. But many oil analysts in the consuming

[14] *On the Chilean and Bolivian nationalizations, see my* Copper Is the Wage of Chile, *and* Bolivia: The Price of Tin: Part I, *American Universities Field Staff Reports, West Coast South America Series, Vol. XIX, No. 3, 1972, and Vol. XXI, Nos. 1 & 2, 1974.*

[15] *P. H. Frankel,* Essentials of Petroleum *(London: Cass, 1969), second edition, p. 97.*

countries now believe it would be more tragic for humanity than for the OPEC countries for the price of a barrel of oil to fall back to the pre-1970 price of $2, thus stimulating a return to wanton consumption that would hasten the exhaustion of the world's limited petroleum reserves. A return to low oil prices also would undermine the shaky financial structure supporting worldwide oil exploration, into which consuming countries poured upward of $10 billion in 1974.

Given future market uncertainties, now may be a good time for Washington to enter into long-term price and supply arrangements with Venezuela, which could thus continue as a pioneer in developing new relations between producing and consuming countries. While Venezuela's unsuccessful quest for hemispheric preferences has been forgotten in the upward surge of prices over the past few years, such favored access to the U.S. market, coupled with price guarantees, could be extremely helpful to her should oil prices again become unstable. Extending preferences and guarantees to Venezuela, which could be done unilaterally by Washington, would be in the U.S. interest in that they would stimulate Venezuela to expand her oil production capacity despite worldwide economic uncertainty, and to remain an extremely valuable supplier. In addition, price and market guarantees could be coupled with technical and educational support to the nationalized oil industry to give Venezuela more economic autonomy and stability over the long term.

This kind of cooperation is certainly not going to be achieved through economically meaningless and politically counterproductive reprisals such as the denial to OPEC members of most-favored nation status under the new U.S. foreign trade statute, a provision that has led Venezuela and Ecuador, the two Latin-American OPEC members, to force cancellation of the Buenos Aires hemispheric foreign ministers' conference in March.

In the end, the United States must meet the challenge posed by President Pérez's letter to President Ford. If not for reasons of sympathy or justice, then a decent respect for the future price and supply of a wide range of raw materials should dictate a new departure in U.S. policy toward nationalized industries. This would mean a reversal in U.S. economic diplomacy, since these industries traditionally have been treated as pariahs by international aid agencies. However, the stability of supplies of oil, copper, tin, iron, bauxite, and even bananas will depend, to a considerable degree, on the performance of nationalized industries in Latin America. To ensure a rational flow of these products into world markets, it may be in the self-interest of consuming countries to provide facilities in Latin America for the training of people from these nationalized enterprises in such varied skills as management, marketing, cost accounting, and specialized engineering operations. If the United States could provide continual training for more than a decade for police and counterinsurgency operatives in Latin America, then Washington surely could support, along with other industrialized countries, a public sector manpower training program implemented by some international agency. Beyond this kind of training, it may be advisable to provide design, engineering, and capital assistance to these industries to expand their capacities, especially in the processing of raw materials, and reduce the polarization between producing and consuming countries that is at the heart of the oil crisis. In this connection, perhaps as counterpoint if not refutation of former President Nixon's public expressions of support for the military dictatorship in Brazil, it might not be amiss for Ford to voice solidarity with Venezuela's democratic institutions and with her economic defense of the hemisphere's more vulnerable republics.

CUBA: TIME FOR A CHANGE

by Abraham F. Lowenthal

For the first time in years, the United States and Cuba have a chance to break the deadlock which has kept such close neighbors so far apart. The outcome of the San José meeting of the Organization of American States (OAS) this July means that the United States is now free to determine its own stance toward Cuba. For its part, Cuba is ready to compromise to achieve rapprochement with the United States. "Normalization"—mutually respectful and profitable diplomatic, commercial, and cultural relations—is at last possible, perhaps within two or three years.

The road to normalization will be long and cannot be one-way. Traveling it successfully will require patience, skill, and flexibility on both sides. Neither country desperately needs improved relations, though each nation would gain substantially, both in bilateral terms and in the broader framework of inter-American and international relations. Each country will encounter formidable internal problems as it moves toward nonhostile relations. Each (especially the United States) must contend also with allies who will be unenthusiastic about a U.S.-Cuban rapprochement. But the will to face internal and external difficulties to achieve normalization exists in Havana, both at intermediate and at high levels of government. In Washington, a similar spirit prevails at intermediate levels in the executive, and is gaining increasing strength in Congress.

Despite some signs in Havana and in Washington that normalization is desired, however, U.S.-Cuban relations are still logjammed, if not icebound. Each side waits for the other to make concessions before direct negotiations begin. Cuba has already taken several significant steps toward the negotiating table, but the United States has yet to respond clearly; ambiguous, even contradictory, signals emanate from Washington instead.

To move beyond the impasse, therefore, the U.S. government should clearly demonstrate its interest in normalization. The United States should take the next symbolic step by lifting at least part of its longstanding blockade of Cuba and by expressing its intent to end the remaining sanctions as soon as direct negotiations with Cuba permit. And Washington should act now, before the electoral campaign deprives the Administration of flexibility.

These are the main conclusions I draw from recent and extensive conversations in Havana and in Washington. I would not pretend, of course, that 11 days in Cuba and two days in Washington this June make me an authority. But the more interviews I have, the more clearly these conclusions emerge.

The Revolution Is Here to Stay

Recently published reports about CIA involvement in attempts on Castro's life remind us how intensely hostile relations between the United States and Cuba became in the early 1960s. The captured Sherman tanks at Giron (the Bay of Pigs) impressed that point on me most vividly. Over 200 Cuban soldiers died there in 1961 in defeating a heavily armed force, trained by the CIA, convoyed to Cuban waters by U.S. Navy destroyers, and aided (however ineffectively) by temporary U.S. air cover.

Despite its humiliation at the Bay of Pigs, the U.S. government continued its ardent efforts to topple the Castro regime. American radio broadcasts wooed the Cuban populace, periodic U.S. airdrops supplied anti-Castro groups in the Escambray mountains, and American intelligence operatives reportedly helped carry out sabotage operations. But all these tactics failed.

Even in retrospect, the triumph of Castro's movement was impressive. The few surviving veterans of Moncada and *Granma* had only an outside chance to oust Batista, much less to purge the island of U.S. influence. The American presence in Cuba—once described by a Cuban nationalist as "no more independent than Long Island"—was overwhelming. But, however implausibly, the Cuban revolution did triumph. Cuba's political, educational, and economic systems have been transformed. Many of its national habits and values have been profoundly altered. After several false starts, Cuba's economy seems to be on a successful course: national income is going up, the balance of payments was favorable in 1974 for the first time in 15 years, and heavy investments in infrastructure, public health, and education are beginning to pay off. Above all, perhaps, Cuba's historical relationship with the United States has been thoroughly overturned.

A fundamental reversal of Cuba's revolutionary achievements is most unlikely. The regime faces no serious threat from within. A large share of the country's dissidents were among the approximately 650,000 persons who left after 1959, mostly bound for the United States. Half the island's current population has been born since Fidel took power. The populace is fully mobilized, mainly through the Committees for the Defense of the Revolution, in which 80 per cent of adults are said to participate. Finally, the government has shown its will and capacity to control and even suppress dissent. There is, therefore, no need for an obtrusive military presence in Cuba, nor for the obvious surveillance of foreigners which marks the Soviet Union. The traffic control posts outside each Cuban town still remain, but no one bothers to stand guard inside the booths. The revolution is here to stay.

A Policy of Restrained Hostility

And yet the U.S. government, at its highest levels, seems never to have fully accepted the presence of a Socialist state in Cuba. True, Washington's attempts to subvert the Cuban government were slowly abandoned, but only as it became clear that Castro's hold is firm, and as U.S. dealings with the Soviet Union sharply reduced the military security problems Cuba poses for the United States (and limited what the United States can do to Cuba). But even after dropping its direct efforts to end the Castro regime, the U.S. government tried hard to isolate Cuba. The policies of diplomatic nonrecognition and "economic denial" which the United States pressured its allies to support were avowedly aimed at thwarting Cuba's "export of revolution" and at forcing Cuba to cut its military ties with the Soviet Union. More important than those two stated goals, however, was the desire to undermine Cuba's appeal as a development model by minimizing the successes of the Castro government and by limiting Latin-American access to Cuba. And there was long a fourth reason, a wishful thought (especially among many Cuban immigrants) that the Cuban revolution would eventually abort, if only the United States did not recognize or support it. These four reasons—reinforced by personal pique and by psychological stress, no doubt—have undergirded U.S. policy toward Cuba since the mid-1960s, a policy of restrained hostility.

In September 1975, none of these four concerns provides a defensible basis for U.S. policy (if, indeed, they ever did). Yet America's hostile policy, symbolized by the total embargo, continues.

Cuba began to disengage from its previously active attempts to "export revolution" in 1968 after Che Guevara's storybook failure in Bolivia. By 1969, Cuba was supporting the reformist Peruvian military regime, even though the Peruvian junta was led by army officers who only a few years before had commanded counterinsurgency units to combat the spread of Cuba's influence! By 1971, Cuba was being sharply criticized by rebel leaders like Douglas Bravo of Venezuela for failing to provide effective support to revolutionary movements. By 1975, Cuba had re-established diplomatic relations with Venezuela, which had proposed the OAS expulsion of Cuba in 1964; Cuba has also developed correct to cordial relations with Argentina, Colombia, Panama, and a number of Caribbean states. All these countries seem reasonably confident that Cuba is neither engaging in nor planning armed subversion in Latin America. The U.S. government, which maintains constant air surveillance of Cuba, is in a position to be sure of this as well. Cuba's extensive military build-up over the years has been defensive in character; short-range fighter-interceptors, rather than bombers, compose most of Cuba's air force purchases, and Cuban military training emphasizes defense of the island, not attacks on others.

As for Cuba's relations with the Soviet Union, U.S. efforts to isolate and punish Cuba have done absolutely nothing to limit the considerable (though hardly visible) Soviet presence in Cuba; on the contrary they have surely increased Cuba's incentive to remain close to Moscow. The United States has a legitimate interest in trying to limit Russia's capacity to use Cuba as a base for hostile actions. But the 1962 missile crisis showed conclusively that the main actors can and will deal with each other directly. That lesson was reinforced in 1970 when a sharp American reaction to Soviet naval movements and construction activity at the port of Cienfuegos led the superpowers to clarify (or perhaps to extend) their agreement that bars Russia from introducing a strategic offensive capability into Cuba.

Normalizing U.S. relations with Cuba will not immediately weaken Cuba's links with the Soviet Union. But there is absolutely no reason to believe Soviet influence will increase with normalization, and there is some reason to think it may decline over time. One can reasonably speculate, at least, that Cuba's capacity to act independently of the Soviet Union should expand if Cuba enters a triangular relationship involving both superpowers.

The long-standing U.S. aim to isolate Cuba in order to limit its appeal to Latin America is both forlorn and misguided. It is forlorn because Cuba has already broken down the blockade. Not only has Cuba in recent years established or re-established relations with innumerable countries of Latin America, the Caribbean, Africa, Asia, and Europe; it has also joined the Latin American Group at the United Nations, been elected to the U.N. "Committee of 24," hosted several important international meetings, and become an obligatory stop for distinguished statesmen and aspiring politicians from all parts of the world, near and far. It is misguided because Cuba's appeal in most of Latin America has been, and is, strictly limited. Cuba's revolution may have shattered the myth of "geographic fatalism," but the "second Cuba" feared by U.S. officials a decade ago never appeared, and shows no sign of doing so. Highly placed Cuban authorities freely concede that a second Socialist revolution in the Americas is not easily foreseeable. The Colossus of the North has nothing to fear from Cuba's full entry onto the hemispheric stage.

Finally, the unstated hope that the Cuba issue will eventually disappear simply cannot be sustained. Not even the Cuban community in Miami still really holds on to the belief that the revolution will be reversed. Richard Nixon, whose involvement with Cuban exiles eventually did him in, apparently maintained to the end his conviction that the present Cuban leadership could be ignored. Gerald Ford, the fifth American president to rule since Fidel took over in Havana, should not cling to this illusion.

"No Virtue in Perpetual Antagonism"

The long-time U.S. policy of restrained hostility toward Castro's Cuba is clearly being eroded, as was signaled by Secretary Kissinger's statement in March 1975 that the United States sees "no virtue in perpetual antagonism" between this country and Cuba. But various pronouncements, including President Ford's subsequent interview with Pierre Salinger in June, suggest that the U.S. government may delay undertaking any significant shift in the U.S. posture. The Administration's view has long been that "it takes two to tango," and that the United States proposes no move toward the dance floor until it is convinced that its putative partner is willing. Even after the OAS meeting at San José, therefore, the U.S. government waits, either because it feels it has no real interest in rapprochement with Cuba (beyond having partially defanged the Cuba issue as a problem in inter-American relations), or because it is not sure whether the Cuban regime really wants normalization, or because it does not wish to give up—or appear to give up—any "bargaining chips" without gaining something concrete in return.

An impasse has thus been reached; the Cubans want the United States to drop (or at least clearly to begin to drop) its obviously hostile blockade of Cuba as a precondition to discussing other bilateral issues. The U.S. government waits for a "change in Cuban attitudes"; Cuban gestures to date are dismissed as not dealing with "basic issues."

This impasse should be broken now. Moving beyond the impasse will require some elegant steps in a minuet (if not a tango), a minuet which has already begun. A less hostile tone in diplomatic discourse and public statements between the two governments has been noted, for instance. So have a few American gestures, primarily the slowly evolving U.S. position on the Cuban issue within the OAS forum, the liberalized restrictions on the travel of Cuban diplomats posted at the United Nations, and the decision to permit a few Cubans to enter the United States for cultural or religious purposes. But, despite some Administration indications to the contrary, all the major steps toward normalization so far have been taken by Cuba: the 1973 hijacking agreement (belatedly recognized this June by Assistant Secretary William D. Rogers as having been a significant gesture by the Cuban government); the invitations extended to important members of Congress from both parties and to congressional staff persons; the treatment accorded visiting journalists and scholars; the content of various Cuban government statements, especially Castro's television interview with Dan Rather in October 1974 (with his skillful, if subtle, praise for Presidents Kennedy and Ford and for Secretary Kissinger and his careful distinction between the American people and U.S. government policy) and his remarks to Senator George McGovern in May 1975; the release of several U.S. prisoners; the invitation to exchange baseball teams; and the announced intention to return a $2 million hijacking ransom confiscated some years ago by the Cuban government. Thus, the logical next step, if our government genuinely desires normalization, would be for the United States unambiguously—if only partially—to begin ending the embargo of Cuba, the continuing embodiment of official American hostility.

Why the United States Should Act Now

Arguing persuasively that the U.S. government should set in motion the dynamics of rapprochement by beginning to lift its embargo of Cuba requires showing: (1) that it is in our national interest for normalization to occur; (2) that the Cubans themselves now seek normalization and are therefore willing to compromise to achieve it; and (3) that there is no reason to think that the United States will achieve normalization on more favorable terms by further delay.

Normalization of relations with Cuba—on negotiated terms which are responsive to legitimate U.S. concerns—would be in our national interest for several reasons. First, ending official American hostility toward Cuba would help make it clear that the United States is adopting the new approach toward Latin America persuasively recommended by the recent report of the Commission on United States-Latin American Relations (the "Linowitz Report"): an approach "respectful of the sovereignty of the countries of the region and tolerant of a wide range of political and economic forms." As the Linowitz Report emphasizes, the United States—in its own self-interest—should cooperate with the countries of Latin America to build a more equitable, stable, and mutually beneficial structure of international relations. Efforts by the United States to make the "management of interdependence" a positive fact, not merely an ambiguous slogan, will depend for their success in part on securing the active help of the Latin-American countries, nations which share our primary interest in improved economic security and which exert increasing international influence.

No "new dialogue" to achieve this vital objective will have even a remote chance to succeed, however, if the United States appears to prolong its overbearing attitude toward Latin America. We can no longer expect to veto change in Latin America and elsewhere in the Third World. The days of unquestioned U.S. domination of the hemisphere are over. U.S. policy toward Cuba thus takes on a special significance, as it often has in the past, as a test of this country's attitudes and assumptions. A creative attempt to resolve outstanding problems with Cuba and with Panama would be understood in Latin America as testimony—far more eloquent than official rhetoric or state visits—of this country's desire to improve its hemispheric relations. And failure by Washington to change its policies in these key instances could convey exactly the opposite message.

The second set of reasons for the United States to seek normalized relations with Cuba involves economics. Given the size of the U.S. economy, no one would contend that the benefits the United States would gain from eventual trade with Cuba are overwhelmingly significant in aggregate terms. The Cuban market could be very attractive, however, for specific U.S. corporations trying to recover from a prolonged international recession. Cuba might import from the United States fairly substantial quantities of such products as automobiles and automotive equipment; agricultural commodities (corn, rice, wheat, cattle and poultry feed, vegetable oils, and fertilizers); farm machinery; food processing, textile manufacturing, construction and port equipment; computers and computer technology; and general know-how in agriculture and specific industries. A significant market for spare parts of U.S.-produced goods also appears to exist. Cuba's imports of consumer goods are rising, too, and American products are still the standard by which Cubans shop. Cuban officials emphasize that import decisions will be based on the quality and price of goods, on credit terms, and on delivery date; their repeated mention of the last criterion suggests that their experience with the distant and centrally planned economies of Eastern Europe may make Cuban managers long for the day when they will be able to call Miami or Chicago and obtain rapid delivery of needed items.

Trade with Cuba would not necessarily be one-way. Cuba's major exports—sugar and nickel—are products the United States imports; Cuba's known reserves of nickel, a raw material in scarce supply, are among the world's largest. Cuban cigars are still remembered in the United States with fond nostalgia. Cuba's hoped-for expansion of the tourist trade would find its greatest potential source of customers in the United States. A major Cuban project, supported by the United Nations Development Program, promises to achieve a breakthrough in lowering the cost of producing paper from bagasse (a sugar by-product), thus opening up the possibility that Cuba could help alleviate this country's paper shortage. Though none of these prospective Cuban exports to the United States is of crucial importance, each would be of some benefit.

A more speculative but potentially very important benefit of a U.S.-Cuban rapprochement would be that it might help Cuba lessen its dependence on the Soviet Union. Cuban officials explicitly reject this as a possible motive for their interest in improving relations with the United States; they invariably refer, as do numerous billboard posters, to Cuba's "unbreakable" bonds of friendship with the Soviet Union, the only foreign country singled out for mention in the draft constitution now being discussed in Cuba.

"Cuba wants and expects normalization, is striving to achieve it, and *is* ready to compromise to gain rapprochement with the United States."

My own guess, however, is that Cuba's official line "doth protest too much." Cuba's foreign trade statistics are suggestive in this regard. In 1957, the United States accounted for 64 per cent of Cuba's foreign trade. Although diversifying its international relations was a leading aim of Castro's movement from the start, 13 years of revolutionary foreign policy had, by 1972, succeeded only in reversing the statistics; 64 per cent of Cuba's trade in that year was with the Socialist countries (and overwhelmingly with the Soviet Union). Only since 1972 has Cuba been able to diversify its trade pattern more extensively; in 1974 (admittedly an exceptional year, due to the record high price of sugar), Cuban trade with non-Socialist countries climbed to nearly 42 per cent. 1975 and 1976 may see some slippage, but Cuba's commercial agreements since 1973 with Argentina, Canada, Spain, France, England, Italy, and West Germany —agreements for lines of credit totaling over $3 billion—suggest a keen desire to move away from its nearly exclusive reliance on the Comecon countries for both imports and exports. Cuba's sugar sales to Japan have been extraordinarily high for several years. Normalizing relations with the United States is part of this long-term strategy. And lessening Cuba's dependence on the Soviet Union should be a key aim of U.S. policy, for Cuba's only plausible threat to the United States is as an instrument of potential Soviet ambitions.

In sum, normalized relations with Cuba on negotiated terms which protect legitimate U.S. interests would be desirable. Arguing that these relations should now be actively sought by the United States depends on showing, however, that Cuba's interest in normalization is sufficiently strong to warrant thinking that direct negotiations would lead to reasonable compromises on outstanding U.S.-Cuban problems.

Cuba Wants Normalization

Perhaps the most important impression I obtained on my visit was that Cuba wants and expects normalization, is striving to achieve it, and *is* ready to compromise to gain rapprochement with the United States.

Officials and others with whom I talked were willing to guess, for instance, that most well-informed Cubans think normal diplomatic and commercial exchanges with the United States are possible within two years, and certainly within five. But Cuba is not merely waiting for history to take its course. The number of Foreign Ministry personnel working on the United States has nearly doubled in the past year, and the professional competence of Cuba's America-watchers is impressive. One Foreign Ministry specialist asked detailed questions about the Kansas City reforms in the Democratic Party's convention delegate selection process, for instance, and three members of the University of Havana's government-linked study group on the United States grilled me on the role of nonprofit institutions in U.S. foreign policy-making. The skillful campaign Cuba is waging to influence American opinion clearly expresses Fidel's interest in normalization.

With regard to each of the major issues outstanding in Cuban-American relations, I came away from Havana with a sense of Cuban willingness to bargain flexibly, provided that the United States is willing to do so.

On the difficult issue of compensation for expropriated American companies (and of possible Cuban counterclaims, which Cuban officials have indicated might amount to three or four times the U.S.-certified claim of $1.8 billion), a fairly detailed conversation with Carlos Rafael Rodriguez, Cuba's First Deputy Prime Minister, convinced me that Cuba is prepared to reach a realistic settlement. Such a settlement would involve not only recognition of the principle of compensation (which Cuba has already paid to several European countries) but some net transfer of funds from Cuba to the U.S. government, with our government acting as trustee for the expropriated firms. The Cuban desire not to pay "a single cent" to any American company could easily be taken into account by an arrangement similar to the one the United States and Peru devised to resolve the imbroglio involving the expropriated International Petroleum Company (IPC); a U.S. government claims commission could distribute a lump sum Cuban payment according to criteria decided by the United States alone. Exactly how much Cuba would pay the United States obviously remains subject to detailed negotiations. The price of sugar would be one relevant factor in these negotiations, and a specific understanding regarding Cuban access to the U.S. market would clearly be another.

As for Cuba's aim to oust the United States from the anomalous and unneccessary Guantanamo naval base, Cuba is deliberately letting this issue remain on a back burner until a later stage in the normalization process, after we have dealt with the Panama problem. Cuban officials understand that their chances of ending the U.S. presence at Guantanamo will increase if an American withdrawal cannot easily be represented in the United States as unseemly capitulation. Cuba seems prepared to wait, therefore, until the Guantanamo issue can be discreetly resolved in a mutually satisfactory manner.

Regarding nonintervention in the affairs of other countries, Cuban policy pronouncements and Cuban practice over the past several years appear nearly to coincide—something that cannot be said about our own government's statements and actions. Assurances against foreign intervention should not be difficult to secure from Cuba on a reciprocal basis.

"The embargo no longer serves to isolate Cuba; the country being isolated is the United States."

The one "sleeper," potentially the most difficult issue between Cuba and the United States, concerns the future of Puerto Rico. Cuban officials openly express their support for Puerto Rico's independence movement but claim that their support is restricted to "legitimate" activities and does not include terrorism, armed subversion, or other internationally proscribed acts. (I know of no hard evidence to the contrary, though it would not surprise me to learn of some.) Whatever the current facts, I suspect that trends in Puerto Rico will bring that territory's problematic status to the fore in years to come. If Cuban-American hostility continues unabated, Cuba's incentive to exploit this country's Puerto Rican problem will heighten. If the United States and Cuba normalize their relations, Cuban sympathy for Puerto Rican *independentistas* may still produce continuing friction. In that case, however, tacit or perhaps even explicit limits on the character and extent of Cuban activity should be possible to work out. Mutual restraint of propaganda efforts should be feasible, for instance, and mutual control of subversive groups should be possible.

Cuban assurances that its links with the Soviet Union will not be threatening to the United States are unlikely to be made public, but the tacit mutual understandings which have evolved since 1962 regarding the Soviet military presence in Cuba and U.S. restraint of anti-Castro Cuban exiles can probably be reinforced and made more explicit. The United States can probably not exact in advance a specific commitment from Cuba to reduce the Soviet military presence on the island (though such an arrangement may be feasible in the larger context of U.S.-Soviet negotiations). What can be accomplished, however, is to create conditions in U.S.-Cuban relations which would encourage Russian withdrawals from the island. To the extent that Cuban-American tensions are reduced, the Cuban desire to reduce Russia's presence should increase.

The desire of Cubans on the island and in the United States to be able to exchange visits from time to time is another item on the bilateral agenda. No commitments have yet been made by Havana, but the Cuban authorities understand that one way to reduce Cuban refugee opposition to normalization will be to ease the agonies of divided families by allowing such visits to take place.

Other pending issues range from Cuba's postal debt on the one side and blocked Cuban assets in the United States on the other to U.S. concerns about Cuba's violations of fundamental human rights, particularly in the cases of political prisoners, believed in Washington to number several thousand. Some questions can surely be settled early in the normalization process; Cuba's track record in resolving specific problems in its negotiations with France, Spain, and Switzerland is encouraging in that regard. Other problems—the plight of political prisoners is a painful example—may well seem as far from satisfactory solution three years from now as they do today. What can be said, however, is that the leverage the U.S. government can exert on an issue like this, limited at best, is even less in a situation of mutual hostility than it would be under conditions of some openness in U.S.-Cuban relations.

The Time Is Now

Our government's bargaining strength will not improve if the United States continues stubbornly to prolong the hostile posture symbolized by the continuing embargo. On the contrary, the embargo was for some years a wasting asset, even on its own terms; by now it is undoubtedly a mounting debit. The embargo no longer serves to isolate Cuba; the country being isolated is the United States, whose policy and practice toward Cuba is every day further removed from the realities of the 1970s. Indeed, it is ironic (or worse) that the United States continues to impose its coercive Cuban embargo while bitterly protesting OPEC and particularly Arab oil diplomacy. Our pleas for an end to raw displays of commodity power might be more convincing if the United States ended its own politically motivated sanctions against Cuba.

There are reasons to think that the point of greatest U.S. leverage in its negotiations with Cuba may well be now. Cuba's first five-year plan, covering the period 1976-1980, is currently being drafted; assumptions about the availability of U.S. goods might affect immediate Cuban decisions with operational consequences two or three years from now. Unless the United States acts soon to make it clear that normalized relations are being sought, Cuba may well find itself forced to make commitments which will severely limit American access to a market in which the United States would otherwise have considerable competitive advantage. And this would, in turn, sharply reduce Cuba's incentive to compromise.

Similarly, international economic and political circumstances make this a good time to break the impasse in Cuban-American relations. Having enjoyed the benefits of record high sugar prices and having seen these prices fall back down to about 12 cents a pound in mid-1975, Cuba would undoubtedly value the increased economic security that improved relations with the United States would afford. If the United States drags its feet, however, Cuba will either find itself in a stronger bargaining position in the future (assuming that sugar prices stabilize at about 20 cents a pound, as many experts predict) or else more dependent than ever on the Soviet Union; in neither case will the United States be more likely than it is at present to reach advantageous compromises with Cuba.

A final reason why the United States should act now is the imminence of the Panama issue as a congressional and political focal point. A positive and flexible American posture toward Cuba would clearly reinforce the stance the Administration is taking on the Canal issue. At the same time, importantly, it would defuse criticism of Washington's fruitless policy on the Cuban issue without giving away anything of real consequence prior to detailed negotiation. The Cuban issue would be taken out of the limelight and allowed to percolate on the back burner through the election campaign, while greater public attention could be devoted to the potentially explosive Panama question.

Despite all these reasons to end the embargo, some well-informed Washingtonians feel that the U.S. government may not act soon. The reason most often cited is an alleged White House perception that a positive U.S. gesture would risk adverse domestic political consequences outweighing any national or international gain. The problem is said to be compounded by the relative lack of sustained high-level attention which the Cuban issue can command from top decision-makers beset with accumulating domestic and international problems. The President and the Secretary of State are said to believe that the costs of our long-standing Cuban policy are not demonstrably great and will decline now that the OAS action has taken place. The presumed benefits of normalization are thought to be remote and speculative, while its domestic political costs may seem immediate and concrete, especially for a President bent on winning his first national election. The President is thought to fear that significant numbers of the American electorate would interpret even a partial end to the Cuban embargo as a sign of national weakness.

I hope, and suspect, that this analysis underestimates President Ford's capacity for creative leadership in foreign affairs. An alert President concerned with the national interest and not primarily with partisan political advice will recognize the scope he has for a well-conceived Cuban policy. By now the American people as a whole are ready for U.S.-Cuban rapprochement. 63 per cent of Americans polled by Gallup in October 1974 favored normalization; the percentage may well be higher now after the visit in May of Senator George McGovern and a flock of journalists, including Barbara Walters. According to a State Department analysis, 79 per cent of the leading newspapers which had expressed themselves by June 1975 favored normalization. Senators Kennedy and McGovern among Democratic leaders, and Percy and Javits among Republicans, have proposed a U.S. initiative to end the embargo.

The President need not fear that such a largely symbolic gesture of the Administration's interest in negotiating with Castro's Cuba will be understood as a sign of weakness. On the contrary, an Administration decision to begin the normalization process could very persuasively be presented as an example of President Ford's realism, and of his refreshing willingness to cut unnecessary losses, in contrast to three Presidents before him. The President inherited a number of bad policies; one important measure of the Ford Administration will be its capacity to end anachronistic and unjustified measures.

Indeed, if the Administration does not seize the initiative on Cuba during the six months after San José, it might find itself on the defensive in the electoral campaign, vulnerable to what could be a telling criticism that it has not adjusted to a changing world but rather has prolonged Cold War attitudes which no longer have any place (if they ever did) in hemispheric relations. A Republican Administration which has sought détente with the Soviet Union, promoted negotiation in the Middle East, and wants to travel to Peking in search of better understanding might appear to be hung up over outmoded concepts or hostage to special interest groups if it shied away from talking with Cuba. The political costs of this image could turn out to be much greater than the resentment thought likely to be stirred up among some Cuban immigrants by a conciliatory U.S. government attitude toward Castro, especially if the Cuban community is—as several observers believe—far less monolithic in its opposition to U.S.-Cuban rapprochement than it is usually represented.

But perhaps the whole Cuban issue is simply not worth the time of the highest U.S. government officials, faced with the Indochina debacle, the Korean powder keg, the Middle East conundrum, the crisis of democracy in India, and Communist gains in southern Europe. U.S. government officials working on Latin-American affairs undoubtedly have a hard time getting the President and the Secretary of State to focus for long on the question of normalizing relations with Cuba, a relatively small country which poses no urgent or critical problem for the United States.

Our top officials cannot, of course, afford to spend much time on the Cuban issue, nor on any of a number of other potentially important foreign policy problems from Angola to Zaire. No one individual, not even Henry Kissinger, can be expected to deal with every problem. But the process of foreign policy-making must not be limited by the attention span of the Secretary of State. Kissinger has assembled at State perhaps the ablest group of individuals ever to work together on U.S. policy toward Latin America. These officials seem ready to face the fascinating challenge of protecting U.S. interests on the road to normalization. The time has come for the President and the Secretary of State to give them a chance to do so.

What Should We Do Next?

If and when our highest officials decide that the United States should unambiguously express its interest in negotiating rapprochement with Cuba, how should the Administration proceed?

The natural way to begin undoing the embargo, which hopefully may even have occurred by the time this article appears, would be to lift coercive sanctions affecting third countries, sanctions all the more offensive now that the formerly multilateral character of the embargo has been ended by the OAS vote at San José. The President should determine that it is no longer in the national interest to deny foreign aid to nations which aid or trade with Cuba, or whose ships enter Cuban ports. Restrictions on bunkering in U.S. ports by foreign vessels engaged in trade with Cuba should also be dropped. Constraints against trade with Cuba by subsidiaries of U.S. corporations operating in foreign countries, already relaxed on an exceptional basis in cases involving Argentina and Canada, should now be removed entirely. But these welcome (if overdue) measures to end U.S. conflict with third countries will not be understood—in Havana, in Washington, or anywhere else—as clearly indicating a U.S. government desire to improve bilateral relations with Cuba;

they will only signify that the United States does not wish its Cuba policy to affect relations with other countries. Before direct negotiations to settle outstanding issues in U.S.-Cuban relations begin, Cuba can reasonably expect some evidence of American good will to match its own recent gestures, some indication that the U.S. government hopes that the results of negotiation with Cuba will permit eventual normalization.

Such an expression of official U.S. interest in improved relations with Cuba could come about in any of several ways. The Secretary of State could make a major public pronouncement on Cuba, or the President could do so. Kissinger could even show up in Havana as he did in Peking. A flamboyant display, however, would needlessly rile up domestic critics and might create false expectations of rapidly improved relations. A much more advisable tack would be for the Administration to signal, clearly but unobtrusively, that it seeks to begin serious negotiations with Cuba.

As Castro himself has suggested, our government could easily advance this process by making it legal for U.S. firms to sell food and medicine to Cuba, thereby ending a unilateral and gratuitous sanction imposed despite a specific exemption of these items in the 1964 OAS resolution. Castro has already said Cuba would regard such a gesture as a "positive act"; Cuba would probably respond to it, perhaps by releasing one or more of the U.S. citizens still held in Cuban jails for political crimes. The President might then undertake any or several of a whole spectrum of measures. He might, for instance, suspend the current travel restrictions on U.S. citizens bound for Cuba, restrictions of dubious legality and even less effectiveness, in any case. He could order that Treasury Department asset controls be modified to allow personal remittances and other modest financial transactions to take place. He could enable Cuban journalists from Prensa Latina, the Cuban-sponsored wire service, to work in Washington, presumably in return for a Cuban agreement to allow the major U.S. wire services to reopen their Havana offices. He could make it clear—as contradictory decisions in 1975 do not—that the United States would welcome cultural and athletic exchanges with Cuba.

All these measures—and others of similar scope—should be undertaken by the Ford Administration soon, before the 1976 electoral campaign makes such an initiative a hostage of the vociferous and geographically concentrated Cuban immigrant minority. Though such actions would probably be understood in Havana as an important earnest of the U.S. government's interest in normalization, they would not significantly weaken our government's leverage in detailed negotiations with Cuba on specific, bilateral issues. Cuba's main incentives to compromise—access to the American market for its exports and access to American goods on terms comparable to those on which products from other countries are available—would still be withheld by the United States, pending the outcome of direct negotiations.

A U.S. initiative to break the current impasse would enable this country to move toward normalizing its relations with Cuba without sacrificing any legitimate American interest. It would allow the next 18 months to be used constructively: to expand contacts, to broaden communications channels and patterns, to foster trust (or at least to reduce distrust), to assess more accurately the costs and benefits of normalization, and quietly to begin detailed negotiations. Some of the thorniest problems in U.S.-Cuban relations would probably not be resolved until after next year's Presidential election. Beginning the process now, however, would enable both countries to create some momentum toward settlement rather than needlessly deepening mutual resentment. Seeking peaceful acceptance of America's most recent revolution would be a worthy task for the United States during its bicentennial year.

PANAMA PARALYSIS

by Thomas M. Franck & Edward Weisband

After 10 years of on-again, off-again negotiations, beginning with the Johnson-Robles agreement of September 24, 1965, the United States and Panama have reached the "fish or cut bait" phase in efforts to rewrite the 1903 treaty cutting a 10-mile-wide swath—372 square miles run by the United States "as if sovereign" and "in perpetuity"—across the isthmus. But with agreement at hand, Congress appears to be balking.

Thirty-seven senators cosponsored a resolution that "The government of the United States should maintain and protect its sovereign rights and jurisdiction over the canal and zone, and shculd in no way cede, dilute, forfeit, negotiate, or transfer any of these sovereign rights. . . ."[1] The House of Representatives, on June 26, 1975, voted by 246 to 164 to deny funds to "negotiate the surrender or relinquishment of United States rights in the Panama Canal." With great difficulty this was converted, in October, into a joint Senate-House "sense of Congress" resolution that the negotiators should "protect the vital interests of the United States in the Canal Zone."

Not only have the opponents of the treaty been first out of the starting gate, but they have entered an impressive and determined string of seasoned contenders. Congresswoman Leonor Sullivan, for example, chairs the House of Representatives' Committee on Merchant Marine and Fisheries which must report out the essential enabling legislation. Sullivan has made it clear that she will sit "forever" on any such bill. "I've told them again and again," she says, referring to the State Department, "the House will never enact a law to give away the zone. . . . If the 1903 Hay-Bunau-Varilla Treaty isn't honored, no treaty is worth anything. They'll be wanting to renegotiate the Louisiana Purchase next." Among other potential opponents with key committee posts are Senators Sparkman, Eastland, Symington, and McClellan.

At least one opponent of a new treaty, Senator Barry Goldwater, has recognized that "getting their hopes up and then getting it killed is bound to cause trouble with Panama." Ambassador Ellsworth Bunker, the chief U.S. negotiator with Panama, agrees. If the treaty is rejected, he says, "we would likely find ourselves engaged in hostilities with an otherwise friendly country, a conflict that, in my view, the American people would not long accept."

Despite such warnings, the ritual preliminaries for a deadly U.S.-Panama game of "chicken" are already in place. President Omar Torrijos has recently declared that if his country's volatile students, radicals, and nationalists use violence against the zone—as they did in 1959 and 1964—"we will have two alternatives, to smash it or to lead it, and I'm not going to smash it." A substantial number of members of Congress, however, see this as a bluff. Some agree with Congressman Larry McDonald, that "these threats, if one could call them that, are coming from U.S. officials, not from any organizations in Panama. Apparently, some of our public officials will stoop to anything in their efforts to weaken the United States. As for Mr. Bunker, someone should remind him that he represents the United States of America and that his proper posture, particularly when confronting a country ruled by a Marxist-oriented military strongman, is proudly erect, not cringing on his belly."

In a small foretaste of confrontation, on September 23, 800 Panamanian students hurled Molotov cocktails and rocks at the U.S. embassy in Panama City. They were reacting to Secretary of State Kissinger's reported remark at a southern governors' con-

[1] *U.S. Senate Resolution 301, 93rd Congress, 2nd Session, March 29, 1974.*

ference that the United States must retain the right to defend the canal "unilaterally" and "indefinitely" (or, according to a later version, "for a long time"). This represents the continuing ambivalence of the administration, badgered by congressional hawks and fearing the growth of the Reagan-led right wing in a presidential election year.

The Two Options

Despite these ambiguities, there are now only two directions for the U.S.-Panamanian relationship to go. One leads toward a U.S. withdrawal—phased, to be sure, over years—from its three isthmian roles: as guardian of the Canal Zone, as commandant of the military bases and training schools, and as operator of the canal itself. This is the *de-escalation* option.

The other direction points toward a firm, unrelenting reassertion of Washington's intention to retain long-range control over all three U.S. roles in Panama. The exercise of this *escalation* option would have to be accompanied by the dispatch of enough additional military forces to deal decisively with any local rioting and attempts at sabotage. It might also involve a series of substantial carrots, such as the return of some "spare" lands and construction of a high-level bridge and a third-lock system, as well as other public works to help divert Panamanians from political to economic concerns.

In practice, there are no other alternatives. That is the hard fact from which President Ford tends to shrink. And the choice of alternatives can no longer be postponed or temporized away. Some authorities have called for the canal's "internationalization." This third option, however, is no longer viable. It has been rejected by the Panamanians, as has a related proposal to place the waterway under Latin-American, regional, or OAS (Organization of American States) control. Under pressure of Panamanian "whirlwind diplomacy" around their capitals, Latin-American states (a few, like Brazil, with less enthusiasm than meets the eye) have fallen into step behind Panamanian claims to sole control. The Security Council, too, has demonstrated, during its March 1973 meetings in Panama, that there would be no significant support in the United Nations for any solution other than a bilaterally negotiated transfer from the United States to Panama. By the unprecedented step of re-electing Panama to the Security Council as representative of their region only two years after the expiration of its previous term, the Latin Americans have again given Panama the means to use this world forum to press for an unqualified acknowledgment of their sole sovereignty over the zone. Finally, the February 7, 1974 Kissinger-Tack Agreement on Principles set its sights on a bilateral solution in which, at a time to be agreed, "Panama will assume total responsibility for the operation of the canal. . . ." It is on this basis that the recent talks have proceeded between Foreign Minister Tack and Bunker. They have created a firm expectation that a decision will be made soon and in a bilateral framework.

A Bad Year

Ideally, 1976 is not a felicitous choice for the year of Panama. The U.S. withdrawal from Vietnam has rendered this country sore and preoccupied with its loss of credibility in the world. It has also left the State Department, and Kissinger in particular, with less clout to exert in Congress on behalf of a Panama treaty. Even among the Washington foreign policy establishment and the White House, in the words of one U.S. negotiator, "Panama is always sixteenth on any list of the 15 top issues." As a presidential election year, 1976 leaves the president and members of Congress particularly vulnerable to political passions. And passion, in this instance, is mainly the prerogative of those who oppose "giving away the canal." Most of these are southern Democrats and midwestern and southwestern Republicans who are the mainstay of President Ford's increasingly vulnerable right wing. Those Americans who see the need for satisfying what they recognize as a natural Panamanian desire for territorial integrity and decolonialization are, for the most part, liberal Democrats who are unlikely to vote for Ford no matter what his policy on Panama. Nor are they imbued with the kind of zealousness over this cause that manifests itself in public rallies and congressmen's mailboxes. Robert Dockery, staff counsel of the Senate Foreign Relations committee, has observed that "no year ever seems to be the year for Panama."

It appears that those within the Ford Administration who have favored postponing a final settlement until after the 1976 elections are getting their way. Six months of 1975 were frittered away by infighting between the State Department and the Department of Defense. When negotiations were resumed in September, Bunker returned to Panama with instructions which were bound to create another stand-off. The most hopeful timetable, now, does not provide for action on a treaty by Congress before November 1976. It is less clear that Panama's volatile students can be restrained that long unless there are good prospects for a highly favorable treaty.

The protracted negotiations have revealed a pattern for settlement which can protect essential U.S. interests while satisfying all but the most radical minority of Panamanians. Such a treaty, over a short transitional period, would phase out the quasi-sovereign status enjoyed by the United States in the zone, together with its incidents, such as commercial, judicial, and police services. The United States would yield title to the bulk, i.e., more than half, of zonal territory. A canal authority, probably an incorporated agency of the U.S. government but with increasing Panamanian participation, would run the canal for a fixed period, terminating around the end of the century, after which it would relinquish operating rights and titles to Panama. While they endure, these operating rights and titles would be immunized by treaty—to the extent law can protect against politics—from premature Panamanian abrogation. The authority's senior officials would be subject only to limited Panamanian jurisdiction.

By separate but related treaty, there would continue to be U.S. bases in Panama, perhaps half a dozen in number, but fewer than at present, established and operated under lease and status-of-forces agreements very similar to other U.S. overseas base arrangements. This base agreement would run for a decade or slightly more beyond the end of the agreement governing U.S. operation of the canal itself. The United States and Panama would jointly undertake the defense of the canal. The Latin-American counter-insurgency training program in Panama would be phased out, implicitly if not explicitly. Tolls would be allowed to rise to give Panama annual revenues in the $50 million-plus range. While these are not all terms to which the parties have already agreed, a final treaty, if there is one, will probably not depart much from these basics.

A treaty cannot, however, come into effect until after a national plebiscite in Panama and until the U.S. Senate has given its "advice and consent" by two-thirds majority. In addition, since U.S. property is to be disposed of, the participation of the House of Representatives is probably necessary under Article II, Section 2 of the Constitution.[2] That these bodies will go along is far from a foregone conclusion. Except in a major crisis, congressional foreign policy tends to be made not by the "silent majority" but by small groups of congressmen representing committed minorities of Americans with deeply held convictions and intense loyalties to one side of an interest conflict. In the case of the Panama Canal, there is keen articulation by opponents of "surrender" which is not matched by the majority either of members or of citizens.

[2] *See* Disposal by Treaty of United States Property Rights in Panama, *Congressional Research Service, Library of Congress.*

The Panama Lobby

The Panama lobby in Congress and in the nation, which opposes such a treaty, consists of three interest groups and one amorphous but potent ideological constituency. Best organized among these are the labor groups like the Canal Zone Central Labor Union and Metal Trades Council (affiliated with the AFL-CIO), representing the preponderance of U.S. employees of the Canal Company and zone government, and the Panama Canal Pilots Association, which consists of approximately 200 U.S. and three Panamanian citizens. It is a much-quoted shibboleth on Capitol Hill that "the canal pilots won't work for the Panamanians." As for the U.S. employees of the zone government and Canal Company, Panama-ization presents them with the threat, at best, of loss of privileges and, at worst, with diminution of career prospects.

Second are transnational corporate interests. AIMS, the American Institute of Merchant Shipping, has a primary stake in keeping tolls low and the canal open, which is the status quo. U.S. corporate investors in the zone—such as ITT, which owns Central American Cables and Radio, Inc., as well as Transoceanic Communications, the zone-based communications system—are beginning to register their unease at the prospect of coming under direct Panamanian jurisdiction, although they are keeping a low profile.

The third organized interest group is the U.S. military establishment. At its periphery, this includes the Veterans of Foreign Wars. The key factor, however, is the Department of Defense—in particular the Department of the Army, which has traditionally had the main role in running the zone—and the Joint Chiefs of Staff. It has always been clear that Congress would never approve any treaty with Panama over the opposition of Defense and the Joint Chiefs of Staff and this, throughout the negotiations, has given them a sort of veto. This was held carefully in reserve until late spring, then used very effectively.

That story of last summer's interdepartmental guerrilla warfare has been widely chronicled by the media, in large part because Defense strategy, masterminded by Army Secretary—and more recently Ford Presidential Campaign Manager—Howard Calloway, called for it to be played that way. While Bunker and Assistant Secretary William D. Rogers kept an agonized public silence in accordance with interdepartmental etiquette and a prior agreement, Defense emissaries and "spokesmen" began to appear everywhere—in *Washington Post* interviews and at National Security Council and congressional offices—expressing their concern that the treaty, as it was shaping up, would not protect the national defense interest. They fretted that State was willing to settle for a 25-year tenure while the Army needed 50 years plus a strong renewal option and that State was willing to concede land and water areas of the zone that the Army needed to defend and sustain itself. This was not the view of all, but only of some of the hawks in Defense who saw the issue in terms of presidential primaries.

The conflict over these issues was resolved in a series of National Security Council meetings in July and August, culminating in a new set of instructions personally approved by President Ford. The result, in the unanimous opinion of the scribes, was a famous victory for the State Department.[3]

On September 4, in a news event staged with the loving care of a Canossa, Assistant Secretary Rogers flew down to Panama with the chairman of the Joint Chiefs of Staff, General George S. Brown, and Deputy Secretary of Defense William P. Clements, Jr.,

[3] *For one such account see Stephen S. Rosenfeld, "The Panama Negotiations—A Close-Run Thing,"* Foreign Affairs, *October 1975, pp. 10-11. Our analysis of these events, however, varies from that of the Rosenfeld article, which implies that Defense did not want a treaty with Panama and that the president's new instructions to Bunker in August constituted a victory for the State Department. We disagree with both of these assertions.*

for a carefully orchestrated one-day meeting with Torrijos. This culminated in a statement by Brown at Panama City airport: "I assured General Torrijos that the Joint Chiefs and the Department of Defense were committed to working out a new treaty and that we fully support Ambassador Bunker's efforts."

When Bunker returned to the talks in September, the Panamanians had high hopes, fanned by erroneous press reports, of that State Department victory. But the victory was really a compromise. And Bunker's cautious opening gambit—offering a 50-year base agreement with option to renew—seemed a terrible letdown. Since then, however, State has signaled that this is far from being its final offer and has urged the Panamanians to come back with an offer of their own.

Besides the specific interest groups there is a larger, amorphous ideological constituency opposed to the treaty. It is composed mainly of unorganized U.S. voters whose interest in the canal is primarily symbolic and who see its surrender as yet another retreat from superpower commitment. Much of this opposition comes from the South and Southwest, is confined to a certain generation, reflects the mystique of Teddy Roosevelt, and was learned in school by persons now in their forties and fifties who used the "imperial America" class of textbooks. The building of the canal, to some people, was the moon-walk of the 1910s. The staffs of members of Congress opposed to concessions insist that no subject engenders a more continuously heavy stream of mail overwhelmingly opposed to surrendering any of the legacy of McKinley and Roosevelt.

In addition to these interest groups lined up against the treaty, there is the ever present Kissinger Factor and the divinely ordained War Among the Branches. A prime source of congressional opposition to the direction of the current negotiations stems from the usual resentment felt by members at being excluded from the State and Defense Departments' bargaining with a foreign power. In 1967, after an earlier set of negotiations, it was bitterly pointed out that the draft treaties were not communicated to congressmen, while they were circulating freely on the streets of Panama City. In 1974 and 1975, similarly, U.S. negotiators—with the exception of the State-Defense imbroglio described above—have strictly adhered to their commitment to secrecy while the Panamanians have been less inhibited. As a result, even liberal members of Congress and pro-de-escalation staffers of congressional committees concerned with foreign relations complain that "Bunker has made no effort to keep us informed. When he does come up here, we arrange to hear him in secret session but he still tells us nothing." Most of what Congress knew about the negotiations—some of it inaccurate—was learned from published versions of interviews given by Foreign Minister Tack or official leaks in the Panamanian press. On September 24, Ambassador Gonzalez-Revilla, the deputy Panamanian negotiator, in an "off-the-record" discussion at the Council on Foreign Relations (which promptly found its way into *Washington Post* and *New York Times* news stories), detailed what had and what had not been agreed to date. Inevitably, these leaks put the direction of talks in a light most favorable to Panama, thereby further arousing the concern of Congress. This is accentuated by a notable and as yet inchoate coalition of anti-Kissinger and anti-secret diplomacy attitudes that unites the conservative and liberal wings of both Houses.

The antitreaty forces focus on the importance of the canal (1) to American trade and (2) to American defense. They argue that these interests are too important to be entrusted to the stewardship of an unstable foreign government. Protreaty advocates can rebut these assertions of the canal's importance and of the vulnerability of American interests. But ultimately, if the argument is to be won by the protreaty forces, it will have to be shifted to other, higher ground of their own choosing.

Trade

The trade issue raised by those who opposed de-escalation relies in part on an assertion that canal tolls will skyrocket if the United States does not retain firm control over the waterway's operations. One reply to this is that even with the United States still operating the canal, tolls—which remained virtually constant until last year despite the rise in almost all costs since the canal opened in 1914—will have to climb very substantially to permit reasonable upkeep and modernization as well as the inevitable increase in fixed annuities to Panama. The 20 per cent increase in tolls granted last year is only a beginning, since income still barely covers operations and maintenance and does not provide for improvements.

The proposed treaty does not envisage Panama supplanting the new Canal Company as toll-collector for approximately 25 years. But even if the power to fix charges were to revert to Panama tomorrow, the elasticity of tolls would still be limited. The real inhibitor of a toll increase is not U.S. control but the economics of the alternate routes, or the canal's "traffic sensitivity." In the case of United States intercoastal traffic as well as in the case of exports and imports beginning or terminating at either coast, the most obvious and commonly used alternative is transshipment across its own territory. For other cargo, the route around Cape Horn offers an option which becomes attractive either when a ship exceeds a certain tonnage or after tolls have increased above a threshold. Although the traffic sensitivity to toll increases varies from commodity to commodity, a recent expert study shows that when tolls are increased beyond 150 per cent, "the revenue impact of the higher toll rate is more than offset by the decline in traffic volume." For bananas, total predicted toll revenues decline after the charges are increased by only 25 per cent. For sugar, iron ore, scrap metal, coal, and crude petroleum, the anticipated revenue shrinkage point is reached when tolls increase beyond 50 per cent. For seven other commodities that point is 100 per cent and for 10 more it is 150 per cent, or possibly higher.[4]

The Maritime Administration of the Department of Commerce points out that a 200 per cent increase in canal tolls would raise prices of products shipped via the canal by less than 5 per cent. A 75 per cent increase would cause a 1.8 per cent rise in commodity price, assuming demand remained constant.[5]

Rates are only one aspect of U.S. concern over the canal's availability for commercial shipping. Still, it is no longer the commercial lifeline—at least not for the United States—that it once was. It remains important, but its importance to other countries is far greater and is increasing. Three-quarters of Nicaraguan ocean cargo goes through the canal compared to about 17 per cent of U.S. seaborne commerce, putting America tenth in order of dependence on the route. In comparative terms, the canal is far more important to at least nine Latin-American states.[6] It is almost as important to Japan, South Vietnam, Taiwan, Korea, Mexico, and New Zealand as it is to the United States and it is of considerable, if smaller,

[4] *It has been pointed out that, at the 1972 level of tolls, a dry-bulk carrier of 12,500 dwt. could break even by sailing about 1,000 extra miles in order to avoid the canal tolls, but a 37,500 dwt. carrier could afford to travel an additional 1,600 miles and a 67,500 dwt. carrier, 3,200 miles. See J. E. Howell and Ezra Solomon,* The Economic Value of the Panama Canal, *prepared for the Panama Canal Company (Palo Alto, Calif.: International Research Associates, 1973), pp. 20-22, 23.*

[5] *U.S. Department of Commerce, Maritime Administration,* The Panama Canal in U.S. Foreign Trade: Impact of a Toll Increase and Facility Closure, *May 15, 1974, pp. 7-9.*

[6] *Ibid. Comparative percentages of cargo taken through the canal are as follows: Chile (34.3 per cent), Colombia (32.5 per cent), Costa Rica (27.2 per cent), Ecuador (51.4 per cent), El Salvador (66.4 per cent), Guatemala (30.9 per cent), Nicaragua (76.8 per cent), Panama (29.4 per cent), and Peru (41.3 per cent). The U.S. percentage is 16.8.*

importance to the Philippines, Canada, and a number of other Latin-American countries.[7] Further, since foreign trade constitutes only 10 per cent of U.S. gross national product (GNP), its vulnerability is even further diminished in comparison to Latin-American, Western European, and Asian states that must "trade or perish." Less than 1 per cent of our GNP passes through the canal.[8] The U.S. intercoastal trade, dominant in the canal's early days, now accounts for only 2.9 per cent of all cargo shipped through the canal.

This analysis suggests that collective bargaining with Panama by all canal users might be at least as effective as U.S. control in keeping the canal open, neutral, and economically viable. Certainly it is not only, or even primarily, the United States which ought to be concerned about toll stabilization and other terms of use. Panama, after all, needs the canal even more than its users. Its leaders have long referred to it as "our sole natural resource." Even if speculative mineral exploiting schemes pan out, the canal will remain central to Panama's economy for decades. And with Panama setting the tolls, the Latin-American, Japanese, and Western European user states would have a common interest with the United States in exerting leverage to keep tolls down rather than, as at present, being united with Panama in opposition to U.S. "colonialism."

Also, as the comparative dependence of the U.S. economy on the canal declines, so does the number of cargo vessels physically able to pass through it. Already, not only oil supertankers but many cargo ships carrying other bulk or containerized commodities are too large. The advantage of the larger ships is that their speed is such as to cut the costs of the longer voyages on alternate routes. Thus, a considerable portion of the coal now shipped from the eastern United States to Japan travels in huge cargo ships via the Cape of Good Hope route at prices which are competitive per ton with the same load sent via Panama.

Still, the canal is certainly important to the U.S. economy, and if it were closed to shipping, as compared to merely being subject to a moderate rise in tolls, there would be a pronounced negative impact on the economy. The coal of West Virginia, the grain of the Middle West, the cotton and textiles of the Southeast, and the oil for the northeastern states remain significant users of the waterway. But closure of the canal to U.S. ships or cargo, for whatever reason, is conceivable only if Panama were prepared to go to war with Washington.

How Strategic A Value?

Is the canal a cornerstone of hemispheric defense strategy? This important issue breaks down into two others: How important is the canal itself to U.S. global naval strategy? How crucial is the Southern Command's (CINCSOUTH) headquarters base to U.S. strategic interests in Latin America?

The strategic value of the canal to the United States has rapidly diminished in recent years. The military itself assumes that in the event of a future war, the use of the canal would be denied the United States either by air attack or by sabotage. The present locks, dams, and power systems, a government study has found, "make the present canal a vulnerable target. In certain situations, the canal could be closed for two years."[9] This was, for a time, the principal argument in favor of building a new sea-level canal, which would be far more resistant to bombing or sabotage. That project, however, is now thought to be so fraught with ecological dangers and burdened with

[7] *Ibid.*

[8] *1973 figures based on statistics in statement of General David S. Parker, governor of the Panama Canal Zone and president of the Canal Company, in U.S. House of Representatives, Committee on Merchant Marine and Fisheries, 93rd Congress, 1st Session,* Hearings on the Panama Canal, *series no. 93-19, July 17, 1973, p. 3.*

[9] *Report of the Atlantic-Pacific Interoceanic Canal Study Commission, December 1, 1970 (Washington, D.C.: Government Printing Office, 1971), p. II-6.*

astronomical costs as to be excluded by both Washington and Panama.

U.S. bidexterity has also diminished the waterway's strategic coin. While the present canal was initially favored by Roosevelt because the Spanish-American War had demonstrated the need for naval mobility, the emergence since the start of World War II of virtually separate U.S. navies on each ocean has downgraded this consideration.[10] This is further evident from the construction of more than 24 U.S. aircraft carriers that cannot traverse it. During the Vietnam war the carriers *Enterprise, Independence, Boxer,* and *Annapolis* were deployed from the east coast but could not go via the isthmus. Nuclear submarines, too, cannot run the canal except by surfacing.

On the other hand, the Vietnam war did demonstrate the residual strategic importance of the canal, if not in moving naval vessels, then in transporting supplies. Ships that take the canal route rather than circumnavigating Cape Horn can save 8,000 miles. Between 1965 and 1970 (the years of maximum use), the number of U.S. warship transits rose from 284 to 1,068 before again declining. It has been estimated that closure of the Panama Canal "would approximately double the requirements for ships to support operations in the Pacific."[11] Nevertheless, the United States has increasingly switched to cross-continental land transport to bring strategic goods to the Pacific coast. The land transport option could seriously strain existing rail and road facilities in a large-scale emergency. On the other hand, if up to $10 billion were saved by not having to modernize the existing canal, or build a new one, some of this money could be spent on needed improvements in domestic public transportation. More immediately, the resupply of U.S. forces in Korea and Japan is logistically better accomplished through the ports of Seattle and San Francisco.

The Defense Department is concerned not only with the canal as a logistic resource, but with many other defense facilities—$760 million worth—not directly related to the canal operation: airfields, dry docks, a communications and command center, and a jungle warfare school. But CINCSOUTH facilities are barely sufficient to defend the canal against Panamanians, let alone engage in hemispheric missions. The approximately 6,500 troops, including noncombat support forces, currently deployed in the canal area are insufficient to play a major role in a Central American military operation. They would certainly be unable to do so if they were simultaneously defending the whole zone against angry Panamanians. Ultimately, too, the only way for the United States to defend the canal against agitators is alongside the Panamanian troops.

Yet even the most avid congressional advocates of no surrender shy away from recommending large-scale military escalation—estimated at 50,000 to 100,000 U.S. troops—that would be required to make the Canal Zone riot-, sabotage-, and guerrilla-proof.

Any realistic appraisal of U.S. forces likely to be stationed in Panama must conclude that these forces can only be deployed as a tripwire, not as a Maginot line. A tripwire strategy involves the commitment of just enough forces, over just enough real estate, to ensure that a potential aggressor cannot achieve his objective (capturing the canal) without confronting the United States. A few thousand troops located in base areas—perhaps one at each end and one toward the middle of the canal—would be sufficient for that limited purpose. The aggressor could overrun the bases, but he would then have to deal with Washington's virtually unlimited retaliatory capability. Bases sufficient for this purpose are an integral part of the agreements now being negotiated with Panama.

[10] *"The Navy has always operated on the assumption that in a major war the Panama Canal would be denied them, and, in effect, the United States today possesses a two-ocean Navy"* [Panama: Canal Issues and Treaty Talks *(Washington, D.C.: Center for Strategic Studies, Georgetown University, 1967), p. 51*].

[11] *Report of the Atlantic-Pacific Interoceanic Canal Study Commission, op. cit., p. II-5.*

None of this is to deny the legal and practical validity of the argument made by critics of de-escalation that base lease agreements are subject to premature unilateral termination by the host country and that the effective use of leased bases can be restricted in specific crises (as happened, for example, when the Thai government objected to the use of U Tapao base during the rescue of the *Mayaguez*). Yet, it should also be recognized that, militarily, the strength or vulnerability of U.S. bases in Panama will first and always depend on the number and types of forces deployed and second on the acquiescence of the local population. And if our objective is to provide residual U.S. forces and reinforcements with a legal status that is defensible—morally, if possible, but with force, if necessary—against the possibility of reneging by Panama, then a better stand can surely be made on a clear, definitive, and openly arrived at 1976 base agreement that reconciles minimal U.S. and Panamanian strategic interests than on a 1903 treaty negotiated on Panama's behalf by a dubiously accredited Frenchman with a $40 million personal stake in its outcome, the meaning of which has been bitterly contested since 1904.

The Basic Issue

Proponents and opponents of the de-escalation option each essentially perceive the Panama Canal Zone quite differently. The pro-status quo forces see the zone as a continental parcel of U.S. territory, acquired in perpetuity like Hawaii or Puerto Rico, encumbered only by the obligation to return it to Panama in the unlikely event that the United States decides to give it away to anyone. But this is just a fancy way of saying the zone is a colony. It is run by the U.S. Army, has no elected representation in Washington and no legislature in the zone itself, and is not likely to acquire any. Why should we now doubt the necessity of decolonizing the zone? The British, French, Dutch, Belgian, Spanish, and, most recently, Portuguese empires have all been wound up—as was our own Philippine presence. Does the United States want to be perceived as the world's last colonial power, stubbornly clinging to an enclave which actually cuts an independent country in half and leaves it bereft of a single deep-water port of its own?

In his efforts to save the zone for the United States, Congressman Dan Flood has recently introduced legislation to give its U.S. inhabitants an elected delegate in Congress. But unlike Puerto Rico, which is similarly served, the zone is mostly inhabited by a small group of stateside government employees and military personnel who have been posted to the Panama Canal to do a job. They are not by any stretch of the imagination the stuff of which indigenous commonwealths are made.

The presence of U.S. Canal Company employees, support service operators, and 6,500 troops with an equal number of dependents in the Canal Zone—America's *pieds noirs,* living at a suburban stateside standard of living—creates friction in a Panamanian economy "just down the block" in which the per capita income is about $700. At the other end of the pay scale, U.S. minimum wage laws apply to local employees, thereby creating a different kind of distortion and tension. An unskilled Panamanian laborer in the U.S. zone must now be paid at a rate equal to that earned in Panama by a fully trained schoolteacher.

Against this may be set two facts. First, the level of U.S. aid to Panama has been the highest, per capita, of any country in the world and disbursements amounted to $227 million in 1972. More significantly, since 1936, successive U.S. presidents, often against the recommendations of their defense and commerce advisers, have sought to ameliorate and, most recently, to terminate the colonial relationship. The Hull-Alfaro agreement of 1939 and President Eisenhower's concessions in the 1955 Chapin-Fabrega agreement made some significant concessions to Panamanian sensitivity.

These were not, however, directed to the fundamental fact of a U.S. colony cutting Panama in half, focusing instead on the right of the army to intervene outside the zone in Panama, on the size of the annuity, and on the Canal Company's purchasing and commercial licensing policies: changes that were essentially cosmetic. By 1959, the anticolonial agitation to be found in any Third World area had begun in Panama. In 1964, students clashed with U.S. forces in the zone over efforts to fly the Panamanian flag alongside The Stars and Stripes. Panama called an emergency session of the OAS under the Rio Pact, alleging an "unprovoked armed attack."

Through the efforts of the OAS Peace Committee, diplomatic relations and negotiations were resumed on April 3, 1964. In a landmark concession, President Johnson, on December 18, 1964, instructed the U.S. negotiators to seek an entirely new agreement with Panama that would terminate the 1903 treaty and would "recognize the sovereignty of Panama" while seeking to retain, for a fixed period, U.S. rights to operate and protect the canal and to administer those areas essential to that limited purpose.

In the decade following President Johnson's recognition that there was a colonial regime, that it was a relic of an earlier era, and that it ought to be ended, there have been painstaking negotiations—and even more painful *lapses* in negotiations—in an effort to enunciate the elusive formula that would give the United States narrow, functional rights for a transitional period while returning to Panama the attributes and, increasingly, the functions of sovereignty. These efforts have now climaxed in the Bunker-Tack round of talks.

Whether one regards the purpose and direction of these talks benevolently depends, ultimately, on how one would prefer the United States to act in, and be perceived by, the world. It is this which, for more than a decade, has been the fundamental issue. And it is on this that protreaty advocates must now take their stand if a mutually acceptable treaty is to be negotiated and ratified by Congress within 24 months—the limit, in the opinion of most observers, for avoiding a bruising confrontation.

In such a confrontation, the United States could only lose—even if it won over Panama. It would appear to the whole world as yet another contest between justified nationalism and imperial America. No doubt the United States has important interests in the canal. But politics, the art of the possible, has demonstrated to the post-World War II world that essential interests can be protected without—often, nowadays, *only* without—recourse to colonialism. Real U.S. self-interest demands not that we teach Panama to mind the United States—they already know from decades of big-stick interventionism which is the stronger republic—but that we expand the underexploited but potentially large areas of interdependence.

Perhaps most important to the strategy of those who will work to enlist Congress and public opinion on the side of the deescalation option is to move the debate away from the important but inconclusive concern with shipping costs, toll elasticity, and defense logistics toward this more basic issue. In the words of one senior Army Department negotiator, "For those of us who really care about the Army, My Lai was an awful blow. We know what that's done to our reputation. The last thing in the world we want now is to be ordered to start shooting into a crowd of Panamanians." Ultimately, what is at stake in the Panama debate is America's global role and image.

ATOMS FOR BRAZIL, DANGERS FOR ALL

by Norman Gall

> The weight of Brazil in world affairs increases every day. In a world full of disturbances and contradictions, the conduct of your country, Senhor Minister, appears as a factor of stability and equilibrium.—*Toast by the West German foreign minister on the eve of the signing of the Brazil-German nuclear sales agreement, June 1975.*

The Deal

The 1975 nuclear deal between Brazil and West Germany is momentous in several ways. It is a major step toward diplomatic independence by two steadfast postwar allies of the United States in response to the upheavals in the world energy economy in the mid-1970s. It calls for the largest transfer ever made of nuclear technology to a developing country. This complex umbrella agreement threatens to establish a new kind of commercial rivalry for international sales of power reactors that could accelerate nuclear weapons proliferation in the final decades of this century. If fully implemented over the next 15 years, it would give the German reactor industry desperately needed export sales and fuel supplies. It also would meet Brazil's projected demand for atomic energy through 1990 and provide much of the technological base for Brazil to make nuclear weapons if she wished. The deal thus would satisfy the long-standing ambitions of both countries for greater nuclear "self-sufficiency" and would contribute toward realization of Brazil's dream of becoming a major power.

The Brazil-German agreement was negotiated in the months following the Indian nuclear explosion of May 1974. That event had a special psychological impact among developing countries, particularly Brazil and Argentina, the rival "near-nuclear" neighbors which both refused to sign the 1968 Treaty on Non-Proliferation of Nuclear Weapons (NPT). A *New York Times* editorial headlined "Nuclear Madness" spearheaded U.S. reaction to the deal. It called the agreement a "reckless move that could set off a nuclear arms race in Latin America, trigger the nuclear arming of a half-dozen nations elsewhere and endanger the security of the United States and the world as a whole."[1] The official Soviet reaction was more cautious in expressing concern for nuclear proliferation, reflecting Moscow's perennial suspicion of Germany's intentions in the nuclear field while avoiding language that might disrupt her own growing nuclear trade with Bonn. More than any other event in the development of commercial nuclear power, the Brazil-German deal has led to intense questioning of the safety and viability of the international industry as presently organized. Some of the more important issues were raised in a speech by Senator Abraham Ribicoff a few days after the accord became public knowledge:

> Hard economic times and the high price of oil have combined to establish a desperate need to sell and a desperate need to buy nuclear power reactors. Nothing less than balanced international payments and energy self-sufficiency are at stake. The resulting cutthroat nuclear competition is leading to the spread of plutonium reprocessing and uranium enrichment facilities. The capability to produce nuclear explosives is spreading "like a plague" in the words of the Inspector General of the International Atomic Energy Agency, who is responsible for detecting the diversion of peaceful nuclear materials to weapons development. . . . In truth, the United States must assume a major share

[1] The New York Times, *June 13, 1975, p. 36.*

of the responsibility for the present nuclear proliferation problem. We pioneered the civilian nuclear power technology, made it available to other nations through our atoms for peace program, and still clearly dominate the worldwide nuclear power industry. Closer attention should have been given to safeguards over the years, particularly to safeguards conditions on the re-export of U.S. nuclear technology by nations like France and West Germany.[2]

Giant Reactors

The centerpiece of the deal is the sale to Brazil of between two to eight giant reactors, together worth from $2 billion to $8 billion, that would accelerate her nuclear energy program toward the goals of 10,000 megawatts of electricity generating capacity by 1990 and of producing 41 per cent of her total energy supply by 2010.

The basic design of the power plants to be built by the West German consortium Kraftwerk Union (KWU) was developed by Siemens—senior partner in KWU and Germany's largest producer of electrical equipment—under license from Westinghouse, the world's largest reactor manufacturer. Westinghouse suspended these licensing arrangements in 1970, after KWU was formed to compete with Westinghouse in the international market.

The agreement, signed in Bonn on June 27, 1975, provides for creation of several mixed companies for joint Brazil-German participation in all phases of the nuclear energy industry, from prospecting for uranium ore in Brazil to the construction of reactors and the manufacture of components. The deal also calls for intensive training of Brazilian professionals in nuclear technology and heavy participation by Brazilian industry, which would enable Brazil eventually to become an exporter of nuclear fuels and equipment. The deal would generate contracts for some 300 German firms and "now assures for the first time the stability" of 13,000 jobs in KWU's own offices and factories. A leading German weekly observed that "the federal government already had invested DM 15 billion ($5 billion) in nuclear energy research out of tax moneys—of which at least half was for basic research—and now this was finally to pay off."[3]

To obtain these benefits for West Germany, Bonn has assumed the entire financial risk for the first two plants through a consortium of five big banks lending $1 billion at concessionary interest rates. Half the debt will be financed at 7.25 per cent by the Kreditanstalt für Wiederaufbau, a development bank formed to distribute Marshall Plan aid. The Kreditanstalt will draw one-third of its contribution at 3 per cent interest from a special revolving fund left over from the Marshall Plan used to finance German exports.

The Dangers of the Deal

Bonn's commitment to provide Brazil with a uranium enrichment plant and a facility for reprocessing spent fuel, from which plutonium could then be extracted, raises a major political issue. These plants could be used, alternatively, for the preparation and recycling of reactor fuels, or for the production of nuclear weapons.

In response to widespread criticism of the deal's dangers, West Germany obtained Brazil's reluctant agreement to a framework for international inspection that goes far beyond the safeguards required by the International Atomic Energy Agency (IAEA) to detect any diversion of nuclear equipment or materials for weapons production. These safeguards would cover not only the life of

[2] *U.S., Congress, Senate,* Congressional Record, *94th Cong., 1st sess., June 3, 1975, p. S9323. The first general disclosure of the deal came a few days earlier in Robert Gillette, "Nuclear Proliferation: India, Germany May Accelerate Process,"* Science, *May 30, 1975. Also see Lewis H. Diuguid, "Brazil Nuclear Deal Raises U.S. Concern,"* Washington Post, *June 1, 1975, p. 1.*

[3] *Heinz Michaels, "Querschüsse aus den USA,"* Die Zeit, *June 20, 1975. Also see "Atomwirtschaft: 12,000,000 Mark für Deutschland,"* Wirtschaftswoche, *June 27, 1975, p. 13.*

the agreement but also the useful life of all installations built under it and any application of technical know-how acquired from the Germans to any other nuclear facilities built in Brazil.

These new "know-how" safeguards, to be applied for the first time in the Brazil-German deal, apparently now are becoming standardized in international sales of nuclear technology as a result of an agreement reached, at U.S. initiative, by the principal supplier nations, known as the "Secret Seven,"[4] at a series of secret meetings in London throughout 1975.

However, nobody seems to know how these technology safeguards will be implemented after enrichment and reprocessing plants with weapons-making potential are delivered to countries such as Brazil, whose military regime for the past decade has had a programmatic commitment to carrying out "peaceful" nuclear explosions. Since there is no intrinsic distinction between a "peaceful" and a military nuclear device, the spread of these plants throughout the world could create a series of de facto situations clearly beyond the control of the international inspection machinery. This machinery is operated by the underfinanced and understaffed IAEA, which is empowered only to report violations to the U.N. Security Council and has no enforcement mandate.

The text of the Brazil-German accord makes it contingent upon a safeguards agreement with the IAEA, "assuring that these nuclear materials, equipment, and installations, as well as the special fertile and fissionable materials produced in them, processed or used, and the respective technological information, are not used for nuclear weapons or other nuclear explosives." However, the semiofficial commentary published with the text in the Brazilian press said: "For Brazil, this does not represent a commitment to forgo nuclear devices in the future. . . . One can presume that this does not rule out the possibility of Brazil developing her own technology based on knowledge acquired by Brazilian technicians who become familiarized, in time, with the jet-nozzle process."[5]

THE DEAL IN A NUTSHELL

> *Uranium exploration and mining:* Initial exploration of two areas totaling 73,000 square kilometers. Guaranteed delivery of 20 per cent of any ore to German utilities, with proportion increasing later. NUCLEBRAS (the new Brazilian state nuclear energy corporation) share, 51 per cent in joint company.

> *Uranium enrichment:* Construction in Germany of a pilot plant by 1981, with an industrial-scale plant to be built later in Brazil, using experimental jet-nozzle technique being developed by Germans. NUCLEBRAS share, 75 per cent.

> *Fuel fabrication:* Pilot plant, then commercial plant built by Germans. NUCLEBRAS share, 70 per cent.

> *Reprocessing of spent fuel:* Construction of pilot plant under technical assistance agreement between NUCLEBRAS and German consortium. NUCLEBRAS share, 100 per cent.

> *Power plants:* Two 1,300-megawatt pressurized water reactors by 1985, and option for six more by 1990, with increasing participation by Brazilian industry in construction and component manufacture to reach 70 per cent by 1980 and 90 per cent by 1990.

Looking beyond the dangers of nuclear weapons proliferation in exports of the "complete fuel cycle," the Brazil-German deal reflects the centrifugal forces in the postwar international power structure that have been gaining momentum in recent years. At the height of U.S. influence, the principal

[4] *The United States, Canada, France, Great Britain, Japan, the Soviet Union, and West Germany.*

[5] *From the Portuguese text of the agreement and commentaries published in* Jornal do Brasil, *June 28, 1975, p. 11.*

supports of the Western system were the American command of strategic nuclear weaponry, the role of the dollar in assuring monetary stability, and U.S. control of critical fuel supplies through the overseas petroleum reserves held by the major oil companies and through the commitment of the U.S. Atomic Energy Commission (AEC) to provide enriched uranium for the West's nuclear power plants. Now all of these elements of U.S. power have declined in importance, forcing adherents to this power, such as Brazil and West Germany, to make bargains for themselves in a much more uncertain world.

The Impact of the Energy Crisis

Brazil's nuclear deal with West Germany must be viewed in terms of the impact of the energy crisis on Brazil's rapid economic growth that has created a dominant role for her in South America. Under the pressures of the energy crisis, Brazil has reached into the South American heartland to make arrangements for critical energy supplies with two of her weaker neighbors, Bolivia and Paraguay. These two deals are for natural gas from Bolivia and for a huge binational hydroelectric dam, Itaipú, to be built jointly with Paraguay. Both were negotiated over the opposition of Brazil's traditional rival, Argentina, which during the 1950s and 1960s developed a long lead over Brazil in nuclear technology and has been suspected of attempting to fabricate nuclear weapons of her own.

While Brazil's ambitions and geopolitical rivalries will be discussed more fully later, it is worth stressing here that Brazil has been moving toward a new and still undefined role in world affairs in the tense climate created by the quadrupling of oil prices in 1973-1974. As the *developing* world's leading oil importer, Brazil has been in deep balance-of-payments trouble since the 1973 Middle East war. Consequently, she has adopted a new "ecumenical pragmatism" in her foreign policy by which she has moved closer to the Arabs diplomatically and has sought to diversify her export markets and her sources of energy, technology, and foreign investments.

Explaining these policy departures in a lecture at Chatham House, London, in October 1975, Foreign Minister Antonio Azeredo de Silveira said: "During the cold war, a rigid alignment with the leader of the Western bloc was required of the nations of the developing world that share the basic values of the West. The reason for this or, if you prefer, the pretext was that the future of the entire system we belonged to was at stake and that unity was the price of survival." Observing that "these realities no longer apply to the final quarter of this century," Silveira explained that "an emergent power, with a wide range of interests in many fields, cannot allow rigid alignments, rooted in the past, to limit her action on the world stage." He voiced hope that the Brazil-German nuclear deal could lead to a "horizontal interdependence."

In Washington, the deal led to prolonged analysis of U.S.-Brazilian relations. Partly as a result of these deliberations, Secretary of State Kissinger visited Brasilia in February and signed an agreement committing the foreign ministers of the United States and Brazil to an annual exchange of visits for consultations on world problems, an arrangement that Brazil had sought actively for two years. At a dinner in his honor, Kissinger pronounced an official blessing over Brazil as ". . . a nation of greatness—a people taking their place in the front rank of nations. . . . My country welcomes Brazil's new role in world affairs."

The German Connection

The "horizontal interdependence" between Brazil and West Germany stems from the peculiar nature of Germany's own energy crisis. With no oil or uranium of her own, West Germany is now heavily dependent on petroleum imports and has staked her energy future on the world's largest per capita investment in nuclear power. This means construction of some 40 power stations that would raise the nuclear share of her electricity supply from 7 per cent in 1974 to 45 per cent in 1985, an increase from 4 million to 88 million tons per year coal equivalent.[6]

In implementing these plans, West Germany thus far has relied on supplies of enriched uranium sold by the U.S. government, the main nuclear fuel supplier to power plants throughout the non-Communist world. Consequently, West Germany's energy position was severely compromised by the one-two punch delivered in 1973-1974.

First came the oil price rises that accompanied the Arab boycott. Then came an important event that was little noticed in this country outside nuclear industry and government circles—the suspension by the AEC of the signing of all new contracts for future supplies of enriched uranium because, in the surge of reactor orders in the early 1970s, projected commercial demands for enriched uranium were outstripping the capacity of the three AEC enrichment plants (the newest of which was built in 1956). In addition, the AEC retroactively classified as "conditional" enrichment contracts for 45 foreign reactors scheduled to begin operation in the early 1980s, including two in Brazil and 10 in West Germany.[7] It is still not known who will supply the enriched uranium for the first two KWU plants.

Testifying that the enrichment cutback was a trigger to the Brazil-German deal, the top State Department science official told Congress: "We have run out of capacity. We saw that coming. We did not take action."[8] According to a spokesman for Westinghouse which is building Brazil's first nuclear power plant and was negotiating to build more:

> We thought... that we pretty well had that business locked up until the question of contracts between Brazil and the U.S. government for the slightly enriched uranium for fuel came to a sudden halt, and the Brazilians were denied firm contracts for the slightly enriched fuel, and at that point, any further industrial discussions between ourselves and the Brazilians ceased and Brazil started discussions with West Germany, with the results that were recently announced.[9]

While it is not at all clear that Westinghouse had Brazil's future reactor orders "locked up" by July 1974, many specialists see the U.S. cutoff of future enrichment commitments as having created both a reason and an opportunity for Brazil and West Germany to act together to implement separate strategic aims. Brazil has long expressed interest in "self-sufficiency" in the the nuclear fuel cycle for civilian and/or military purposes, while West Germany has wanted to make inroads into the fast-developing international nuclear energy market that has been dominated by U.S. manufacturers.

West Germany has been driven to search for new export markets and for critical fuel supplies by the loss of direct control of most of the world's known oil reserves by the major Anglo-American oil companies, and the inability of the U.S. government to maintain its open-ended commitment to fuel the world's nuclear power plants. This

[6] *"West German Energy Outlook,"* The Petroleum Economist, *June 1975, p. 208.*

[7] *U.S., Congress, Joint Committee on Atomic Energy,* Future Structure of the Uranium Enrichment Industry: Hearings *(Washington, D.C.: U.S. Government Printing Office, 1974), pt. 3, vol. II, phase III, p. 1351. For a detailed and perceptive account of the international enrichment crisis in the 1970s, see Edward F. Wonder,* International Uranium Enrichment Cooperation: The American Case *(Ottawa: The Norman Patterson School of International Affairs, Carleton University, mimeograph, December 1975).*

[8] *Testimony by Myron B. Kratzer, acting assistant secretary, Bureau of Oceans and International Affairs, State Department, U.S., Congress, Senate, Committee on Foreign Relations,* International Organization and Security Agreements: Hearings, *July 22, 1975.*

[9] *Testimony by A. L. Bethel of Westinghouse, U.S., Congress, House, Committee on Interior and Insular Affairs,* International Proliferation of Nuclear Technology: Hearings, *July 22, 1975 (Washington, D.C.: Government Printing Office, 1975), pt. 3, p. 67.*

search has led Germany to act as a catalyst of the nationalist ambitions of such countries as Brazil, Iran, and South Africa in trading her technology for fuel supplies.[10]

West Germany's efforts to capture the Brazilian reactor market began in June 1968, shortly after Siemens won the Atucha I contract to build Latin America's first nuclear power plant in Argentina. Foreign Minister Willy Brandt, during a visit to Brazil, publicly expressed German interest in supplying Brazil with nuclear technology. A few months later a former vice minister of foreign affairs, Pio Correa, was hired as president of the Siemens subsidiary in Brazil. A bilateral agreement for scientific and technical cooperation was signed in 1969. A key role in these negotiations was played by the new president of NUCLEBRAS (the new Brazilian state nuclear energy corporation), Paulo Nogueira Batista, who then became the minister-counselor of the Brazilian embassy in Bonn to implement the accord.

Brazilian technicians were sent to Germany for training in nuclear engineering, and in 1971 a formal working relationship was established between Brazil's National Council for Nuclear Energy (CNEN) and the Center for Nuclear Research in Julich, whose representatives were to help in promoting exports of German nuclear technology. Visits of German scientists to Brazil under this agreement led to rumors, reported in the London *Sunday Times,* "of Germans conducting nuclear research in areas that would be ruled out if it were attempted on German soil." The Soviet defense ministry newspaper *Red Star* interpreted the scientific agreement as a German attempt to draw Brazil into its "atomic diplomatic game" and to encourage Brazil to reject the NPT.[11]

Apparently, intensive negotiations with the Germans did not begin until after the U.S. cutoff of future contracts for enriched uranium in July 1974. A number of important Germans visited Brazilia in mid-1974 on secret business, among them State Secretary of Technology Hans Hilgar Haunschild, former Defense Minister Franz Josef Strauss, and State Secretary for Foreign Affairs Hans George Sachs.[12] Agreement on the Brazil-German deal was reached on February 12, 1975. The U.S. ambassador in Bonn was informed a week later, and a general outline of the agreement filtered into the American trade press within a few days.[13]

Meanwhile, the 38-year-old head of the "international section" of the Julich nuclear research center, Klaus Scharmer, defended Germany's new relationship with Brazil:

> Brazil has the capacity—and will use it —to produce components and even build nuclear installations on her own. Only a partner that knows this aptitude can maintain fruitful contact for a long period. We thus saw that to try to sell installations to Brazil on a turnkey basis would be an unwise policy. We must combat the "development gap" that tends to grow between countries that are more and less developed. We must try to hasten the advance of the underdeveloped.[14]

U.S. Objections

The 1975 nuclear deal readily evokes memories of the U.S.-German rivalry for the Brazilian market that began before World War I and reached its climax during the arms race of the 1930s.[15] In both Ger-

[10] *See Robert Gerald Livingston, "Germany Steps Up,"* FOREIGN POLICY 22.

[11] *H. Jon Rosenbaum and Glenn M. Cooper, "Brazil and the Nuclear Proliferation Treaty,"* International Affairs, *January 1970, p. 88.*

[12] *Política Nuclear: Os projetos, as alternativas e o misterio,"* Visao, *September 9, 1974, pp. 27-28.*

[13] *The dates were given in* Frankfürter Allgemeine, *June 5, 1975. Translation from* German Press Review, *June 11, 1975, p. 3. First news of the negotiations appeared in* Nucleonics Week, *February 20, 1975.*

[14] *"Depois da vitóriapolítica, desafió talvez mais difícil,"* Visao, *July 7, 1975, p. 16.*

[15] *See Stanley J. Hilton,* Brazil and the Great Powers, 1930-1939: The Politics of Trade Rivalry *(Austin: University of Texas Press, 1975).*

many and Brazil, U.S. objections to the nuclear deal were widely interpreted as reflecting the disappointment of American suppliers who had sought the contract. While U.S. newspapers and politicians urged the Ford Administration to pressure Bonn into rescinding or modifying the Brazilian deal, Washington's negotiating position was severely undermined by its inability to offer other nations an alternate source of reactor fuel.

Chancellor Helmut Schmidt expressed surprise that the Brazil deal had not been mentioned by the Americans at a high level. Thus, two days before the accord was signed in Bonn, Schmidt told a press conference that "some of this excited discussion—some of it also in a segment of the American press —would appear rather clearly to go back to the very tangible interests of major industrial firms in the United States."

The German press took the same tack with much greater vehemence. "In order to get contracts the Americans fight in the international competition with heavy gloves," said the liberal, pro-Western *Die Zeit* of Hamburg. "No matter where a plant is being planned, American diplomats agitate as if they were employees of the American firms." One German official complained that "our strongest competitors are actually not Westinghouse or General Electric. The strongest competitor is the American Export-Import Bank. . . . Even when we try to lower the burden of interest through all sorts of tricks, the Eximbank comes in with 2 per cent less."[16]

Leading German papers claimed that American reactor salesmen in Iran, Yugoslavia, and Argentina spread rumors that KWU's financial difficulties would prevent it from making promised deliveries, and suggested that reliable supplies of reactor fuels might not be available if U.S.-built power plants were not ordered. Further questioning of American motives occurred in January 1975, while negotiations for the Brazilian deal were in their final stages, when the United States objected, in NATO councils, to a West German reactor export to the Soviet Union as part of a package deal that would have included Soviet sales of electricity to Germany.[17] A leading German economic weekly gave this view of the intensifying competition:

> With the Brazil deal, KWU is breaking into a new market that previously was firmly in the grip of U.S. companies. Westinghouse and GE are trying to protect their shrinking market position in various ways: hard sell by sales managers and U.S. government permission, wherever possible, to apply massive political pressure to those who issue the contracts. Just as the U.S. aircraft industry managed to check foreign airplane producers, the U.S. reactor industry is blocking competition from other countries.[18]

Geopolitics of Uranium

On top of the intensifying competition for export markets, the disorder in the international reactor industry has been compounded by the new uncertainty about the future U.S. capacity to export enriched uranium, thus creating a new geopolitics of uranium supplies. After the AEC cutoff in 1974 of new enrichment contracts, the Soviets have become important suppliers of enriched uranium to Western Europe. Moreover, the West Germans have been trying to diversify their sources of uranium by providing their own enrichment technology, the experimental Becker jet-nozzle process, to two potential uranium suppliers, Brazil and South Africa. The Germans are reported to have secretly assisted the South Africans, with exchanges of visits by key officials,

[16] *Heinz Michaels, "Querschüsse aus den USA,"* Die Zeit, *June 20, 1975, and "Atomwirtschaft: 12,000,-000 Mark für Deutschland,"* Wirtschaftswoche, *June 27, 1975, p. 13.*

[17] *The deal foundered over Soviet-German disagreement on Bonn's insistence that the electric power lines from the reactor pass through West Berlin en route to West Germany.*

[18] Wirtschaftswoche, *op. cit.*

to develop something very similar to the jet-nozzle technology the Germans will be providing Brazil under the new deal; in October 1975, a West German air force general was forced to resign when news leaked out of an undercover trip he made to South Africa that included a visit to a nuclear research center.[19] Two months later, *The Economist* reported that Iran, which is South Africa's main oil supplier and has an ambitious nuclear program of her own, may also finance commercial development of South Africa's jet-nozzle process in return for guaranteed supplies and access to the technology.

Similarly, one of the main hopes for both sides in the Brazil-German deal is that German geologists will help discover substantial uranium reserves that they believe to exist in Brazil. (While she has large proven deposits of thorium, a fertile material that can be made into reactor fuel and bomb material, no commercial technology has been developed so far for the use of thorium in power plants.)

Brazil has greatly intensified her uranium exploration since 1969 but with uncertain results. What was initially reported in mid-1975 to be a major find of 50,000 tons of uranium ore, in the pre-Cambrian rock of the Brazilian shield in the sprawling inland state of Goias, was modified two months later by an official estimate of only 1,500 tons. German geologists are now fanning out over the northern Amazon basin to seek new uranium deposits, with 80 per cent of their exploration expenses subsidized by Bonn. This is because Brazil's present proven reserves are far from enough to pay, in any significant degree, for the huge transfer of nuclear technology that is envisioned for the next 15 years.

Meanwhile, German firms have found valuable deposits in Namibia (South-West Africa) and are also exploring for uranium in Austria, Algeria, Australia, Canada, Indonesia, Nigeria, Spain, Switzerland, Togo, and the United States. Defending Bonn against criticism of the Brazil deal, Munich's leading newspaper observed that "the temporary export stop of the United States of uranium products made strikingly clear the dependence not only of the Federal Republic but also of the entire Western world on American fuel for nuclear reactors."[20]

Enrichment: The Gordian Knot

Uranium enrichment involves a scale of industrial activity without precedent. The U.S. government's Oak Ridge gaseous diffusion plant contains more than 1,500 machines, each the size of a railroad car, spread over more than 100 acres of factory floor. The electricity needed to drive these machines costs $500,000 a day. They are cooled by up to 90 million gallons of water daily, evaporating in huge clouds that form over the Tennessee Valley. To build such a plant today would cost $6 billion.

As long as these huge costs and the U.S. domination of gaseous diffusion technology prevented other nations from entering the business, the United States has been able to use her control of supplies of enriched uranium as a way to prevent nuclear proliferation. This leverage was applied by encouraging other nations to depend on U.S. enrichment services, on the condition that all fuels, and the plutonium therein, be monitored against diversion bilaterally or by international inspection. These controls have become less effective with the multiplication of reactors throughout the world and the spread of enrichment capacity, with new technologies, to other countries. The Brazil-German deal is the first major consequence of the accelerated scramble for alternate sources of reactor fuel, issuing from the inability of the United States to sign contracts that would commit U.S. sources to a major investment in expanded enrichment capacity.

---

[19] *Robert Gillette, "Uranium Enrichment: With Help South Africa Is Progressing,"* Science, *June 13, 1975.*

[20] Sueddeutsche Zeitung, *June 5, 1975.*

In seeking the "complete fuel cycle" in exchange for a commitment to export enriched uranium to West Germany, Brazil originally had asked Bonn to provide the new gas centrifuge technology, which is said to use much less energy than the gaseous diffusion process used in the United States. But this proposition was vetoed by the Dutch, who share control of the centrifuge process with Britain and West Germany as partners in URENCO, the European enrichment consortium, now building a centrifuge plant in the Netherlands.

Instead, the Brazilians had to settle for the experimental jet-nozzle process which is mechanically simpler than the two other technologies but consumes more electricity: nearly twice as much as the gaseous diffusion process and 20 times more than the centrifuge. While simpler mechanically than the other processes, the jet nozzle poses formidable technical problems of its own.

To separate the fissionable U-235 from the nonfissionable U-238 in gaseous form under enormous pressures, uranium hexafloride gas (mixed with hydrogen) is pumped through a long slit, forming a rapidly moving sheet of gas. The gas strikes a curved wall, where centrifugal forces carry the heavier U-238 (making up 99.3 per cent of the gas) to the outer surface of the sheet. The isotopes are separated along paring blades with tolerances of 0.00005 (five hundred-thousandths) of an inch that must remain accurate, stress-resistant, and stable under these pressures.

The jet nozzle process, in laboratory tests, has been so energy-intensive that only a few nations, such as Brazil or Switzerland, have enough cheap hydroelectric power to use it economically. Moreover, the industrial-scale engineering problems are still unsolved. The prospects of the jet nozzle competing with the centrifuge process in Europe were so dubious that in May 1974 Bonn's research minister ordered a cutoff of federal subsidies for development of the jet nozzle, only to have the order reversed under industrial and bureaucratic pressure. Development of the jet nozzle has continued as a technology for the export trade.[21]

One of the striking features of the deal is that NUCLEBRAS will actually finance development of the experimental German jet-nozzle enrichment process now in the pilot plant stage, into an industrial-scale operation. If sufficient uranium discoveries are made in Brazil, or if ore can be shipped economically from abroad, Brazil could become an important exporter of enriched uranium. But a huge commitment is needed to bring this technology into industrial production. Last year, for example, the South Africans disclosed that merely to bring their version of the jet-nozzle process to the pilot plant stage, they were employing 1,200 persons and had spent $148 million since 1970. Brazil has few scientists and technicians available for this scale of nuclear research. To build a full-scale enrichment plant in Brazil, an investment of billions of dollars would be needed. Her available human and financial resources are already overcommitted, and there must be serious doubts as to whether Brazil can sustain or justify such an effort on a process that is still unproven.

The International Reactor Industry

The increasing cost and uncertainty of oil supplies has stimulated ambitious plans in several countries for new atomic power plants that would increase the nuclear portion of the West's electrical generating capacity from 2 per cent to 15 per cent in 1985. But unexpected increases in both capital costs and time needed to build these plants have caused suspensions and cancellations of orders from utilities. The added capital outlays have tended to nullify the lower operating costs that are the nuclear plants'

[21] *See Robert Gillette, "Nozzle Enrichment for Sale,"* Science, *May 30, 1975; James J. Glackin, "The Dangerous Drift of Uranium Enrichment,"* Bulletin of the Atomic Scientists, *February 1976; and Jonathan Kwitny, "Enriching Venture,"* The Wall Street Journal, *November 20, 1975.*

main commercial advantage. Inflation will be pushing the aggregate price tags of the West's nuclear power plants to between $1 trillion and $1.5 trillion by the early 1990s.[22]

At the same time, strong public opposition to nuclear power has spread from the United States to France, Germany, Japan, and Sweden, compounding the inflation and delay. Foreign demand for nuclear power plants has grown far faster than U.S. demand, with 50 per cent more nuclear generating capacity already existing abroad. Both U.S. and European reactor manufacturers have responded to inflation and delay at home by competing fiercely for export sales in third markets, especially in developing countries with authoritarian regimes that need not worry about public opposition.

According to separate projections by the IAEA and AEC, the market for nuclear power among developing nations is likely to be concentrated in a handful of countries. The IAEA estimated that more than half the installed nuclear generating capacity by the year 2000 will be absorbed by only four nations: Brazil, India, Iran, and Mexico, and that 70 per cent of the same market will be concentrated in eight countries.

However, a more detailed study subsequently commissioned by the AEC found even this limited market potential to be "too optimistic," due to extremely loose forecasts of electricity demand, ignorance of costs, shortages of foreign exchange, and the inability of many national electricity systems to absorb the output of large nuclear plants. This independent study, by Richard J. Barber Associates of Washington, stresses the importance of the sales push of companies and governments in developing this market:

> Nuclear reactor system vendors have acknowledged, more or less openly, that many of the initial nuclear plants sold both domestically and internationally under "turnkey" arrangements were (and apparently still are, in the case of new reactor types) "loss leaders" for which the reported prices paid by utilities significantly understated the true cost of building the plants. Governments have clearly subsidized domestic and international power sales of their vendors by means of no-interest or low-interest loans, loan guarantees, absorption of research and development costs, preferential access to and pricing of fuels and reprocessing services, etc. The amount of such subsidies is often concealed, thus distorting the true cost of the power station. . . . The German government, for example, underwrote the success of Siemens' sale to Argentina by giving the Argentine government a five year no-interest loan, a subsequent very low interest loan, and balance-of-payments considerations. France managed to sell a reactor unit in Spain in return for loans covering 90 per cent of its cost and agreeing to represent Spanish interests in the Common Market. It is common knowledge in nuclear industry circles that German, U.S., and Canadian vendors "lost their shirts" on their initial sales to Argentina, India, and Pakistan.

Until the Brazil-German deal was negotiated, there had been little official concern or public discussion as to the economic wisdom and military implications of the drive to export, and even give away, nuclear reactors.

The plutonium for India's 1974 nuclear explosion was diverted from the unsafeguarded "Cirus" research reactor donated by Canada in 1956, for which the AEC supplied heavy water. India's first nuclear power plant, built by General Electric (GE) was financed with a $74 million U.S. foreign aid loan at 0.75 per cent interest over 30 years after a 10-year initial grace period, with additional support coming from the AEC and the Ford and Rockefeller foundations.[23]

[22] *"The Case Against Nuclear Power,"* The Economist, *May 10, 1975, p. 84.*

[23] *Pan Heuristics,* Moving Toward Life in a Nuclear Armed Crowd *(unpublished report to the U.S. Arms Control and Disarmament Agency).*

With her own scientific community building on the technological base provided by the United States and Canada, India has created an immense network of nuclear facilities of all types. The "Cirus" reactor is located at the Trombay laboratories, near Bombay, which alone employs 10,400 persons, including 2,400 scientists. During construction of the plutonium separation facility at Trombay, senior Indian scientists repeatedly visited the AEC reprocessing plant in Idaho, under the "Atoms for Peace" program, for extensive interviews with staff members on the technical problems of extracting plutonium from spent fuel. Today India manufactures her own rockets and solid fuel propellants, and plans to launch rockets by 1979 capable of putting a 1,200-kilogram payload into orbit, or of delivering nuclear warheads anywhere in Asia. India's example has not been lost on other ascendant powers. While several countries are now trying to acquire nuclear technology with bomb-making potential, Brazil and India are the only two developing countries carrying out space programs with their own launching facilities.[24]

However risky and unprofitable the export trade in nuclear technology now may seem, this is precisely the direction in which the industry keeps moving.[25] German and French reactor manufacturers, still marginal in the international industry, have fought for survival, seizing on the 1974 U.S. enrichment cutoff as an opportunity to win power plant sales by offering such "sweeteners"—with bomb-making potential—as the technology for uranium enrichment and for plutonium separation from spent fuel.

Competing U.S. firms cannot legally offer these "sweeteners," but the pressure for them to do so is very great as escalating costs and political complications have shrunk the domestic market: In 1975, only seven nuclear power plants were ordered in the United States, compared with 18 abroad, and a U.S. deal to build eight nuclear plants in Iran is stalled in a dispute over Iran's insistence on the right to reprocess her own spent fuel. In November 1975, the Shah told *Business Week*: "In atomic energy you are asking us for safeguards that are incompatible with our sovereignty, things that the French or the Germans would never dream of asking."[26]

Two months later, a Westinghouse representative complained to Congress: "The U.S. government is proposing to attach a permanent veto power over nuclear fuel processing in Iran, as a precondition for sale of U.S. nuclear reactors. Other vendors from Germany and France are already selling nuclear reactors to Iran without such conditions. The result is obvious—the U.S. has sold no reactors to Iran, despite an Iranian desire to buy a large number."[27]

These broader economic and political considerations make the implementation of the Brazil-German deal a critical indicator of the future course of the international reactor industry. The compulsion to export is deeply felt in this high-risk, capital-intensive, heavily-subsidized industry. The instability is such that even West Germany's huge "complete fuel cycle" deal with Brazil was

[24] *Robert Gillette, "India: Into the Nuclear Club on Canada's Shoulders,"* Science, *June 7, 1974. For a detailed Canadian account of India's nuclear development, see Barrie Morrison and Donald M. Page, "India's option: the nuclear route to achieve goal as world power,"* International Perspectives, *July-August 1974.*

[25] *France, for example, arranged in 1975 to build reprocessing plants in South Korea and Pakistan. While the South Korean deal was canceled in early 1976, thanks largely to U.S. pressure on Seoul, the Pakistan deal subsequently was approved by the* IAEA *and is going through. Prime Minister Zulfikar Ali Bhutto has vowed that Pakistan would match India's nuclear capacity even if Pakistanis had "to eat grass" to mobilize the resources. Industry sources estimate that for a reprocessing plant to be economically viable for civilian uses, it must reprocess spent fuels from at least 20 reactors. Pakistan has only one nuclear power plant.*

[26] *"Recession's Impact on Iran: Interview with Shah Mohammad Reza Pahlavi,"* Business Week, *November 17, 1975, p. 57.*

[27] *Testimony by Dwight J. Porter of Westinghouse, U.S., Congress, Senate, Government Operations Committee,* Nuclear Proliferation: Hearings, *January 29, 1976.*

not enough to dissuade AEG Telefunken from trying to withdraw as Siemen's partner in KWU, citing 1974 losses of $287 million.[28] Explaining West Germany's overseas sales drive, a KWU spokesman told a Brazilian journalist:

> We have to export. KWU has the capacity for construction of six reactors a year, and would be very satisfied if it could build three of them in Germany now. We can't export to France or Spain because the American competition is very strong. We were able to sell one reactor each in Argentina, Holland, Austria, and Switzerland, and have begun to build two in Iran.[29]

However, nobody has determined the real cost of these exports, nor the real benefits likely to accrue to customers and suppliers, nor whether these big deals will provide any real guarantees for the industry against an increasingly uncertain future. Nor is it clear whether any economic gains could outweigh the mounting dangers of nuclear proliferation.

The Rivalry

While the world energy crisis and the instability of the international reactor industry created the conditions for the Brazil-German nuclear deal, Brazil's "great power" aspirations and the peculiar nature of her own energy crisis provided the incentives. Moreover, Brazil's nuclear rivalry with Argentina made the risks of not seizing upon this opportunity unacceptable from a military point of view.

Although achieving power and prestige in proportion to her size long has been a major aim of Brazilian foreign policy, these ambitions have only been taken seriously since the military seized power in April 1964. Tightly restricting mass consumption and civil liberties while providing incentives and guarantees that attracted large amounts of foreign investment, a succession of military regimes set the stage for the so-called Brazilian "miracle."

This was a surge of rapid economic development crowned by a growth rate averaging 10 per cent yearly in the 1968-1974 period, a "miracle" that was a conspicuous beneficiary of low oil prices and of the radical expansion of the world's money supply and trade in the postwar decades. As industrialization advanced by giant strides, Brazilians began to see themselves emerging from the role of a "key country" in the global strategy of the United States to become an important military-political force in their own right. During the visit to Washington in 1971 of President Emilio Garrastazu Medici (1969-1974), those aspirations were encouraged by President Nixon's oft-quoted blessing: "As Brazil goes, so goes South America."

While Brazil's relative geopolitical position has been strengthened greatly by the political disintegration of Argentina in the 1970s, Argentina one day could recover sufficiently to inhibit Brazilian maneuvers in South America. At the same time, the energy crisis has become a crucial factor in Brazil's future growth and influence. While Brazil today is the world's fifth-largest country in area and seventh-largest in population, there is no other continental nation so deficient in economically useful deposits of fossil fuels.

Brazil's main energy asset at present is the immense hydroelectric potential of her great rivers, which is being harnessed at an impressive rate. Hydroelectric production has increased thirteenfold over the past three decades and tripled since the mid-1960s, leading to fears that the water-flow potential near the major cities may be exhausted before the turn of the century. This is being given as the main economic justification for Brazil's embarking on an ambitious nuclear power program, even though electricity de-

[28] *"AEG to Pull Out of Kraftwerk Union, Either Partially or Completely,"* Nucleonics Week, *November 7, 1974, p. 1.*

[29] *"Depois da vitória. . . ."* Visao, *op. cit., p. 16.*

mand is unlikely to continue growing at the rate of recent decades. According to NUCLEBRAS president Nogueira Batista:

> By 1980, our hydroelectric resources would be exhausted in the southeast and the Sao Francisco Valley. We will still have at that time only the hydroelectric potential of the Amazon (90,000 megawatts), a good deal of which is in the region's north (far from markets). . . . The fact is that the installation of our nuclear reactors near the centers of consumption will enable these energy resources to be used right there without costly and wasteful long-distance transmission.[30]

The Impact of India

The Indian nuclear explosion of May 1974 had a major impact in both Argentina and Brazil. For some time these two countries had viewed each other's activities in the nuclear field with suspicion. After May 1974 it became a topic of common table talk among the elites of both countries to speculate about who would get the bomb first. Indeed, the Argentine magazine *Estrategia* praised the Indian peaceful nuclear explosive (PNE) as showing "how an underdeveloped and technologically dependent country can attain objectives based exclusively on her own appreciation of the priorities of national defense."[31] The same article added:

> The projections of Brazil's demographic growth place Argentina at a disadvantage that will tend to widen markedly over the next 30 years. Despite all the distortions of her growth, Brazil will become an important power, causing Argentina, if she does not adopt pertinent policies, to find it increasingly difficult to overcome Brazil or even maintain a situation of relative equilibrium. . . . Argentina is, for the moment, ahead in nuclear technology. The Atucha power reactor, using natural uranium, is now operational and the project for the new reactor in Rio Tercero assures [Argentina] an advantage for at least the medium term. . . . Argentina and Brazil both are theoretically capable of producing an atomic bomb. This would mean, above all, a *political* decision. [emphasis in original]

The present nuclear rivalry of Brazil and Argentina dates from the early postwar period. Initially, Brazil supported U.S. efforts to control the development of atomic energy by secretly agreeing in 1945 to limit her thorium exports to consignees "in the United States or . . . designated or approved by the United States" in return for annual U.S. purchases of specified amounts of thorium ore.[32] However, Brazil's rivalry with Argentina soon led both countries to try to acquire technology developed in the unsuccessful German atom bomb project.

Shortly after the Argentine National Commission for Atomic Energy (CNEA) was formed in 1950, President Juan Peron appointed Ronald Richter, an émigré Austrian nuclear physicist who had done fusion research in Nazi Germany, as director of a new research facility on a remote island in a lake in southern Argentina. The facility was launched with considerable publicity.[33] Twenty months before the first U.S. thermonuclear (hydrogen) explosion, Peron gave a press conference to tell the world: "On February 16, 1951, in the atomic energy pilot plant on the island of Huemul, in San Carlos de Bariloche, thermonuclear reactions were carried out under controlled conditions on a technical scale." Peron then turned the press conference over to Richter, who told the reporters: "I control the explosion. I make it increase or diminish at my

[30] *Mauricio Dias, "Entrevista: Paulo Nogueira Batista,"* Veja, *July 23, 1975.*

[31] *Luis Garasino, "Explosión Atómica en la India: Proyección Eventual en América Latina,"* Estrategia, *May-June 1974, p. 91 and p. 97.*

[32] *From a recently declassified document, in U.S. National Archives Record Group No. 77. For an account of Anglo-American efforts to control world uranium and thorium supplies, see Martin J. Sherwin,* A World Destroyed: The Atomic Bomb and the Grand Alliance, *(New York: Alfred A. Knopf, 1975), pp. 104-105.*

[33] *John R. Redick, "Nuclear Proliferation in Latin America," p. 7 (unpublished manuscript).*

desire."[34] Twenty months later, Richter was suddenly fired and jailed when Argentine scientists found that he was experimenting with gas discharges using high-voltage capacitors, an activity not unrelated to fusion research but falling far short of his claims.

A Secret Deal

These strange experiments in the south of Argentina may have led to a much more serious effort by Brazil to obtain German nuclear technology during the postwar allied military occupation. In 1953, Admiral Alvaro Alberto, the first president of Brazil's National Research Council, visited Germany and met with Paul Haarteck, Otto Hahn, and Wilhelm Groth, scientists who had played key roles in the abortive Nazi atom bomb projects. According to a recently published report, Groth, who pioneered the centrifugal enrichment process, told Alberto: "Allocate the necessary funds and we will make the prototypes. Then we'll all go to Brazil and make the equipment there."

A secret deal was made to ship three gas centrifuges for uranium enrichment to Brazil. Three Brazilian chemists were sent to Germany for special training in the handling of heavy gases, while Groth quietly ordered components from 14 different German factories. Alberto later told a parliamentary inquiry that "Germany was a country occupied by the victorious powers, and if it were discovered that they were planning to produce enriched uranium, this would lead to an international crisis."

The secret was uncovered only when the centrifuges were ready for shipment. After the machines were seized on orders from James Conant, U.S. high commissioner to Germany, the Brazilian government then turned to France in an attempt to obtain gaseous diffusion technology, again unsuccessfully. In a confidential memorandum to Brazil's national security council, the U.S. embassy in Rio "frankly" observed, that this "German adventure in Brazil . . . could be considered as a potential threat to the security of the United States and the Western Hemisphere."[35] The embassy also urged Alberto's dismissal, warning that "the subject of atomic energy is and may continue to effect [sic] the political and economic relations between Brazil and the United States."[36] Alberto, now a national hero and a pioneer of Brazil's shrewd policy of "specific compensation" (trading natural resources for technology), resigned his post in frustration in 1955.

The nuclear programs of Brazil and Argentina accelerated after 1955, when both countries signed agreements with the United States under the "Atoms for Peace" program, making available newly declassified scientific information and providing for the training of nuclear scientists and technicians. While Brazil obtained her first research reactors under this program, Argentina steadfastly pursued an independent nuclear development policy to avoid international controls where possible and dependence on the virtual U.S. monopoly over supplies of enriched uranium.

Argentina Moves Ahead

With her own uranium reserves, a large pool of trained manpower, and a relatively advanced industrial base, Argentina soon moved well ahead of other Latin American nations in developing a nuclear energy program. In 1958, Argentina became the first Latin American nation to operate a research reactor. In 1968, her CNEA began operating the region's first, and so far only, chemical

---

[34] *Text of press conference in* La Nación, *March 25, 1951, p. 1.*

[35] *While U.S. official documents concerning this episode are still classified, Portuguese translations of them have been published repeatedly in Brazil over the past two decades. I am quoting here from the texts translated in Juárez Távora,* Atomos para o Brasil *(Rio de Janeiro: Jose Olympio, 1958), p. 347.*

[36] *The English original is quoted in Moniz Bandeira,* Presenca dos Estados Unidos no Brasil *(Rio de Janeiro: Civilazacao Brasileira, 1973), p. 369n.*

processing plant—on a pilot scale—for reclaiming plutonium from spent reactor fuel, and in 1974 Argentina started up Latin America's first nuclear power plant.[37]

"The CNEA in 1957 made a fundamental decision: not to import research reactors but to build them in Argentina," the CNEA scientist Jorge Sabato wrote in a detailed account of Argentina's progress. "In this way we would not only have, in these reactors, a tool for training and research, but their construction would also allow us to develop our own capacity for nuclear engineering. . . . In 1957, the CNEA also decided not to import fuels. These should be manufactured in Argentina. And so it (gradually) occurred. The development of our own nuclear engineering capacity was very important in the realization of our own feasibility study for Atucha I,"[38] the 320 megawatt power plant, fueled with natural uranium, that went into operation in 1974 near Buenos Aires. By the early 1970s Argentina was operating six major centers for nuclear research and many of her scientists and engineers had received advanced training in the United States and Europe.

Argentina's nuclear program was developing so rapidly that the twelfth Pugwash Conference meeting in the Soviet Union in 1969 was told that Argentina was mobilizing her physicists to produce nuclear weapons within 15 years.[39]

In February 1968, the CNEA announced that it had chosen Siemens of West Germany from among 17 bidders from five nations to build the Atucha I nuclear power plant. Although U.S. suppliers had underbid the Germans, CNEA's choice of a system using natural uranium, rather than the enriched uranium fuel of U.S.-designed reactors, enabled the Argentines to employ their own uranium reserves and to do so without obligatory international controls.

Explaining Argentina's rejection of the U.S. bids, Sabato wrote that "the fundamental disadvantages of the enriched uranium design is that at the moment only one country (the United States) provides commercial uranium enrichment." Natural uranium reactors also have a military advantage over enriched uranium reactors: They are especially prolific in producing weapons-grade plutonium that can be separated chemically from spent fuel. Natural uranium reactors also are designed for frequent and easy replacement of fuel rods while the reactor is running, not feasible in enriched uranium plants, making inspection against secret diversion of plutonium for weapons production much more difficult.

The military implications of Argentina's decision to build a natural uranium power plant were not lost on the Brazilians. Early in 1974, while Atucha I was being readied for operation, a nuclear engineer published an article in Brazil's official military journal that has been widely and repeatedly quoted in the Argentine press. It said:

> The Brazilian people need to be proud of their country for other, more serious reasons than football and carnival. International prestige is, evidently, a national objective. . . . The relationship between Security and Development is very well known. Undeniably, it will be impossible to be a power without the required military protection. A simple agreement like Itaipú would be impossible if one of our neighbors had 20 kilos of plutonium.[40]

The Argentines, meanwhile, have become deeply concerned over Itaipú, the world's largest hydroelectric dam, which the Brazilians are building, with some Paraguayan assistance, on the border of the two coun-

[37] *Robert Gillette, "India and Argentina: Developing a Nuclear Affinity,"* Science, *June 28, 1974, p. 1351.*

[38] *Jorge Sábato, "Energía Atómica en Argentina,"* Estudios Internacionales, *October-December 1968, p. 342.*

[39] *Walter Sullivan, "Pugwash Parley in Sochi Told of Argentina's Nuclear Plans,"* The New York Times, *October 27, 1969, p. 19.*

[40] *Elvé Montiero de Castro, "A Energia Nuclear no Brasil,"* A Defesa Nacional, *January-February, 1974, p. 63.*

tries. Itaipú is only about 10 miles north of the Argentine frontier in a region that, over the centuries, has been a theater of recurrent geopolitical rivalries, first between the Spanish and Portuguese empires and later between Argentina, Brazil, and Paraguay.

The dam has become a symbol in Argentina of Brazilian penetration and domination in areas of the continent where Argentina used to have great influence. Argentina opposed the Itaipú dam on grounds of environmental impact and international law, and has mustered majority support for her position at recent international conferences, but that has not affected the progress of the project.

The NPT

Argentina and Brazil refused to sign or ratify The Treaty on Non-Proliferation of Nuclear Weapons (NPT) on similar grounds. During the 1968 U.N. debate on the proposed NPT treaty, Argentina said she "cannot accept remaining subordinate to a continuing dependence on the great powers in nuclear technology for peaceful ends, especially when our country has laid the foundations for a nuclear technology needed for economic development." Coining a phrase that was subsequently heard often in the nuclear proliferation debates, the Argentine delegate said the NPT would "disarm the unarmed" while imposing no restrictions on the superpowers' arms race.[41] The Brazilians have seen the NPT as an attempt to "freeze" the international power structure to contain emergent powers such as Brazil.

Shortly after taking office, President Arthur da Costa e Silva argued: "The development of scientific research in the field of nuclear energy includes, inevitably, at a certain stage, the use of explosions; to veto access to the use of explosions would be equivalent to impeding the development of the peaceful uses of nuclear energy."[42] In December 1967, as Argentina's CNEA was preparing to announce its final decision on the design and contract for Atucha I, Costa e Silva approved a National Security Council report that recommended, as permanent objectives, "transfer of nuclear technology to our country; obtaining in the shortest time our independence in the production of nuclear fuels; creation of an infrastructure of support for the nuclear program; and formation and training of teams competent in the different (specialized) areas."[43] In 1967, Brazil's National Council for Nuclear Energy (CNEN) commissioned a study of the feasibility of building an atom bomb, concluding that such a project, if attempted, would take 15 years.[44]

Brazil's Nuclear Development

Brazil's nuclear development had been slowed by a number of false starts. At the end of the 1950s, President Juscelino Kubitschek (1956-1961) had decided on construction of a 150-200 megawatt power reactor using enriched uranium following the U.S. model that dominates the industry today. In 1961, however, the seven-month government of President Janio Quadros, in developing its independent foreign policy, reversed these plans and opted for a natural uranium reactor along the lines of the first reactors then being developed in France. This project continued under President João Goulart (1961-1964) as Brazilian technicians went to France for training and French nuclear engineers went to Brazil to begin preparations for construction of the

[41] *José María Ruda, "La posición argentina en cuanto al Tratado sobre la No Proliferación de las Armas Nucleares,"* Estrategia, *September-December 1970, January-February 1971, p. 79.*

[42] *Quoted in James W. Rowe, "Science and Politics in Brazil," in Kalman H. Silvert (ed.)* The Social Reality of Scientific Myth *(New York: American Universities Field Staff, 1969), p. 91.*

[43] *Quoted in "Política Nuclear: Os projetos, as alternativas e o mistério,"* Visao, *September 9, 1974, p. 25.*

[44] *H. Jon Rosenbaum, "Brazil's Nuclear Aspirations," in Onkar Marwah an Schulz (ed.),* Nuclear Proliferation and the Near-Nuclear Countries *(Cambridge, Mass.: Ballinger, 1975).*

reactor. However, this project was, in turn, cancelled by the military regime that seized power in 1964, while the French, a few years later, abandoned their efforts to develop a natural uranium reactor in favor of U.S. enriched uranium technology.

Subsequently, Brazil seriously weighed the possibility of buying a Canadian Candu natural uranium reactor of the type which is to be used in Argentina's second nuclear power plant and was used in India to "cook" the plutonium used in the 1974 nuclear explosion. Brazil also has repeatedly asked Westinghouse to help her develop a new technology to use her huge thorium reserves as reactor fuel, assisting the experiments of the Brazilian "Thorium Group" in Belo Horizonte. Westinghouse, a contractor to the U.S. Navy's classified research program to develop a reactor based on the thorium fuel cycle, declined Brazil's request on the grounds that it could not commit the resources to develop thorium technology, and because, as presently conceived, a power plant using thorium would need an initial charge of weapons-grade uranium, and would not be economically competitive.

Yet Brazil's quest for "self-sufficiency" has continued, through her 1972 contract with Westinghouse for her first nuclear power plant and, more importantly, through her giant deal with West Germany embracing the whole fuel cycle.

A Decisive Step

News of the Brazil-German deal had such a psychological impact in the Western Hemisphere that its main political effect may have been achieved long before the final details of the complex agreement are worked out and construction begins in 1977-1978 on the eight-year project to build the first two power plants. The commanding general of the First Army in Rio de Janeiro said the nuclear accord "constitutes a decisive step that reinforces the country's sovereignty," and predicted that Brazil would "be transformed into a great power." Foreign Minister Silveira, after signing the agreement, said that "Brazil has gained new technological and political status on the world scene with the nuclear agreement," adding: "Both of our two countries must pray that nobody throws an atomic bomb at our heads while we are working at carrying out these agreements. Because we won't be the ones to throw it."

Argentina's present inability to check Brazil's initiative in the nuclear field parallels her inability to counter Brazilian geopolitical initiatives in the interior of South America, and is easily understood in view of the political disorder that has escalated steadily over the past two decades in Argentina. Under these conditions, it is not surprising that Argentina's own nuclear program would be paralyzed by her present financial difficulties.[45] In addition, many of Argentina's nuclear scientists have left the country. Many are working now in Brazil. The former head of CNEA, Admiral Oscar A. Quihillalt, is now serving in Iran as adviser to the Shah's atomic energy commission at a reported monthly salary of $10,000, assisted by seven other Argentine specialists.

In July 1975, the present head of CNEA visited Tripoli to sign a nuclear cooperation agreement between Argentina and Libya, while at home Argentina is engaged in an expansion of her pilot facilities for the reprocessing of spent fuels. With reserves of trained manpower and critical energy supplies greater than Brazil's, Argentina's capacity for maneuver can only increase if the new regime stabilizes the country. An expanded nuclear program would have great symbolic value in such a comeback. The Argentine military's concern about the deal may be contained in *Estrategia's* admonition:

> Given the available facts, *it is possible to affirm that* [*Brazil*] *has taken the firm decision to join the Nuclear Club, that is,*

[45] *See Mark Gayn, "No safeguards yet, Canada building A-plant in Argentina,"* The Toronto Star, *July 22, 1975, p. 1.*

to make an atom bomb under the concept of peaceful uses . . . the decision to manufacture the nuclear explosive and the opportunity, are critical for Argentina, since our neighbor's nuclear device, without a counterpoise, will affect our Security palpably and decidedly. (emphasis in original) [46]

The Future

This likely peril is being instituted by an ally in our backyard (while) the U.S. government is heavily committed in West Germany's backyard to defend them against a likely peril. . . . I say of all the countries in the world that should not have done it is West Germany. . . . The present government in Brazil may be very amenable to the United States. . . . But we are living in a changing world where governments are being toppled over day by day. How do we know that we will not have another Castro in some other country in Latin America? Once that happens and they have the facilities to make the bomb, then we have something else to worry about. . . . I might conclude by saying this: If this agreement goes through at this time in this fashion, it will make a mockery of the Monroe Doctrine.—*John O. Pastore (D., Rhode Island), chairman of the Joint Congressional Committee on Atomic Energy, on the Senate floor, June 3, 1975.*

The senatorial thunder that greeted the news of the Brazil-German deal seemed to treat it as a kind of stab in the back from two of the closest postwar allies of the United States, as well as one more sign of the erosion of U.S. power and influence. However, an outsider might have been surprised by the strange failure to foresee these developments by those statesmen who promoted "Atoms for Peace" and arranged for this torch to be passed from one generation to the next.

In January 1976, David E. Lilienthal, the AEC's first chairman (1947-1950), told the senators that "we, the United States, our public agencies and our private manufacturers, have been and are the world's major proliferators." Not only did the United States let the genie out of the bottle, but her salesmen have proselytized the genie's magic powers as a "safe and cheap" source of energy supplies. While the Soviet Union has been far more responsible and cautious in purveying the "peaceful uses" of atomic energy, the U.S. government has, in the words of a Brookings Institution study by Jerome Kahan, "actively encouraged the sale abroad of U.S.-built reactors by providing extensive technical assistance, attractive financing through the Export-Import Bank, and long-term supplies of enriched fuel at stable prices. During this period, foreign firms entered into licensing arrangements with U.S. firms in order to acquire the capability to produce reactors."

In view of the results of these policies we might well ask, with Mark Twain, "Shall we go on conferring our Civilization upon the peoples that sit in darkness, or shall we give those poor things a rest? Shall we bang right ahead in our oldtime, loud, pious way, and commit the new century to the game; or shall we sober up and sit down and think it over first?"

Problems Ahead

There are problems ahead at every level—technical, strategic, political, and moral. Apart from the military potential of commercial nuclear power, the industry still must solve such problems as the long-term fuel shortage, safe disposal of large amounts of deadly radioactive waste materials, danger of terrorist theft of plutonium extracted from spent fuel, and rapid escalation of reactor construction costs.

As inflation and delay have raised the price of reactors from $300 per kilowatt of capacity in 1970 to $1,135 in 1975, the nuclear industry has been hit hard by recent cancellations of orders for at least 12 new power plants by U.S. utilities and post-

[46] *Juan E. Guglialmelli, "Y si Brasil fabrica la bomba atomica?"* Estrategia, *May-June 1975/July-August 1975, pp. 13-14.*

ponement of 133 more. Consequently, there are pressures for increased government subsidies, which is a hallowed tradition in the nuclear industry throughout the world.

At the same time, enormous capital investments will be required for the next phases of development of the U.S. nuclear industry, anticipated for the late 1970s. These would be the expansion of enrichment capacity and large-scale separation of plutonium from spent fuel rods to obtain additional reactor fuel. These new phases of the industry's development involve physical as well as financial risks that are becoming the focus of intense political debate.

". . . it would be worth considering restructuring the international industry into a single cartel-consortium of producing governments using a standardized reactor technology. . . ."

The Ford Administration has proposed federal guarantees of up to $8 billion for construction of uranium enrichment plants by private industry. The leading candidate for a franchise and guarantee for commercial use of this highly classified technology, presently restricted to a government monopoly, is Uranium Enrichment Associates (UEA), a consortium organized by Bechtel of San Francisco, the world's largest private engineering firm and a specialist in construction of nuclear power plants. In recent years, Bechtel has hired two former Nixon cabinet members, George Schultz and Casper Weinberger, as well as Robert Hollingsworth, a former AEC general manager.

Bechtel's salesmanship in the nuclear field led to one of the more picturesque diplomatic episodes to emerge from the Brazil-German deal. In April 1975, four State Department officials made a trip to Bonn, where they tried to persuade the Germans that enrichment technology should not be sold to Brazil because of the proliferation danger. Upon their return they learned that Bechtel had offered Brazil the same kind of technology two weeks before in a last-ditch effort to stop the German deal.

In a letter to Brazilian Minister of Mines and Energy Shigeaki Ueki, dated March 21, 1975, a Bechtel executive had written: "There has been a most recent decision by the Energy Research and Development Administration [(ERDA) a successor agency to the disbanded AEC] to encourage UEA to seek potential sites for enrichment plants outside the U.S.A. One of the locations which is most promising is Brazil, with the abundant hydro potential in the Amazon Basin." Because of ERDA's support, the Bechtel letter added, UEA "can offer Brazil the entire gamut from development of the mine, ore processing, enrichment, fuel processing, through the design of and construction of the nuclear power plants themselves."

Because enrichment activities are confined by U.S. law to a government monopoly operating within the country, and exportation of classified technology is prohibited, the Brazilians previously had been turned down in repeated efforts to get U.S. help in developing their own enrichment capacity. Under State Department pressure, Bechtel withdrew its offer three weeks later, informing the Brazilians in a letter that "it develops that within some United States circles there has been some concern about misinterpretation."

In view of the enormous government subsidies given, one way or another, to private nuclear energy companies in industrialized countries, the Brazil-German deal shows that "businesslike" competition between these subsidized national companies really amounts to competition between the national governments themselves in a highly dangerous sphere of activity. Because of the military potential of the "peaceful" uses of atomic energy, many developing countries are lured into ordering nuclear power plants they cannot afford, which will lead to heavy downstream losses for the already hard-pressed international reactor industry. On the other hand, the desperate need to sell reactors will lead each manufacturer to satisfy clients' demands for "sweeteners" that can be used in weapons making, such as enrichment and reprocessing plants. This will turn each sale into an act of political and diplomatic significance for the client and his neighbors and, in effect, what may be regarded as a military alliance between buyer and seller, lasting at least as long—perhaps a decade or two—as the time needed for the facilities to be built and the manufacturer paid off.

In response to the Brazil-German deal, the U.S. proposed a standardization of the conditions of export sales of nuclear power plants. Foreigners viewed this initiative coolly. They saw it as a maneuver to deny them their first big chance to enter the international reactor business, and to preserve the commanding U.S. position in the field.

At the "Secret Seven" meetings in London of supplier nations, the United States sought agreement on prohibition of the export of reprocessing plants, except under rigidly prescribed conditions. However, U.S. sources later said that France and West Germany would agree only to consultations and safeguards inspection agreements before exporting sensitive equipment and materials. This would have the effect of fabricating a paper umbrella of unenforceable guarantees as a license to create a series of dangerous de facto situations throughout the world.

Who Owns Nuclear Technology?

Because of the fuzzy economics of the nuclear industry and its clear military potential, the illusion that these companies can be run as a "business" may soon evaporate. More and more questions will be raised about the wisdom of parceling out to competing sets of corporate executives a costly technology, developed at public expense, that owes its origin, and most proven use, to achievements in destruction and terror.

Apart from the bomb itself, the electricity-generating reactor was first developed for military purposes in the U.S. Navy's atomic submarine program. The submarine reactor was then "scaled up" to generate electricity commercially by Westinghouse and GE with research and development funds provided by the AEC. To the degree that further development of commercial nuclear energy is justified to prevent the collapse of industrial society, then much more rigid controls should be imposed to restrain the economic and military anomalies, which are in the nature of the beast, from getting out of hand.

Rather than continue to stimulate "free" competition in the nuclear industry, it would be worth considering restructuring the international industry into a single cartel-consortium of producing governments using a standardized reactor technology to minimize diversion of materials for weapons purposes, licensing technology and exporting power plants only under the strictest nonproliferation controls. The standardization of reactor technology, in addition, could significantly reduce costs.

Brazil's Energy Options

While Brazilian officials have spoken of building 63 nuclear power plants by the turn of the century, the deal with West Germany contains firm orders for only two reactors. The size of the initial commitment may reflect some uncertainty about the growth rate of Brazil's future energy demand and about the performance of the German contractors. But the real issue is Brazil's capacity to pay for per capita energy consumption approaching the level of the developed nations.

Brazil's impressive postwar growth was intimately related to the expansion of the world economy and the low price of oil, especially in the 1960s and early 1970s. The Cinderella Year of the Brazilian "miracle" was 1973, when the national product grew by 11.4 per cent. Imports, exports, and the internal money supply all grew by half and oil imports by 46 per cent in that one year.[47] The 1973 Middle East war signaled an abrupt slowdown in this expansion. Over the previous generation Brazil's energy budget had quadrupled, while shifting from a wood-burning to a predominantly oil-burning and hydroelectric economy.

But even with this growth, Brazil's per capita consumption of commercial energy, while 60 per cent greater than the developing countries as a whole, was less than one-third of the world average and one-tenth that of the industrialized nations.[48] Petroleum imports created roughly half the cumulative current account deficit of $14 billion that Brazil incurred in 1974-1975. Present plans call for Brazil to spend around $65 billion through 1985 to develop her own energy resources—mainly offshore oil and hydroelectric and nuclear power, but also including shale, coal, and various forms of solar energy. This $65 billion is roughly equivalent to her whole national product for the Cinderella Year of 1973.

One of the ironies paving Brazil's new nuclear road is that Brazil could easily become a theater of major technological breakthroughs in using nonconventional energy sources, especially solar energy. Apart from the fact that her deposits of oil-bearing shale are second in size only to those of the United States, Brazil is in an excellent position to use photosynthetic transformation of solar energy to produce liquid and gaseous fuels, such as alcohol, methane, and hydrogen, which are both light and easily transportable.

Brazil already has adopted a plan to mix alcohol and gasoline to run her automobiles, which she did three decades ago during the World War II shortages, and is developing a car engine fueled entirely by alcohol. The alcohol would come from sugar cane or from new plantations of cassava on soils of low fertility occupying just 1 per cent of Brazil's total area to meet the country's fuel needs. Some scientists now view the Amazon jungle, with the high density and humidity of its vegetation, as one of the world's most efficient natural systems for conversion of photosynthetic energy. They calculate that the Amazon biomass might be industrially converted into methane at costs competitive with today's oil prices.

Such innovations could be extremely beneficial and could be the focus of international support and cooperation. In an editorial written shortly after the Brazil-German deal was signed, *Science* magazine observed:

> It is to be hoped that in solving its own energy problems Brazil will come to choose to exert world leadership not in facilitating nuclear proliferation but in providing the tropical countries with examples of how best to harvest and utilize solar energy.[49]

Whose Responsibility?

The centrifugal forces operating in the international nuclear energy industry, which have made it possible for Brazil to become a vessel of nuclear proliferation and Argentine scientists to become roving agents of the same process, can only be checked if governments assume direct responsibility for the industry. The salesman's vision of commercial nuclear energy as a boon to mankind and, he hopes, to corporate profits must be discarded in favor of a view of nuclear power as a dangerous but necessary device to be used with great caution.

Since the U.S. government funded the research and development effort for commercial applications of nuclear power by American reactor manufacturers, who then transferred this technology under license to government-subsidized companies in Europe and Japan, these governments have a re-

[47] Petrobrás Annual Report, 1973, *p. 29.*

[48] World Energy Supplies: 1970-73, *United Nations Statistical Papers, Series J, No. 18, 1975, p. 19.*

[49] *Philip H. Abelson, "Energy Alternatives for Brazil,"* Science, *August 8, 1975.*

sponsibility for the "business" of nuclear energy. Indeed, the developing countries singled out by disarmament specialists as being in the "near-nuclear" class and acquiring nuclear technology with clear military potential—South Korea, Taiwan, Brazil, and Argentina—are the same ones to which the big U.S. and European private banks are most heavily overcommitted with shaky loans.[50]

Not only does this imply a Western subsidy to these countries of the huge expense of acquiring nuclear power under very loose terms in the past and present, it also means, for the future, an important source of potential leverage for financial as well as technological restrictions on nuclear proliferation.

Disarmament specialists argue, with reason, that controls on "horizontal" nuclear proliferation need the moral sanction that can only be supplied by controls on the "vertical" proliferation of the nuclear arms race between the superpowers. However, as a practical matter, the present structure of the international nuclear industry still makes it possible for "horizontal" proliferation to be controlled by the Western governments themselves.

Curiously, while the moral claim of developing countries for access to "peaceful" nuclear technology has its main juridical support in Article IV of the NPT, it is the nonsigners of the NPT, who exhibited weapon-making intentions or capacity, that are benefiting most from transfers of "peaceful" nuclear technology, often under concessionary or giveway financial terms.

The pressures to export nuclear technology are expected to escalate rapidly in coming years. Inflation, construction delays, and the mounting impact of suspensions and cancellations of reactor orders are rapidly shrinking the home markets for nuclear power plants in the principal industrialized countries.

In 1975, Westinghouse and GE *each* still had a share of the world market almost as large as all other producers combined. However, U.S. domestic orders for nuclear plants peaked in 1972-1973. Even before the suspensions and cancellations of the past year struck the industry, U.S. companies were capable of producing annually almost four times as many reactor pressure vessels and turbine-generator units as the United States would need in 1977.

At this critical moment, Germany emerged as a major competitor in the international nuclear market. Looking over its shoulder to the expected entry of French, Swedish, and Japanese competitors into the crowded and unstable world market, KWU is being driven to grab as many orders as it can before the competition becomes even more fierce and disorderly.

While Bonn's handling of the Brazil deal initially received virtually unanimous support from the German public in the face of U.S. criticism, some voices subsequently have been raised in West Germany to express concern for some of the deal's implications. "It may be that global expansion of the technology necessary for putting together bombs can no longer be prevented, that in the evil competition for nuclear customers the level of prohibition necessarily drops ever lower," *Der Spiegel* observed.[51] "But must the Federal Republic play the role of advance guard?" Karl Kaiser of the German Society for Foreign Policy, an adviser to the ruling Social Democrats, wrote in *Europa Archiv*:

> On the commercial side of nuclear energy expansion we must ask ourselves whether the former policy of unrestricted nuclear know-how and power stations to developing countries should be pursued in the future.

If the international nuclear industry is to maintain its present scale of operations, government subsidies may have to increase rad-

[50] *See Ann Crittenden, "Loans Abroad Stir Worry,"* The New York Times, *January 15, 1976, p. 1.*

[51] Der Spiegel, *March 15, 1976, p. 73.*

ically and competition may become much dirtier. Too much money already has been invested in nuclear energy, and too many specialized careers have been developed by talented and well-paid technicians, for the industry, by itself, to accord anything but secondary priority to the security implications of its activities. Placed beside these economic stakes, the besieged industry seems to regard the prospect of local nuclear wars or accidents as small potatoes.

Ironically, the world has begun to forget the horror of smaller nuclear weapons. Leaders of developing nations widely regard them as symbols and instruments of power, forgetting that the military advantage of their possession, as well as the economic investment in their development, can be nullified rapidly by proliferation. The main strategic advantage of nuclear weapons lies in long-distance strikes requiring an elaborate delivery capability. In local nuclear wars between neighbors, neither party may escape without massive, lasting damage. A high U.S. official involved in the London negotiations among supplier countries recently remarked that the spread of nuclear weapons potential throughout the world, unfortunately, may not be stopped until the next city is destroyed. By that time, however, the spread of this destructive capability may be so extensive that efforts at control may no longer be possible.

In terms of both economic and military potential, the world is rapidly approaching a no-win situation in the development of commercial nuclear power. It is so burdened by inflation, capital shortages, political controversy, and uncertainties over future fuel supplies that, in the United States, *Science* magazine could recently observe: "The nuclear industry is in such trouble that many people are saying, with some truth, that a *de facto* moratorium on future nuclear development already exists."[52] If this paralysis persists in the U.S. industry, it could spread to nuclear energy enterprises in other industrialized countries, which are experiencing comparable problems of their own. The international reactor industry would then be faced with a clear choice between subsidizing—i.e., giving away—exports of nuclear power plants to developing countries on an even greater scale than in the past in order to sustain industrial capacity at home, or scaling down the nuclear energy enterprise to much more manageable proportions.

In this connection, the liberal *Die Zeit*, in its defense of the Brazil-German deal, made two important observations. The first was: "The deceptive distinction between nuclear technology for 'peaceful' and for 'military' uses lies at the core of the nonproliferation policies. In reality this dividing line is almost irrelevant. Whoever achieves a high level of civilian technology is almost automatically on the threshhold of manufacture of nuclear weapons."[53] The second was a suggestion that, "if America were to dismount from its high horse of nuclear monopoly rights," i.e., the dominant U.S. market position, then a step toward closer integration of the industry's goals could be taken through formation of a "loose confederation" of supplier countries that could be known as "NUTEX" (Nuclear Technology Exporters).

This idea is similar to the more recent proposal by Senator Ribicoff for "a cooperative arrangement with other suppliers, including France and West Germany, that will guarantee each supplier a minimum market share of reactor exports."[54] Such an arrangement might be organized along the lines of Atomic Energy of Canada, Limited (AECL), the government company that acts as general contractor for the Candu reactor and parcels out business to the various component manufacturers.

[52] *Luther J. Carter, "Energy Policy: Independence by 1985 May be Unreachable Without Btu Tax,"* Science, *February 13, 1976, p. 548.*

[53] *Joachim Schwelein, "Heisses Geschaft mit dem Atomstrom,"* Die Zeit, *June 27, 1975.*

[54] *Abraham A. Ribicoff, "Trading in Doom,"* The New York Times, *March 26, 1976.*

While this might require the United States to yield a larger share of the international reactor market to other countries, it could bring the compensating advantage of heading off the kind of trade wars that could lead to nuclear wars. It could promote sharing of the financial burdens of such costly undertaking as enrichment, research, and development, and the production of specialized components. It also could end the plague of "loss leader" giveaways of nuclear exports by establishing financial, technological, and safeguards standards for all sales and by placing final control of these transactions in the hands of an international directorate run by governments, which is where the responsibility belongs. The reactor export industry should become an international public utility.

The fact that the international community has been able to stop the use of certain chemical and biological weapons for more than a half-century offers hope that concerted action can still manage the nuclear trade. Any additional cost incurred by this kind of management would be the price of peace. The failure to pay this price may mean infinitely greater costs further down the road.

KENNEDY AND THE CUBAN CONNECTION

by Donald E. Schulz

Conspiracy theories are fashionable; sometimes even fruitful, as in the case of Watergate. So it should not be surprising that recent revelations of the Senate Intelligence Committee and other sources have resurrected a very old question—namely, what connection, if any, did the Castro government have with the assassination of John F. Kennedy?

A current speculation is that the Cuban dictator, having learned of CIA plots against his life, decided to strike back, returning violence for violence, with consequences that are now a matter of historical record. Indeed, the recent report of the task force headed by Senators Schweiker and Hart, while finding no hard facts to support this theory, did uncover some fascinating circumstantial evidence.[1]

We are told, for instance, of the June 1963 decision of the National Security Council's "Special Group" to step up subversive activities against the Havana government and of the subsequent renewal of CIA contacts with a high-level Cuban official, Rolando Cubelas (code-named AMLASH), who proposed the overthrow and assassination of Castro by means of an "inside job." We learn that shortly thereafter, Castro is-

[1] *U.S., Congress, Senate, Select Committee to Study Governmental Operations with Respect to Intelligence Activities,* The Investigation of the Assassination of President John F. Kennedy: Performance of the Intelligence Agencies, Final Report, *94th Cong., 2d sess., 1976, Senate Rept. 94-755. Hereafter referred to as the Schweiker-Hart report. Unless otherwise specified, information in this article comes from the Schweiker-Hart report and U.S., Congress, Senate, Select Committee to Study Governmental Operations with Respect to Intelligence Activities,* Alleged Assassination Plots Involving Foreign Leaders, An Interim Report, *94th Cong., 1st sess., 1975, Senate Rept. 94-465.*

sued a public warning that should U.S. leaders aid "terrorist plans to eliminate Cuban leaders, they themselves will not be safe." This threat, however, was ignored. CIA covert operations were escalated. On October 29, the head of the agency's Special Affairs Section, Desmond Fitzgerald, met with AMLASH. Presenting himself (inaccurately) as a "personal representative" of Attorney General Robert Kennedy, he informed the Cuban that the United States would back the proposed coup. On November 22, the very day that the American president was struck down on the streets of Dallas, a CIA case officer met once again with AMLASH to reassure him of U.S. support for the operation and confirm that explosives and rifles with telescopic sights would be provided. In addition, the Cuban was given a ballpoint pen, fashioned with a special hypodermic needle, which could be used to inject a lethal dose of poison into the intended victim if the opportunity arose.

Neither this nor previous assassination plots against Castro were ever made known to the Warren Commission. Indeed, the evidence strongly suggests that there was an overwhelming predisposition on the part of the White House, the Justice Department, the FBI, the CIA, and the commission itself to accept Lee Harvey Oswald as Kennedy's lone killer, without adequately investigating other hypotheses and leads that might have led to different conclusions.

Thus, almost immediately following the shooting, FBI Director J. Edgar Hoover, the Justice Department, and the White House exerted pressure on senior FBI officials to promptly complete their investigation and issue a factual report upholding the "lone assassin" thesis. In the words of Deputy Attorney General Nicholas Katzenbach:

> It is important that all of the facts surrounding President Kennedy's assassination be made public in a way which will satisfy people in the United States and abroad that all the facts have been told and that a statement to this effect be made now.
>
> The public must be satisfied that Oswald was the assassin; that he did not have confederates who are still at large; and that the evidence was such that he would have been convicted at trial.
>
> Speculation about Oswald's motivation ought to be cut off, and we should have some basis for rebutting thought that this was a Communist conspiracy or (as the Iron Curtain press is saying) a rightwing conspiracy to blame it on the Communists.

No doubt there was here a sincere belief that such findings were in the national interest. After all, the dangers of irresolution were obvious. Speculation, feeding on fear and grief, might inflame public opinion and drive the Johnson administration into taking some rash and hazardous action. Only the previous year, the United States and the Soviet Union had gone to the very brink of nuclear war over Cuba. There was little enthusiasm in Washington for repeating that scenario.

Although understandable, this attitude would taint the investigation with prejudice from the very beginning. The ensuing FBI inquiry would be handled primarily as a regular criminal case, its almost exclusive focus of attention being on Oswald. And while a massive array of data was compiled on the suspect's background, activities, contacts, and the specific act of assassination, nowhere is there evidence that a broader study was ever conducted to explore the possibility of a conspiracy, either foreign or domestic. The result, not surprisingly, was a report that mirrored the prevailing predispositions.

Moreover, once those conclusions were issued, the bureau's reputation was at stake. Hoover himself viewed the Warren Commission as an adversary. The chief justice, he felt, was "seeking to criticize" the FBI and "find gaps" in its inquiry. Needless to say, such defensive reactions were hardly conducive to a healthy working relationship. Technically speaking, the bureau fulfilled its responsibilities to the letter; it supplied the commission with the information requested. But it volunteered very little. And among the items that never reached Earl Warren's desk was a report on the CIA's assassination plots against Castro.

The CIA's performance was similarly suspect. A major difficulty was the extreme compartmentalization of knowledge within the bureaucracy. The desk officer who coordinated the initial investigation was not even aware of the AMLASH operation. Nor, for that matter, was the CIA director, John McCone. Furthermore, those who were aware weren't talking. Whether out of a desire to avoid another "Cuban flap," or to protect the agency from embarrassment and preserve the secrecy of its activities, or because of a failure to draw a connection between the AMLASH plot and the Kennedy assassination, neither the deputy director for plans, Richard Helms, nor Desmond Fitzgerald, nor the case officer assigned to AMLASH volunteered their knowledge to the authorities responsible for conducting the investigation. As a result, information that might well have become an "absolutely vital factor" in the inquiry—according to the desk officer who coordinated the CIA investigation—was never received. By the time the Warren Commission began to issue requests to the agency, the possibility of a "Cuban connection" had been effectively dismissed. Subsequent analyses were directed almost entirely toward the issue of Soviet involvement.

Neither the Warren Commission as a body nor its staff was ever given details of the CIA's Cuban activities. Ultimately, however, this was the responsibility of the commission itself. If its inquiry was flawed and incomplete, this must in large part be attributed to its own lack of imagination and initiative. At least one of its members, former CIA head Allen Dulles, was aware of the general nature of the covert operations being waged against the Castro regime. Assassination plots had been hatched during his own tenure as director, apparently with his knowledge. Yet there is no evidence that he ever told his colleagues on the commission about those activities. Nor was the issue ever pursued in the commission's requests for information to the intelligence community—in spite of Oswald's known Cuban contacts and Castro's warning that U.S.-sponsored terrorism would bring retaliation.

In sum, if a CIA-FBI "coverup" deprived the Warren Commission of vital information, the latter's performance was also far from impeccable. And while the vice-presidential candidate from Pennsylvania may have gone a bit overboard when he declared that "there is no longer any reason to have faith in its picture of the Kennedy assassination,"[2] at the very least it has been demonstrated that the investigatory process was seriously flawed.

Thus, the Senate Intelligence Committee, disbanded on May 31, 1976, recommended that its permanent successor, the Senate Select Committee on Intelligence, continue the inquiry in an effort to explore the leads that have been uncovered and resolve the troubling questions raised. Thus, the House of Representatives on September 17, 1976, voted to compose a special 12-member Committee on Assassinations to "conduct a full and complete investigation" into the deaths of John F. Kennedy and Martin Luther King. And so, apparently, we are to have a reopening of the case—at last.

A Tale of Two Dialogues

In light of these developments, it seems appropriate to recall a little-known campaign of accommodation launched on a covert basis by Washington and Havana in the weeks preceding that fateful day in November 1963. Actually, the origins of this tentative and ultimately ill-fated rapprochement may be traced back to the previous spring, when Castro, as part of a general reassessment of domestic and foreign policy, announced his readiness to normalize rela-

[2] *Statement by Senator Richard Schweiker cited in the* Columbus Citizen-Journal, *June 24, 1976.*

tions with the United States. The primary reason for this initiative was fairly obvious: Nikita Khrushchev, sobered by the chilling experience of the missile crisis, sorely in need of Western trade and technology to help bolster the hard-pressed Soviet economy, desired a reduction of international tension in preparation for a renewed campaign of détente. At the same time, Castro, increasingly dependent on his Muscovite sponsors, found himself obliged to embrace the banner of "peaceful coexistence" in order to secure the economic and military agreements that he needed to assure the continued survival and development of his revolution.

It was not until September, however, that this campaign began to bear fruit. At that time, William Attwood, a special adviser to the U.S. Delegation to the United Nations, informed Averell Harriman and Adlai Stevenson that he had received information from various sources that Castro was unhappy with Cuba's satellite status and was looking for a way out; in short, that he wanted an accommodation with the United States and was willing to make substantive concessions to get it. The message was passed on to the president, who approved the suggestion that a "discrete contact" be made with Carlos Lechuga, head of the Cuban Delegation to the United Nations. Subsequently, such communications were established and a series of meetings held between Attwood and Lechuga to discuss the prospect of negotiations.

In point of fact, by early November, Kennedy had decided to push toward an opening with Cuba in an attempt to take Castro out of the Soviet fold and erase the memory of the Bay of Pigs. Accordingly, a preliminary conference with Lechuga and René Vallejo, Fidel's personal physician and confidant, was sought at the United Nations in order to prepare an agenda for discussions. On November 18, this message was transmitted by telephone to Vallejo in Havana. Shortly thereafter, Lechuga was instructed to set forth such an agenda for U.S. consideration. Ironically, due to a lag in communications these orders were received only on November 23, the day after Kennedy's assassination.[8]

But this was not the whole story. Even as these developments were unfolding, a second dialogue was taking place through an unofficial envoy—the French journalist, Jean Daniel. On October 24, Kennedy had received Daniel in the White House. The subject of conversation was Cuba. The president, it seems, had learned of the Frenchman's forthcoming visit to the island and had decided to seize the occasion to send Castro a message. In essence, this communication came down to a strong hint that the United States could learn to live with a Socialist Cuba in a "normalized" relationship *providing* certain conditions were met. What were those conditions? One, clearly, was an end to Castroite subversion. While expressing sympathy for Latin-American aspirations for justice and progress, Kennedy stressed that those goals would not be achieved through Marxist dictatorship. The United States had a special responsibility to the "Free World" to contain Communist expansionism. As long as the government in Havana continued to export revolution, the economic "blockade" of the island would remain in effect.

Beyond this, not much was definite. The American negotiating stance had not yet been worked out. Moreover, the president's position remained extremely delicate. Cuba was still a highly emotional issue. Even the State Department had serious qualms about the desirability of dealing with Castro. For obvious political reasons, Kennedy could not be too direct.

Nevertheless, Kennedy's remarks were suggestive enough to convince Daniel that Kennedy had had second thoughts about the efficacy of U.S. policy and was seeking a

[8] *William Attwood,* The Reds and the Blacks *(New York: Harper & Row, 1967), pp. 142-146; and Senate Select Committee,* Alleged Assassination plots . . . , op. cit., *pp. 173-174.*

change. He had come to accept the Cuban revolution as a fact of life. The clock would never again be turned back to the days of the Batista regime, when colonialism, economic exploitation, and national humiliation prevailed—with North American complicity. Kennedy acknowledged U.S. responsibility for much of what had happened. It was almost as though the United States had manufactured the Castro movement without even realizing it. Now it would have to pay. Indeed, the function of the Alliance for Progress would be to correct the vast accumulation of similar mistakes currently jeopardizing all of Latin America. The United States now had the chance to do as much good as it had done wrong in the past—providing, of course, that the area did not go Communist.

But could the United States tolerate "economic collectivism"? The issue, of course, had particular relevance for Cuba, and Daniel wanted to be quite sure of Kennedy's position. The reply: The United States already had accepted it—for instance, in Guinea and Yugoslavia. Only three days earlier, the president had had a "most positive" discussion with Marshal Tito. And the attempt to isolate the island economically? Was this a punishment or a political maneuver? Kennedy smiled. Was Daniel suggesting that the blockade was not politically effective? He would soon have the opportunity to see for himself. In any case, the main issue was Communist expansion. Castro had become a "Soviet agent" in Latin America. He had to be contained: "The continuation of the blockade depends on the continuation of subversive activities."

Thus, Daniel, bearing this message and an invitation to revisit the White House upon his return, set off for Cuba. There he found a proud, critical, yet remarkably receptive Castro. Indeed, during the course of a six-hour interview the *líder máximo* found occasion to praise the American president for his sincerity, realism, and "good ideas": Kennedy might yet become a greater leader than Lincoln. He had come to appreciate "many things" over the past few months; might still understand that there could be "coexistence between Capitalists and Socialists, even in the Americas." For their part, Castro and his countrymen wanted nothing more than peace. They were not supplicants; they asked merely to be left alone to concentrate on the socio-economic tasks of the revolution. If the United States could accept Cuban socialism, then "everything can be restored to normalcy on the basis of mutual respect of sovereignty." The issue of subversion would not be an obstacle. Cubans would naturally "feel solidarity" with their revolutionary brethren in other lands. Ultimately, however, each nation had to determine its own destiny, and "if they choose other regimes than ours, this isn't our business."

That was two days prior to Kennedy's death.

Moreover, on the afternoon of November 22, Castro and Daniel resumed their conversation at the prime minister's summer residence on Varadero Beach. In the midst of the questioning, the telephone rang. The call was from the Cuban president, Osvaldo Dorticós, for Castro. The message: Kennedy had just been struck down in Dallas. It was not yet known whether he would live or die.

Stunned, Castro came back and sat down. Three times he repeated the words *"Es una mala noticia."* ("This is bad news.") He fell momentarily silent. Then the speculation began: There was an alarmingly large lunatic fringe in the United States. This could as easily be the work of a madman as a terrorist. Perhaps a Vietnamese? Or a member of the Ku Klux Klan? In any case, Kennedy might still survive. If so, his reelection would be assured. This last was said with visible satisfaction.

But this was not to be. Within a half hour, the news came over the radio: The president was dead.

Castro stood up. Now everything had changed, would have to be rethought. Kennedy, at least, had been an enemy to whom Cubans had become accustomed. Now the assassin would have to be found quickly, "otherwise, you watch and see, I know them, they will try to put the blame on us. . . ."[4]

This did not, of course, come to pass. In spite of an initial flurry of speculation—Oswald was soon discovered to be a Castro sympathizer with some rather tenuous links to the Fair Play for Cuba Committee—the Johnson administration was quick to embrace the "lone assassin" thesis. Subsequently, the Warren Commission was appointed not so much to get at the truth (the president himself would have preferred to stand on the FBI's report) as to stop the "rash of investigations" that was bound to occur should the nation remain unconvinced of Oswald's sole responsibility for these tragic developments.

Concessions for Survival

But what did all this mean? I have recounted the story of the Castro-Kennedy dialogues because it provides an important—perhaps crucial—frame of reference for congressional investigators and the public alike. It is not, of course, proof of innocence. But would Castro have been so intent on coming to terms with a man whom he was conspiring to kill? One may seriously doubt it.

In point of fact, the rapid collapse of the Cuban economy (the 1963 sugar harvest had come to only 2.8 million tons, compared to 4.8 million tons in 1962 and 6.7 million tons in 1961), aggravated by the devastation of Hurricane Flora that autumn, had made a concerted attempt at rapprochement virtually imperative. Castro was now more dependent than ever on his Muscovite sponsors. During his initial visit to the Soviet Union the previous spring, he had committed himself to a drastic modification of his ill-conceived program of rapid industrialization. Thus, sugar would once again be given priority attention by Cuban economic planners. And the foreign exchange earned from its sale abroad would pave the way for the island's eventual industrialization.

By the same token, however, this meant that the Cubans would have to obtain premium prices and a guaranteed market for their product. And although the Soviets had consented to an increase in the price of their purchases for the current year, the kind of long-range agreement that Castro was seeking had not yet been worked out. Only in January 1964, with his return to the Soviet Union, would such an accord be reached. In exchange for Castro's support for "peaceful coexistence" and other matters (including an explicit pledge to "do everything necessary to re-establish good-neighbor relations between Cuba and the United States"), Khrushchev would agree to take 2.1 million tons of sugar in 1965 and a million more tons each successive year until a level of 5 million tons per annum was attained during 1968 to 1970, all at a price of six cents a pound.[5]

In retrospect, it seems unlikely that Castro would have jeopardized an arrangement so critical to the future of his revolution for the sake of a vendetta against Kennedy, especially when the latter was beginning to respond to his covert initiatives at rapprochement. Indeed, the available evidence suggests that Castro's courtship of the American president was motivated by more than the mere necessity of striking a bargain with Moscow. There was also a clear desire to see an end to the U.S. boycott which, in spite of occasional Cuban protests to the contrary, was seriously damaging the national economy. Thus, when Hurricane Flora passed through the southeastern part of the island in October, leaving more than 1,200 casualties and flooding some 2,500 acres of the country's best farmland, Castro

[4] *The testimony of Jean Daniel may be found in* The New Republic, *December 7, 14, 21 and 28, 1963.*

[5] *The text of the communique may be found in* Hoy, *January 23, 1964.*

seized the occasion to issue a public appeal to Washington to lift its sanctions.[6] To little avail. The official position of the State Department remained as inflexible as ever.

No doubt, there was some hope that the normalization of relations with the "colossus" would lead to Cuban participation in the Alliance for Progress. After all, hadn't Castro himself been the *true* father of the alliance? In May 1959, long before the two countries had broken ties, he had called on the United States to make a $30 billion commitment to a 10-year program of economic development for all of Latin America. His proposal had been the object of considerable ridicule. Later, of course, the Kennedy administration launched its own similar plan in an effort to keep the Castroite virus from spreading to other lands. Now, perhaps, the time was approaching when Cuba would be able to share in the wealth that was being redistributed. Hadn't Kennedy hinted as much in his conversation with Daniel? In any case, the renewal of relations would provide a welcome balance to dependency on the Soviet Union.

The courtship of the United States did not end abruptly with Kennedy's death. Castro continued his initiatives, this time in public view.[7] But it was too late. The assassination had terminated Washington's interest in accommodation. For political reasons of its own, the Johnson administration quickly retreated to an uncompromising cold war stance, demanding in effect that Castro divest himself of his dependence on the Soviet Union, even as it made it impossible for him to do so by continuing its policy of isolating Cuba economically and politically from the so-called "Free World." Under these circumstances, Castro's enthusiasm for détente gradually waned, eventually disappearing altogether in the wake of American interventions in Vietnam and the Dominican Republic.

But that is another story. Our concern is with the opportunities, pressures, and constraints with which Castro had to contend during those fateful weeks prior to Kennedy's assassination. And what about Castro's alleged threats against the president? According to Associated Press reporter Daniel Harker, on the evening of September 7, Castro had held an impromptu, three-hour interview at the Brazilian embassy during which he issued the following warning: "We are prepared to fight them and answer in kind. United States leaders should think that if they are aiding terrorist plans to eliminate Cuban leaders, they themselves will not be safe." Moreover, the "CIA and other dreamers believe their hopes of an insurrection or a successful guerrilla war. They can go on dreaming forever." [8]

The gist of this communication has been confirmed by other sources.[9] The issue that remains is how to interpret it. The theory that has thus far dominated public discussion is that Castro found out about the AMLASH-CIA conspiracy and decided to retaliate in kind. My own opinion is somewhat different. I suggest that what was involved here was a simple exercise in deterrence. It is not unlikely that AMLASH had indeed been discovered, if he was not a double-agent to begin with. Even the CIA suspected that he was an unstable individual and a security risk. At the very least, he talked too much. Moreover, the timing of Castro's warning is especially suggestive. It was issued immediately following the resumption of the AMLASH connection, on

[6] *See the report on Castro's television appearance of October 21, in* Cuba Socialista, *November 1963 and his October 31 speech in the Foreign Broadcast Information Service's* Daily Report, *October 31, 1963.*

[7] *See, for instance, Castro's January 2, 1964 speech to the Cuban people, in* Revolucion, *January 3, 1964; the January 1964 Soviet-Cuban communique in* Hoy, *January 23, 1964; Castro's interview with Richard Eder, in* The New York Times, *July 6, 1964; Castro's speech of July 26, 1964, in the Foreign Broadcast Information Service's* Daily Report, *July 28, 1964; and Castro's news conference with foreign journalists in* Bohemia, *August 7, 1964.*

[8] Miami Herald, *September 9, 1963.*

[9] *Most notably, in the* Las Vegas Sun, *March 1, 1976.*

the very day in fact that CIA headquarters received word of the meeting. Castro's choice of the Brazilian embassy as the site of his remarks is similarly provocative. It had been in Brazil that AMLASH had met his U.S. contact. Was this a calculated attempt by Castro to let Washington know that he knew about the operation? At least some members of the Senate Intelligence Committee believed that it was.[10]

By the same token, however, the very fact that the threat was issued in public suggests the improbability of its actually being carried out. If Castro were going to have Kennedy assassinated would he broadcast it to the world? I think not. Certainly, he could have had few illusions as to the impact that such an act, openly proclaimed and recognized, would have had in the United States. The demand for retaliation would have been overwhelming. And although the revolution had survived the CIA-sponsored invasion at the Bay of Pigs, that had been a half-hearted affair conducted through Cuban surrogates. A full-scale onslaught by the U.S. marines was entirely another matter. In perspective, it seems rather unlikely that Castro would have invited such an attack, especially when he had the evidence of the missile crisis to consider. Clearly, the Soviets were not willing to lose Moscow in order to defend Havana.

A more probable interpretation is that the statement of September 7 was intended to deter the United States from pursuing the AMLASH operation and other subversive activities that were rapidly becoming a serious threat to Cuban internal security.[11] That the warning was ignored does not necessarily mean much. Bluff is often a key element in deterrence. In any case, Castro could not have been sure that the United States would back AMLASH until at least October 29, when CIA agents met with the Cuban once again. And even then, their support was couched in such general terms that it was not at all clear whether the assassination would be permitted (Fitzgerald later claimed that he had informed AMLASH that the United States did not do such things) or technical assistance rendered. Only on November 22—too late to have affected the events in Dallas—would those issues be finally resolved.

Speculation and a Lead

Does all this mean that we may discount the possibility of a Cuban connection? The answer is no. For one thing, the evidence presented in these pages, though clearly outweighing anything that has thus far been offered in support of the retaliation hypothesis, remains circumstantial and inconclusive. If the events of recent years have taught us anything, it is that human beings —and governments—often behave in inconsistent and self-destructive ways. Assassination is a highly emotional issue, and Castro is excitable. Under other circumstances, it would not have been surprising had a threat on his life triggered a pre-emptive attack. And even under the very special conditions described above, it is not impossible that Castro did, wittingly or unwittingly, set in motion the machinery of retaliation. All that was really necessary was that Cuban security agents behave in much the same way as their North American counterparts—that is, semiautonomously, initiating and perpetuating cloak and dagger operations without the explicit authorization of their political superiors. If, due to a lack of political control and a prevailing atmosphere of cold war hostility, CIA agents could be engaged in an attempt on Castro's life at the very moment that the American president was secretly exploring the prospects for an accommodation, it is

[10] *This from a source close to the committee, cited in the* Columbus Dispatch, *June 21, 1976.*

[11] *The problem was especially acute in the Escambray mountains of central Cuba, where more than 1,000 guerrillas were waging a determined struggle—with* CIA *support. These and lesser uprisings throughout the island were eventually put down, but only after several years of struggle and considerable human and material cost.*

not difficult to imagine similar distortions occurring on the Cuban side. Might not some overzealous security officials have taken Castro's threat of September 7 for tacit authority to set up a "program of elimination"?

Moreover, it is important to remember that the "Cuban connection" refers not merely to Castroite involvement but also to the possibility that *anti*-Castro forces were responsible for the killing. After all, Oswald had had contacts with both sides. And certainly the exiles had reason to view Kennedy with bitterness. Promises had been betrayed. The thrust of official policy was no longer on "liberating" the island but rather on "containment"—that is, accepting the Castro regime as a fact of life and limiting the damage. Following the missile crisis, the CIA's covert operations had been reduced. Operation MONGOOSE, the plan to use Cuban dissidents and exiles to overthrow the government in Havana, had been terminated. And the FBI and other agencies had begun to bring their power to bear in a serious attempt to restrict the paramilitary adventures of the exiles. Inevitably, this shift toward opposition had given rise to heated emotions. Might such resentments have been translated into direct action against the president? By the same token, if his assassin could be established as a Castro agent, or at least a sympathizer, might this trigger a U.S. invasion and return the exiles to their homeland?[12]

But all this remains speculation. It is possible to imagine any number of scenarios that might have led to the fatal events of November 22. Hence, the importance of the leads uncovered by the Senate Intelligence Committee; for if they offer substantial new evidence or the promise that such evidence might emerge through further investigation, then clearly a major reopening of the inquiry is obligatory.

With this in mind, let us briefly examine the nature of these leads.

Certainly, the most sensational (not to say sensationalistic) of the lot is the case of "D," a Latin American who appeared at the U.S. embassy in Mexico City a few days after Kennedy's death with a story which, on the surface, would seem to lend strong support to the retaliation hypothesis. On September 18, it was asserted, "D" had been at the Cuban consulate, where he had seen Oswald receive $6,500 from two other men, one of whom was Cuban, and had overheard the trio discuss the forthcoming assassination. Subsequently, he had tried on several occasions to warn the American embassy, but to no avail. Eventually, he had been told to stop wasting his time.

This claim created quite a stir. The fact of the matter was that Oswald *had* been in Mexico City in late September and *had* visited the Cuban consulate (in an unsuccessful effort to obtain a Cuban travel visa). Was this mere coincidence? Again, recall the date of Castro's threat against U.S. leaders.

In retrospect, there is legitimate question about the way in which the ensuing inquiry was handled. The Schweiker-Hart report makes a convincing case that the FBI performance was an essentially negative effort, designed to discredit rather than objectively investigate "D" 's allegations. Nor was the CIA's inquiry immune from criticism. This was Mexican national territory. As such, it was the Mexican police who first interrogated the subject and extracted from him a written confession that his entire story was a fabrication. Later, however, when questioned by U.S. authorities, "D" claimed to have been pressured into making this retraction.[13]

Here, some doubt lingers. Was the CIA so anxious to avoid another "Cuban flap" that it too conducted a "negative" investigation? The Schweiker-Hart report does not

[12] *See, in particular, the arguments and evidence presented by Robert Sam Anson, in* They've Killed the President! *(New York: Bantam, 1975), pp. 246-74.*

[13] Report of the President's Commission on the Assassination of President John F. Kennedy *(Washington, D.C.: Government Printing Office, 1964), p. 308.*

go this far, but it does demonstrate that such a concern existed. Moreover, it suggests that the agency was very quick to write off "D" 's story once word of his retraction had been received. Thus, for instance, mention is made of information from a "sensitive and reliable source" that tended to confirm his initial testimony. This report was never satisfactorily explained, though it was later made available to the Warren Commission staff. Similarly, it is noted that on December 2, the Mexican station reported that it had reason to doubt its earlier conclusion that "D" was fabricating. By then, however, headquarters had lost interest.

Yet, loose ends notwithstanding, one must, in the final analysis, agree with the Warren Commission. There are simply too many contradictions to lend "D"'s story much credence. While his claim to have been pressured into a retraction by the Mexican police seems plausible enough, it must be noted that when he was subsequently given a polygraph test by U.S. authorities, the machine indicated that he was probably lying. Upon being informed of this finding, the subject once again altered his testimony, admitting in effect that he must have been "mistaken." Moreover, it was soon established that Oswald had been in New Orleans on September 18, the day that he was alleged to have been at the Cuban consulate in Mexico City.[14] (Though a story later came in changing that date to September 28, when he *was* in Mexico.) Furthermore, the telephone extension number that "D" claimed to have used in his efforts to warn the American embassy would not have given him the individual to whom he had allegedly spoken; in addition, no one at the embassy had any recollection of his calls. Finally, by his own account, part of the mysterious conversation at the Cuban consulate had been conducted in Spanish. Yet Oswald spoke little, if any, Spanish. That he could have participated in such an exchange would therefore seem rather doubtful.[15]

A More Promising Lead

A somewhat more promising lead involves the testimony of a certain Washington lawyer, whose underworld clients had been called upon by an unspecified government agency to participate in a project that was said to have the highest governmental approval. The objective of this program was the assassination of Castro. According to this version, the plot had nearly reached fruition when the Cuban dictator learned of it. By exerting pressure on captured subjects, he was able to find out the full details, whereupon he decided that "if that was the way . . . Kennedy wanted it, he too could engage in the same tactics." Thereafter, assassination teams were dispatched to the United States for the purpose of killing the President.

This story would seem to have some basis in reality. The lawyer's clients had apparently been involved in the CIA's early efforts to enlist mafia support against Castro. But that campaign had been terminated in February 1963, long before Kennedy's assassination. Moreover, the information which these individuals were said to possess with regard to the alleged Cuban retaliation was strictly hearsay—"feedback" provided by sources close to Castro, who had been placed there in order to carry out the original project. In fact, when these same clients were interviewed by the Senate Intelligence Committee they denied recollection of such information or of ever having discussed the matter with the lawyer.

Still, one cannot rule out their initial tale. There are obvious reasons (the foremost being self-preservation) why such men would not want to get involved with a Senate investigation of the underworld.

[14] Ibid., *p. 308.*

[15] *It appears that "D" (real name, Gilberto Alvarado) was an agent of the Nicaraguan Intelligence Service. His intention in manufacturing this tale was to trigger U.S. action against Castro.* Ibid., *pp. 307-308.*

By the same token, the mere fact that the CIA's mafia campaign had been terminated months prior to the assassination does not necessarily mean much. Covert operations often acquire lives of their own. In this case the mafia intermediary, John Rosselli, had simply broken off communication with his Cuban contacts without informing them that the $150,000 bounty placed on Castro's head had been withdrawn. Under such circumstances, the conspiracy could have remained operational long after it had been officially abandoned. And Castro's security forces, had they uncovered the plot, would presumably have had no way of knowing that it no longer enjoyed U.S. sponsorship.

But this is conjecture. The reluctance of the clients to repeat their story to Senate investigators suggests the difficulties likely to be encountered in any follow-up inquiry. Nevertheless, the effort must be made.

Two other less promising leads are the following:

On the evening of November 22, a Cubana airlines flight from Mexico City to Havana had been delayed five hours, awaiting the arrival of a mysterious passenger. At 10:30 PM, this individual arrived in a twin-engined aircraft and boarded the Cubana plane without passing through customs. Subsequently, he travelled to Cuba in the cockpit, avoiding identification by his fellow passengers and by Mexican authorities.

We also learn of a certain Cuban-American, a Castro sympathizer with connections with the Tampa Chapter of the Fair Play for Cuba Committee with which Oswald may also have had contact. On November 23, this person crossed the border from Texas to Mexico, eventually making his way to Havana via a Cubana airlines flight on which he was the sole passenger. Later, the CIA received a report that he was somehow "involved in the assassination."

With the exception of the story of the Washington lawyer, which only surfaced in 1967, information about these episodes was in the possession of the intelligence community as early as December 1963. Yet, there is no evidence that the Warren Commisison was ever provided with the kind of data that would have enabled it to pursue these leads. Who were these individuals and why their strange behavior? The Senate Intelligence Committee's staff contacted the Federal Aviation Administration in an attempt to determine the origins of the twin-engined craft—without success. Records from that time period are no longer kept. As for the Cuban-American, when last heard he was living in Cuba, beyond the reach of U.S. investigators, spending much of his time playing dominoes. That was in September 1964.

In short, the task is formidable. Thirteen years have passed. Leads which once would have been relatively easy to pursue have long ago dried up. Key witnesses have died, disappeared, or are otherwise inaccessible. This is true even of our old friend AMLASH. In March 1966, Cubelas was sentenced to 25 years in prison for plotting Castro's assassination in league with the CIA. Only after a personal appeal for clemency by his intended victim did he manage to escape the death penalty.

Was AMLASH a double agent? There is some reason to think so. Certainly, he was a professional intriguer and opportunist of the first rank. In the early 1960s he had served as Castro's hatchet man at the University of Havana, where he rode around in big cars and lived the sweet life while presiding over the destruction of traditional academic freedoms. In the process, he had apparently acquired strong connections with Cuban intelligence and had begun to cooperate with it in various ways. (This, at least, was the testimony of AMWHIP, a Cuban exile who had been involved in the AMLASH operation from the beginning.) By mid-1965, the CIA considered the risk serious enough to terminate the entire affair. In the words of the chief of special affairs staff counterintelligence, "Fidel reportedly knew that this group was plotting against him and once enlisted its support. Hence, we cannot rule out the possibility of provocation."

Picture, if you will, the following scenario: Castro, having suffered through innumerable attempts on his life in the years since he came to power, suspected that at least some of these plots had the backing of the U.S. government. This was not illogical, in view of the CIA's vast ongoing campaign of violence and subversion against his regime. But he had no proof. The agency was not the only one interested in "eliminating" him. Elements of the underworld, the Cuban exile community, and the counterrevolutionary underground within Cuba itself were also involved in such activities. And the CIA had taken some care to cover its tracks (for instance, by using mafia figures to mediate its contacts with potential Cuban assassins) in order to prevent operations from being traced to their original source. Castro could not be certain of what he strongly suspected.

He decided to find out for sure. Cubelas had earlier established direct contact with CIA case officers. Now Castro would have him draw them out. In the process, he would discover not only whether the agency was involved in such schemes, but whether the Kennedys were aware of and had authorized these tactics.

Thus the resumption of the CIA-AMLASH connection and the latter's proposal for an "inside job," to include Castro's assassination. Thus, also, Cubelas' request for a personal meeting with Robert Kennedy to obtain assurance of U.S. support. And thus Castro's warning of September 7, a move calculated to deter the president and his brother from embracing the very plan that he himself was initiating.

Of course, it must be understood that the purpose of this trap would not have been to lure the Kennedys into engaging in assassinations but (1) to determine whether such operations were in fact part of U.S. policy and (2) to send the president a message that they would not be tolerated. At the same time, the stick of deterrence would be complimented by the carrot of conciliation, as Castro moved through Attwood and other channels to cultivate the soil of rapprochement.

Looking Ahead

The above scenario is largely conjecture. But even should its essential features prove accurate, it does not answer the central question at hand—namely, what happened *after* September 7?

Here, the Schweiker-Hart report is not much help. For all its value as a critique of the investigatory process through which the Warren Commission reached its conclusions, it fails to provide the hard evidence that would make the hypothesized Cuban connection more than fascinating speculation. Nor do the leads that have been uncovered appear to be all that promising. Too much time has passed. There is a strong suspicion that the case will never be satisfactorily resolved.

Hence the reluctance of some legislators to reopen the inquiry. After all, this is a highly emotional issue, with considerable potential for demagogic distortion. One can already discern the beginnings of a sensationalistic brand of journalism, thriving on a mixture of circumstantial evidence, allegation, speculation, and emotion.[16] No doubt a major follow-up investigation would add more fuel to the fire. And certainly no responsible public official would want to stir up potentially dangerous passions without good reason.

On the other hand, one also gets the impression that there is some concern that a serious reinvestigation might turn up something. Who knows, really, what might be found? What political processes set in motion? With what consequences? What, for instance, would be the reaction of the Amer-

[16] *I refer especially to the article by Hank Greenspun in the* Las Vegas Sun, *March 1, 1976, which received considerable national attention.*

ican public and the U.S. government should hard evidence actually be discovered linking Castro—or even pro-Castro Cubans—to Kennedy's death? And where would the Soviet Union and détente fit into the picture?

In short, it would be most convenient to pretend that the Schweiker-Hart report did not exist. Or at least to reduce such inquiries as may now be necessary to a mere "tying together of loose ends." Though Richard Sprague, chief council and staff director for the recently created House Committee on Assassinations, has vowed that "no document" and "no witnesses" will be beyond the reach of his probe, it remains to be seen whether he will be able to keep that promise. The committee's legislative authority ended with the last Congress, and the attempt to reconstitute it under new leadership has already run into heavy opposition.[17] (It seems there may be a conflict between the civil liberties of committee witnesses and some of the investigative techniques proposed by Sprague.)[18]

Moreover, even if these difficulties are worked out, there is still the matter of the budget. A study group of 170 persons has been requested at a two-year cost of some $13 million. According to Sprague, these are the "bare bones minimum" figures for the task at hand. Unlike the Warren Commission, the committee will not have the full-time services of more than 200 agents from the FBI, CIA, and Secret Service. Furthermore, it will be simultaneously conducting two separate investigations (one each for the Kennedy and Martin Luther King assassinations). Inevitably, its staff and budget will have to be formidable if a credible job is to be done. Should the figures requested be significantly cut by the full House, the inquiry may be in trouble from its very inception.

My own opinion is that the case should be reopened, without blinders. We do not need another "negative" investigation, designed to discredit the leads that have been uncovered. Though it found no "smoking pistols," the Schweiker-Hart task force raised serious questions which should be honestly confronted. And even if our congressional sleuths do not come up with clear-cut findings of guilt and innocence, it would be reassuring to be able to believe that they had been open-minded and determined in their efforts. The issue is not only the Kennedy assassination but the integrity of the U.S. government. If, after all of the revelations made and questions raised by the old Senate Intelligence Committee, Congress should fail to meet its responsibilities, wouldn't there be good reason to wonder whether it too had become part of the "cover-up"?[19]

There will, of course, be risks and costs involved; there always are. But this is not 1964. Cold war tensions have abated considerably. The American public has had time to get over the trauma of the assassination. And the temper of the age, strongly anti-interventionist and self-critical, makes another invasion of Cuba improbable, even in the event that incriminating evidence is found. In short, it is difficult to imagine a major international crisis coming out of all this.

Moreover, recent reports out of Havana indicate that the Castro government is not nearly as apprehensive about these developments as might be supposed. Far from viewing a new inquiry as an obstacle to rapprochement or a prelude to and legitimization of future Yankee aggressions, Cuban

[17] *The outgoing chairman, Thomas Downing (D., Virginia), is retiring. The new chairman is expected to be Henry B. Gonzalez (D., Texas). Sprague is the Philadelphia attorney who drew national acclaim for resolving the Yablonski murder case and securing the conviction of United Mine Worker's President Tony Boyle.*

[18] *See David Burnham, "Assassination Panel Is Warned on Its Techniques,"* The New York Times, *January 6, 1977.*

[19] *According to a recent Gallup poll, 80 per cent of the American public now believes that Oswald did not act alone; only 11 per cent still adheres to the "lone assassin" thesis; the remainder are undecided.* The Washington Post, *December 26, 1976.*

officials have stressed a desire that the case be reopened. Their suspicion is that a "Cuban connection" may very well be discovered. It is reasoned that the recent murders of Sam Giancana and John Rosselli might well be connected with their roles in the CIA-mafia plots against Castro. The feeling is strong (though no proof is offered) that there is a link between those intrigues, Cuban exile politics, and the Kennedy assassination.[20]

Regardless, the case is potentially explosive and will have to be handled with a keen sense of responsibility. It must be made very clear that we are only trying to get at the truth. Thus the importance of exploring all of the evidence, both that which supports the retaliation hypothesis and that which does not. I believe that there is a substantial body of reason and circumstantial evidence, admittedly inconclusive, that suggests that Castro was not directly responsible for the killing in the sense that he ordered it done.[21]

The possibility of indirect responsibility is another matter. It is not inconceivable that Cuban security agents or others in or sympathetic to the regime, inspired perhaps by Castro's rhetoric and threats against North American leaders, may have taken it upon themselves to "eliminate" the president. The whole poisonous atmosphere of hatred and fear that pervaded U.S.-Cuban relations during this period was highly conducive to such schemes. The possibility of exile involvement also cannot be overlooked. Thomas Downing, outgoing chairman of the House Committee on Assassinations, has recently come into possession of information that suggests that right-wing Cuban exiles may have sought the president's death in retaliation for his withdrawal of air support at the Bay of Pigs. These materials will bear close scrutiny.

In the end, the "lone assassin" thesis may very well be reconfirmed, for want of other evidence if nothing else. But this is far from certain. So by all means, let there be a reopening of the investigation. And let it be a serious one, designed to uncover new leads as well as follow up old ones. As with the discovery of the Watergate tapes, it may only take one good breakthrough to settle the whole issue. And even if that breakthrough never comes and the case is never resolved, we will have at least made the effort. That is surely worth something.

Then too, in the process, we will no doubt learn more about the conduct of U.S. foreign policy. One thing is certain: The Senate Intelligence Committee only skimmed the surface in its examination of our "secret war" against Castro. Just to set the record straight, the first proposal to enlist the CIA to assassinate Castro was made not in December 1959, as the Senate Select Committee has suggested, but some two-and-a-half years earlier, when the young Cuban guerrilla was still struggling for survival in the Sierra Maestra. The source: The U.S. Ambassador to Havana, Arthur Gardner. Fortunately for Castro, Fulgencio Batista, then president of the republic, declined the offer.[22] Perhaps, had he accepted, he would have remained in power longer than he did.

[20] *Alton Frye, "The JFK Assassination: Curiosity in Havana,"* Ibid., *September 12, 1976.*

[21] *This tentative conclusion, incidentally, is by no means shaken by the recent discovery of a J. Edgar Hoover memorandum quoting a "reliable informant" to the effect that Oswald had told Cuban officials during his September 1963 visit to the Mexico City consulate that he intended to kill Kennedy. According to the informant, this information came directly from Castro and was based on a report that Castro received from Mexico City. But this has been known for some time. In August 1967, Castro gave an interview to British journalist Comer Clark in which he revealed that Cuban officials had heard Oswald threaten Kennedy's life. Unfortunately, at the time Oswald's remarks had been discounted as the ravings of an unbalanced person. In point of fact, it seems that the Schweiker-Hart task force was aware of the Hoover memorandum and chose not to include it in its final report, since Castro had previously admitted this knowledge in public. Again, the question arises: If Castro were guilty, would he have drawn attention to himself by volunteering this information?* The New York Times, *November 14, 1976 and* Columbus Dispatch, *November 14, 1976.*

[22] *See Hugh Thomas,* Cuba: The Pursuit of Freedom *(New York: Harper & Row, 1971), p. 947.*

SOUTH AMERICA LOOKS AT DETENTE (SKEPTICALLY)

by Mariano Grondona

The word détente evokes opposite responses in liberal circles of the United States and Western Europe on the one hand, and in the military or semimilitary systems of the Southern Triangle of Latin America on the other. For the United States and for many in Europe, détente refers to a kind of hope: the possibility of constructing a positive and durable relationship between the democracies and totalitarian states, between capitalism and communism, that perhaps could evolve toward a final convergence of both systems into something resembling universal social democracy.

In the Southern Triangle of Latin America, which is inclining toward a striking political homogeneity, détente refers to a new potential for trade with the East, but also carries with it a measure of alarm and fear. In recent years, the nations of Latin America have experienced conflict which more than once has placed them in a state of crisis, and has raised the specter of Cuba. The anti-Communist regimes throughout Latin America consider détente an ideological cover for possible subversive penetration into their own societies. Or they sometimes regard it as U.S. abandonment of its less important allies.

Henry A. Kissinger provides an earlier example of this phenomenon of opposite responses in A World Restored, *in which he compares the views of the Austrian chancellor, Clemens von Metternich, "the continental statesman," with those of the British chancellor, Lord Castlereagh, "the insular statesman." They agreed on the necessity of Napoleon's defeat, but for distinctly different and almost opposing reasons. Castlereagh, says Kissinger, was not concerned about the kind of political system that the powers on the continent might choose—be it republican or monarchist, nationalist or imperialist—but that no single regime be able to acquire enough power to unite the European continent at the cost of England's preeminence. For Metternich, on the other hand, the type of political system adopted by each of the continental powers was of supreme importance. Seated atop the volcano of an Austrian Empire, suffering from the agitation of the two revolutionary ideologies of the time—liberalism and nationalism—Metternich could not allow this double ferment to boil over on all sides of his nation without the risk of internal turmoil.*

Castlereagh and Metternich opposed Napoleon because he embodied a revolutionary stance. But the revolution that "the insular statesman" struggled against was purely international: alteration in the balance of power in Europe. The revolution that "the continental statesman" fought was the subversion of traditional values and principles started during the French Revolution and exported by Napoleon's troops. Metternich, who had no English Channel to protect him, was not only concerned about preserving the diplomatic status quo in Europe but also the political status quo in his own state.

The contradiction found in Castlereagh and Metternich is now being repeated in our own times. When international communism—that newfangled "Bonapartism"—makes an advance, it is perceived differently by the developed nations of the West than by the pro-Western sectors of developing nations. For the United States and Western Europe, the Allende rule in

Chile, guerrilla warfare in the Río de la Plata region, or the occupation of Angola, were viewed as threats solely to the extent that they constituted significant changes in the international balance favoring the great revolutionary power of the twentieth century. Latin-American and African anti-Communists did not react the same way. This is because those events and processes were threatening to the internal structure of their societies. Kissinger, a new Castlereagh, was able to negotiate Angola in exchange for some other advantage in some other part of the world. His own political system was not in immediate danger. For the anti-Communists in Angola, there was no other spot in the world that they could negotiate in exchange. For that reason, Metternich's philosophy is spreading among the pro-Western forces of Latin America and Africa, who are defending their own territory, their own system, and for whom no other watchword remains open but intransigence.

The governments of the Southern Triangle of Latin America have declared time and again that there is no holy alliance in their region against the influence of international communism. Nevertheless, in the Southern Triangle there still exists what we would call a "holy alliance situation"—mutual assistance among political regimes whose objection to Communist pressures is resolved not at the negotiating tables of the great powers but in actual confrontations, at times bloody.

Opposition between the two views of détente is made even more acute when the Latin-American regimes of the Southern Triangle, in order to fight against Communist penetration, sometimes restrict public freedoms in a way judged intolerable by the Northern Hemisphere. The paradox then arises that the most ardent defenders of what they consider pro-Western principles are criticized most by the Western capitals. Many believe that is what happened to Pinochet; the regimes in Brazil, Bolivia, Uruguay, Paraguay, and Argentina are, to varying degrees, subject to the same fate.

Something similar happened between 1812 and 1822. Castlereagh, whose country was midway between the traditionalism of the Hapsburgs and the liberalism of the French, failed to agree ideologically with Metternich, who was much further to the right. The United States and especially Western Europe have absorbed different degrees of radicalism and socialism. They have moderate regimes, in the manner of Castlereagh's England, that can only look with reproach on the activity of the Latin-American right. In this case, history is repeating itself. The opposition between U.S. and European liberalism and the anti-Communist right that holds sway in the Southern Triangle of Latin America and in the south of Europe (another area where communism is not solely an "external" threat), parallels the contrast between the center of an international system that is secure and flexible, and its periphery where daily life takes on the aspect of a battlefield.

This contrast demands a detailed analysis, because it is the anti-Communist right, and not the liberal center left, that is taking over power in vast areas of Latin America.

A North-South Communications Gap

There is a communications gap between U.S. and European liberalism on the one hand and the predominant trends within the Southern Triangle of Latin America on the other. The relevant factors are:

1. None of the military or semimilitary regimes of the Southern Triangle has formally renounced democratic aspirations. However they all stress the necessity of establishing, prior to the full restoration of a democratic system, a series of preconditions, without which they think the system of elections and parties would quickly degenerate into demagogy or Marxism. These preconditions are: (a) establishment of effective public law and order, and the subsequent elimination of subversive outbreaks, social disarray, and widespread disobedience of the law; (b) consolidation of the financial sector, based on control of inflation and of administrative chaos in state management; (c) establishment of a self-sustaining process of economic development; (d) reorganization of political parties and labor unions. For U.S. and Western liberals, these preconditions are no more than a pretext for indefinitely delaying the restoration of democracy. The Southern Triangle's reply is that in the North Atlantic area, democracy has been the result of a long process that first assured the given conditions for political authority and economic development under efficient monarchies and oligarchies, only later opening up to unrestricted participation by the masses. Latin America, according to this interpretation, is in the earlier stage of development.

2. From the standpoint of the Southern Triangle, democracy is an end, *a goal. Democracy is built out of conditions in themselves authoritarian. From the Northern standpoint, democracy is an end, as well as a means. It is not just the best of available systems, but also the road leading to its own fulfillment. Democracy is like a muscle that is built up through exercise; it seems contradictory to attempt its foundation on nondemocratic premises.*

3. As seen through the eyes of the Southern Triangle, the Communist movement follows a double tactical pathway. Vis-à-vis the developed and strong regimes, it is responsible and even scrupulous in the fulfillment of its obligations. On this level, the Soviet Union arouses interest as a country receiving technology and investment, and as a vast market for imports. In contrast, vis-à-vis "weaker" regimes, communism focuses on efforts to agitate and to penetrate. This is the dominant tactic in Latin America. For an Argentinean, for a Uruguayan, for a Chilean, the word "communism" has connotations decidedly different than for an American or an Englishman. This is because the former sees one side of the coin and the latter, the reverse side. U.S. liberals view South American anticommunism as a type of McCarthyism; South American anti-Communists view détente as complacency and weakness.

4. This semantic wall applies not just to "democracy" and to "communism." It extends also to "socialism." To a supporter of the regimes in power in the Southern Triangle, the word "socialism" signifies "violence." It carries the same connotation for many Socialists of the region. Socialism is a firearm. It is taken or it is seized, but in any case, it implies that other word, "revolution." In the North, on the other hand, the word "socialism" is considered peaceful and evolutionary. It is interpreted in many cases as the final ripening of democracy in the direction of a more just, more humane, and more egalitarian society. Thus the paradox could arise that one and the same person, traveling in Switzerland and Argentina, might be considered a Socialist in one country and an anti-Socialist in the other, without undergoing any fundamental change in values.

5. According to northern liberals, time is working in favor of democracies. If they succeed in keeping the peace, they believe that internal evolution will lead the Soviet Union into harmonious existence with the West. Improvements in living standards in totalitarian states will compel them to gradually loosen political controls. Greater commercial and cultural relations between East and West will bring both systems closer to common political practices approaching the ideals of a social democracy.

The Southern Triangle's view on this matter is different. It is believed that the Soviet Union is a typical empire with an unlimited appetite for expansion. Its leaders, far from becoming "bourgeois" as a function of economic progress, will intensify their preparations for war, develop greater sophistication in exercising political control, and further penetrate the soft spots of the non-Communist world. But this process, apparent since the end of World War II, involves a logic of catastrophe. Just as Hitler did, Soviet Communist rulers only believe in power. The Western democracies provide only feeble verbal protests in opposition to such advances, just like Chamberlain and Daladier, four decades ago. The result will be comparable. At any time, Soviet totalitarianism will cross an invisible line, the line of maximum tolerance. No one knows what the analogue of Poland will be. But it will have one. The Western powers have lost all credibility as far as the Communist leaders are concerned. Their declarations may be forceful at times; their actions however are not. When they finally move from declarations to actions, it may be, as in 1939, too late.

6. The regimes of the Southern Triangle deem themselves bulwarks against Communist penetration. In this sense, they consider themselves staunch allies of the United States. In liberal circles, on the other hand, the opposite view is held. They regard the authoritarianism of the right just as much as that of the left as conspiring against the West's basic ideals. As a rightist regime, by its nature, nurtures a leftist reaction, far from reassuring the West, the regimes of the Southern Triangle are creating the conditions for just such a swing of the pendulum in the opposite direction. When liberal groups pressure the U.S. Congress to suspend military or economic aid to one of the countries of the Southern Triangle, the decision comes as a surprise for the leaders of that country. They ask if the United States is truly aware of its real allies. They reflect bitterly on this, and recall, without any great love or admiration for the superpower they are dealing with, what happened to others who believed themselves to be friends of the United States—the South Vietnamese, for example.

7. We have already seen how, during World War II, Western liberalism favored Marxism as a final option and opposed fascism. Stalin was an ally, and not Hitler. If faced with the same choice, the final option would undoubtedly be the reverse for the military or semi-military regimes of the Southern Triangle. This may also be true as far as the European and U.S. right are concerned. From the standpoint of the Southern Triangle, it is unjustifiable for the international press to pillory Pinochet, while praising Mao and forgiving Castro. It is also unfair to focus only on the violations of human rights in certain countries, without giving recognition to the progress being made in other fields. Such an attitude seems cynical, for while the American press and Congress condemn the regimes of the Southern Triangle, American businessmen, diplomats, and military men deal on an ever increasing scale with those countries. At the worst, the Southern Triangle is fearful that it might be abandoned by the United States if international conflicts so require. No one in that section of the world can forget Vietnam and Angola. It is believed that while the Soviet Union is an unwavering defender of the regimes that place themselves under its protection, this is not the case with the Western world. The Latin-American right suspects that the Western powers have lost their will to resist.

Moreover, Western liberalism is not at a loss for words when it comes to making denunciations. Any incident will serve to reinforce the notion that in the Southern Triangle, far from seeking democracy and fighting subversion, what is really being built up is a new totalitarian system. Thus, the Southern Triangle seems to be overstepping the boundaries of international legality, and, consequently, its rulers take on Nuremberg features.

To many, the gap between U.S. liberalism and southern anticommunism now appears beyond repair. Subjects such as détente and human rights make that gap evident. Diplomats and businessmen may be able to ignore its existence for practical purposes, but its existence and consistency is one of the central facts of inter-American relations. Only a substantial evolution toward the right in the United States or toward the left in the south could modify this divergence in viewpoints.

The conflicting viewpoints of the right-dominated Southern Triangle and U.S. liberalism does not necessarily hamper hemispheric relationships. The majority in the United States Congress, the press, the Democratic majority and the Republican minority represent U.S. liberalism. Other important U.S. institutions and groups, the business community, the Republican or Democratic right, and the military take a different view. As for the Department of State, its liberal leanings are well known; political discretion prevents it from carrying these leanings too far. Similarly, it cannot be overlooked that in the northern areas of Latin America there are regimes with strong leanings toward the liberal viewpoint, such as Mexico, Venezuela, Costa Rica, and Colombia. In the Southern Triangle itself, political parties out of power as well as university and press circles represent varying degrees of liberalism. Inter-American relations and Latin-European relations carry on in this sense a honeycomb of lines crossing each other; ideological alliances transcend national boundaries. There is no such thing as a single Latin America. Nor is there a single North America or Europe, or a single Argentina or Brazil. The problems of détente and human rights crisscross the West free of geographic, economic, or cultural boundaries.

Détente

Détente lends itself to a number of interpretations.

First of all, détente refers to the bilateral relations between the United States and the Soviet Union. Here is the crux of détente. But this aspect does not receive much special attention in Latin America. What worries the rightist circles is anything said about an advance in armaments by the Soviets; for such an advance is considered one more proof of how little disposed Westerners are to take up battle. But the problem of armaments is not a real issue in most of Latin America, in part because there is nothing that can be done south of the Rio Grande to resolve it. Local conflicts in the international arena outside the Latin-American region, such as in the Middle East or Korea, are also of minimal interest.

It is a well known and welcomed fact in all of Latin America that the relaxation of tensions between the Soviet Union and the United States has led to the proliferation of trade and mutual cooperation agreements in all directions. However, outside of brief periods such as the presidential terms of Velasco Alvarado in Peru and Allende in Chile, the main economic, financial, and commercial ties have kept expanding between the United States, Western Europe, Japan, and the Latin-American region.

Although bilateral U.S.-Soviet relations do not capture the attention of Latin Americans, this is not the case with regard to Cuba. In recent years, as a result of the development of leftist and left-of-center regimes in the region—Allende in Chile, Perón in Argentina, Velasco in Peru—Cuba regained a place in intraregional relations. A mini-détente between the United States and Cuba was apparently being contemplated. But Castro's military intervention in Angola produced a complete turnabout in the situation. In the Southern Triangle, it is believed without reservation that guerrillas are supported at least in part by Cuba. It is known that centers for training and outfitting guerrillas remain active on the island. The fact that Cuba may have turned into a military base for the open export of revolution to black Africa provokes fears of similar interventions on our continent.

On the other hand, it is hard for military regimes to maintain normal relations with

Castro's regime. Commercial trade between Cuba and Argentina, for example, is important; Cuba is the principal importer of Argentine automobile engines. The opening of this market led to a significant conflict over the stand of U.S. affiliates in Argentina, which had to decide between abiding by their own country's embargo and their host country's trade policy. With Cuba, it is much more difficult now to maintain the two-way street of ideological conflict and economic cooperation typical of relations with East-bloc countries. For most Latin-American countries, except Chile, it is not too much of a strain to trade with the Soviet Union. Cuba is too close for this type of exercise, and relations will worsen.

Cuban and Soviet penetration in Angola opened a new source of worry for Latin Americans, and, more particularly, the South Atlantic nations. The fact that international confrontation has now reached the southern part of Africa turns the South Atlantic—which until recently had been a forgotten sea—into a potential theater of war operations. Countries like Brazil and Argentina intend to capitalize on their strategic positions in order to be admitted as full or associate members of NATO. *They hope to acquire a "Spanish position"—bulwarks in the rear guard of the Western defense system, just like Franco's Spain. They are confident that this position will allow them to enjoy a status that would be denied if all that mattered were democratic orthodoxy.*

On another level, détente is only possible in a climate of ideological disarmament with the East. That disarmament has already occurred, at least in regard to U.S. liberalism and various forms of Western European socialism. An emphasis on human rights, pacifism, and antimilitarism create the political and ideological climate in the Northern Atlantic that allows for progress on the diplomatic and commercial road of détente. But this same climate has heightened tensions with the rightist regimes of the Southern Triangle of Latin America and, until recently, with those of Southern Europe—The Greece of the colonels, the Spain of Franco, the Portugal of Salazar and Caetano. There is a Social Democratic front in Europe, in power in countries like the United Kingdom, West Germany, Austria, and Portugal, which is applying considerable pressure in France. However, two important changes should be mentioned here. One is the defeat of the Socialists in Sweden, a country that has been in the vanguard in denouncing the rightist regimes. The other is the liberalization of Spain. Just as the change in Sweden may give the Latin-American right a better chance to breathe, the direction of change in Spain is a new cause for worry. Spain has played, and still plays, a significant role in Latin America. Imitation of Spain is a possibility. The political and economic experiences of individual Latin-American nations influence each other. We speak with great ease in this region about the Brazilian "model" or about the Peruvian one. Spain and Portugal are among the very few countries that enjoy the privilege of penetrating this process of emulation and imitation.

But the sheer vigor of the liberal and radical trends that give détente a marked ideological flavor could affect relations between Latin Americans themselves. We have already witnessed the breaking off of relations between Mexico and Chile and Venezuela and Uruguay. We have seen the cooling of relations between Mexico and Argentina and the interruption of the Andean integration process due to the opposition of Chile. These examples are not merely incidental. Ideological coexistence between a liberal North and a conservative South is becoming more and more difficult in this region. Until very recently, it was possible to prevent Latin-American political currents from halting the economic, diplomatic, and cultural convergence of the region. Today, ideological polarization is causing the erosion of political pluralism. A basic principle governing conduct between the Latin-American ruling bodies has been weakened.

There is a crusade in the wind in Latin America. Before very long, moderation could be replaced by intransigence. The nations of the Southern Triangle are closing their ranks when regional security and human rights are discussed. On the other hand, regimes of similar political coloration are accentuating their gestures of solidarity. At the recent meeting that the Organization of American States held in Santiago, Chile, the Southern Triangle voted unanimously to prevent any sanction against the host country. On the other hand, Argentina recently chose as its ambassador to Caracas a member of the Radical Party, attempting to salvage its relations with Venezuela—partly because the expansion of a third country, Brazil, brings together two opposing regimes with strong geopolitical ties.

Another relevant factor is the general impression that organized subversion is rapidly losing ground in the Southern Triangle. Even in countries like Argentina, where its outward manifestations are still considerable, it is believed to be a transient phenomenon—diminishing rather than expanding. In reality, in the Southern Triangle today, the problem is more the excesses of the repressive groups than those of the guerrillas. At the same time, there are signs of infiltration and agitation in the northern parts of Latin America, especially in Colombia. But this case, when considered along with others, raises the question of whether subversion is migrating from the South to the North. Its strategy would be to limit itself in the South to acts of attrition, especially through international denunciations, while more concentrated action is directed against the more open, penetrable regimes in the North of the region. If this assumption is confirmed, how would it affect the present ideological debate?

Until now, the U.S. government has been cautious in approving sanctions against the rightist regimes of the Southern Triangle—more so than certain European countries. Only Chile is on the blacklist, and then only up to a certain degree. But this has already created friction. For example, the temporary detainment of a U.S. priest created diplomatic difficulties between Argentina and the United States; the suspension of military aid to Uruguay was denounced by two high-placed generals of that country. Military aid to Argentina is under attack. These are small incidents, but they could be aggravated should present attitudes persist.

The outcome of the U.S. elections could influence the course of events of détente. No surprises were expected if Gerald Ford had won. But Jimmy Carter, in contrast, has been an unknown factor. We are told that in international affairs, he proposes to bring actions into line with principles—an attitude directly opposed to the pragmatism of Kissinger. But its consequences are difficult to foresee. The Ford-Kissinger policy was "soft on everybody"—on the Soviets, but also on the regimes of the Southern Triangle. Will Carter be "hard on everybody"? The fact is that neither the Soviets nor the regimes of the Southern Triangle are living up to the principles of U.S. democracy. What will it be like in a world where, at the same time, pressure is put on the Soviet Union and the Southern Triangle in defense of human rights? If concern for human rights becomes more crucial in U.S. policy toward the East, will it also make the regimes of the Southern Triangle less acceptable?

A Common Ground

I have devoted much of this article to investigating the differences between U.S. liberalism and the military regimes of the Southern Triangle in relation to détente. I would now like to raise the question of whether there is a possibility of finding a common ground for those two camps.

Two winds are blowing from the East. Soviet power is simultaneously a classical power and a revolutionary power. The Soviet state conducts itself like the rest of the states and maintains normal relations with them. The Soviet Communist Party continues insisting on ideological and political expansion; it is in this sense a destabilizing force.

Those who back détente have made an historical wager on the victory of the state over the party. They believe that if enough time is granted to this evolutionary process, the Soviet Union will behave more and more like a nation that is compatible with the community of nations and less and less like an empire ravenous for world conquest. A rough sketch of Pygmalion's vocation can be gathered from reading some of the speeches that Kissinger delivered during the recent election campaign. The United States, the former secretary of state believes, should show sufficient firmness and patience to get on with the "education" of the Soviet Union about the rules of living together in a civilized community of nations. Once that system has been formed, he will have his dream: a world like post-Napoleonic Europe, ready for 100 years of real peace.

The historical wager in favor of the state against the party is the first premise of the backers of détente. The second is ideological in nature. We might label it "the centrist analysis." The "center," which is opposed to leftist authoritarianism as much as it is to rightist authoritarianism, refuses, in this context, to "bend" either to one side or to the other. It rejects the suggestion that just because the rightist military regimes are anti-Communist, they can become allies. This would be "bending" the center toward the right. The center does not consider itself as a compromise or a crossroads between the left and right. Nor as a moderate form of anticommunism. It wants to be both anti-Communist and antidictatorial at the same time. Or better yet, antidictatorial in an absolute sense, wherever the dictatorship may come from. It believes that rightist military regimes are just as far from its ideology as Communist totalitarianism.

There is even what I have called a final option toward the left. This does not mean that authentic liberals and supporters of détente would accept, in the final extreme, Communist domination. It means that they would accept a renewal of the Grand Alliance of World War II, but not a reverse coalition with those whom they view as successors of Hitler and Mussolini.

This last assumption is not so much ideological as "vital"; a question of sensibilities. The supporters of détente acknowledge that Pygmalion does not limit himself to changing the person he seeks to educate. He too changes, to the point of falling in love with her! Some of those who back détente assume and accept the fact that if in the course of U.S.-Soviet coexistence, Soviet society will have to approach the Western ideal step by step, then Western society will also have to assimilate varied doses of socialism, until both are at a sufficiently close distance to encourage a sincere friendship. Along this line, one can see what Zbigniew Brzezinski and Samuel P. Huntington called the "theory of convergence"—rejecting it in their classic study, Political Power: USA/USSR.

At the heart of this theory there is something we would call "economicism," the supposition that in the final analysis, the economic structure of production determines political behavior. An excellent version of this hypothesis can be found in the well-known works of John Kenneth Galbraith. In this analysis, given the extent to which large corporations, under the control of "technostructures," direct not only the U.S. but also the Soviet economy, the political and international decisions of the two societies will in the end resemble each other and converge.

One final intellectual trend reinforces the supporters of détente; the thesis that ideologies are not as important as nationality. The Soviet Union, China, the United States, it is assumed, are "nations" with permanent objectives and interests above and beyond "ideologies" and "religions." Kissinger's pragmatism is positioned here. Following this approach, the international power game does not differ as much as widely believed from the games of centuries past. For that reason, China is at odds with the Soviet Union. For that reason, it is possible to build up once again a pluralistic international system through patient negotiations, a discreet show of face, mutual concessions and advantages. From this perspective, détente would be but a new manifestation of an art as old as the world: the art of diplomacy.

Two winds are blowing from the East. The supporters of détente are opting for one, its South American critics for the other. The latter maintain that the Soviet state is no more than a cover for the ideological imperialism of the party. To continue playing the game of détente is to grant time to ideological expansion until it may be too late. The South American hawks feel that the course of history will run not for but against Western ideals unless something is done to reverse the trend. From this point of view, what matters today are the left and right, not the center—a mere geometric point without substance of its own. For the center represents the desire not to choose, the refusal to confront reality, i.e., the constant advance of an empire pursuing ambitions at the expense of an "imperial republic"[1] which, like ancient Athens, prefers to continue being a republic rather than take possession of its empire.

The final option of the hawks points naturally toward rightist authoritarianism and not toward Marxism. Pygmalion, according to them, does not teach; to the contrary, he is infiltrated and manipulated. "Economicism" is unacceptable. Politics has its own laws and cannot be reduced to economics. If the Soviet Union receives wheat and technological assistance thanks to détente, the result is not its conversion, its being "bourgeoisied," but rather a freeing of its resources to be used on a new push in armaments or revolution. New missiles or revolutionary aid to Angola are born out of the wheat. Finally, the hawks believe that ideas, not national interest in the classic sense, rule the world. Like it or not, Western nations are confronting the spread of a new secular religion, whose believers are motivated by fanaticism.

The inner ambivalence of the Soviet position (its peace-making and aggressive nature) not only instigates the debate between U.S. liberalism and the military regimes of the Southern Triangle, but also brings to life two incompatible mentalities, whose dialogue may be impossible in the final analysis. Conservatives and liberals everywhere have two different attitudes toward the world and history. A head-on clash between the two can be avoided as long as no issue ever obliges the one group to take a clear stand against the other. Détente is one of those issues. For this reason, in the United States as in the rest of the Americas, détente is an occasion for this latent disagreement to reveal itself. Conservatives and liberals discover that they cannot resolve their differences on détente through discussion.

Different scales of values are involved in this dispute. On one scale, order ranks first; on another, change ranks uppermost. While order is political, change is economic. Order is solid; its boundaries are fixed. Change is fluid; it suggests mixtures and combinations. Circumstances air either one or the other trend. In the Southern Triangle, the conservatives are triumphant because the wind of revolutionary aggression is blowing. In the Northern hemisphere, where the gentle breeze of trade and diplomacy is prevailing, doves fly more freely.

[1] *Raymond Aron,* République Impériale *(Paris: Calmann-Lévy, 1973).*

The polarization of positions between U.S. liberalism and the Southern Triangle has produced new tensions on the issue of détente. The advent of coexistence at the end of the 1950s and the beginning of the 1960s was well received by a Latin America where democratic reformism held sway. The Latin America of Frei, Frondizi, and Belaunde coincided with both the era and spirit of John F. Kennedy, Nikita Khrushchev, and Pope John XXIII. It was the time of the Alliance for Progress. The United States seemed capable of leadership then. But the era of détente of Nixon and Brezhnev, of Kissinger and Gromyko, had from the beginning another flavor—a flavor of diplomatic calculation and politics.

Likewise, the Latin America witnessing this had also changed. Peronism, Peruvianism, and the turnabout to the center-left in nations like Venezuela and Mexico, were taking the region toward a Third World outlook. Governments in Latin America today that are not anti-Communist and military are overwhelmingly partial to the Third World. But this has not resulted in enthusiasm for détente. The expansion of trade in all directions was praised, as was the elimination of ideological barriers to international competition. However, it is feared that if détente advances in the direction of alliance and friendship, it will lead to a division of the world into spheres of influence between the two superpowers. According to this hypothesis, Latin America would remain imprisoned within the grip of U.S. imperialism. According to this view, the true line dividing the world today does not run from North to South separating the East from the West, but rather from East to West separating the North from the South. Whatever the arrangement between the superpowers of the North, this cannot be good news for the South. Hegemonial arrangements would be made at its expense. To the extent that détente opens up this possibility, it is regarded with suspicion.

This prompts a final reflection upon the paradoxes of anti-Americanism in Latin America. If the campaign of liberals for détente and against rightist authoritarianism continues, if sanctions affecting nations like Chile and Uruguay for violation of human rights are extended, then the military regimes of the Southern Triangle acquiesce to varying amounts of anti-Americanism. They like to regard the United States as the bastion of the West. Yet when they observe its contacts with Moscow, its censuring of regimes that are combating communism within their own borders, there is a strong temptation for those in power today in the Southern Triangle to accuse U.S. leaders of abandoning their allies and of forsaking their historical role.

This development will not bring Third World currents any closer to the United States. They do not want alliance with the United States. Unlike the anti-Communists, they are not disillusioned pro-Americans. They want to free themselves totally from any and all influences, and they cannot accept the idea of a division of the world as a condition of détente. Finally, among those who push for sanctions against the regimes of the Southern Triangle, there are the theoreticians of dependence; Marxists or Communists who, for ideological reasons, identify the United States as their principal enemy. As was witnessed a few months ago in the subcommittee of the House Committee on International Relations, several of the principal Communist leaders of Argentina—natural enemies of the United States—testified on the violation of human rights by the Argentine military regime—presumably a friend of the United States. Carl Schmidt once said that one of the decisive problems of politics is to identify one's enemies with certainty. The least that can be said is that such a definition has not been attained between the U.S. Americans and the Latin Americans with respect to détente.

BRAZIL: THE END OF A BEAUTIFUL RELATIONSHIP

by Roger W. Fontaine

The dust has begun to settle, and in the distant haze I see the smoking ruin of a special relationship. The United States and Brazil have ended more than a century of close ties. The destruction followed a trumpet blast from the Carter administration consisting of two shrill notes: human rights and nonproliferation. The underlying motif: morality in foreign policy.

What have we done that's so bad, and why are the Brazilians so angry with us? To answer that properly, we must separate intentions from results. Then, perhaps, we can write ourselves a new policy, before the poisoned relations with Brazil extend into the next generation.

President Carter, whose intentions were lofty if not exactly modest, wanted to restore respect for human rights in Brazil and, more importantly, to prevent that country from acquiring a complete nuclear fuel cycle and hence the bomb. The objectives were laudable; the implementation is another, rather sad matter.

We have alienated a friend and old ally, and we did not get (nor will we likely get) what we sought in the first place. Worse, we have probably increased the chances that Brazil will select the nuclear option by the end of the century. That decision will be made by a generation of Brazilian leaders who have accepted Charles De Gaulle's warning: Don't trust the Americans if your greatness is at stake.

We have also bungled on the issue of human rights. The current trend in Brazil is toward more, not less, authoritarianism, and our ability to stem that disturbing development in Brasília has probably reached a postwar low.

The results of the Carter policy were foreseeable: nothing the Brazilians have done should come as a surprise. But those who make high-pitched moral pronouncements rarely let simple matters like consequences get in the way of their good and righteous cause.

A short history of our new policy toward Brazil should prove instructive. The president made the dangers of nuclear proliferation a central issue during the campaign, and Brazil was soon singled out as a leading target for criticism, because its 1975 agreement with West Germany was to provide the South American giant with a nuclear fuel cycle. The first move of the Carter administration was to place direct pressure on the Germans to cancel the agreement, commencing with Vice President Walter F. Mondale's trip to Bonn last January. That move had the effect of virtually canceling the "memorandum of understanding" which had been signed by the United States and Brazil less than a year earlier. The memorandum formally pledged regular consultations on economic, political, and technological issues affecting both countries, as well as the coordination of all policy in the international arena. Our new approach to nuclear proliferation, of course, fell within the scope of the agreement. The Rio de Janeiro newspaper, Jornal do Brasil, *remarked at the time that a "memorandum is a record of things that cannot be forgotten."*

The Carter administration, however, chose to forget, first ignoring the Brazilians and then, one month after the Mondale visit to Bonn, sending a State Department delegation to Brasília to demand that the West German agreement be modified. To be sure, the United States sweetened this bitter pill with a promise of an "assured" supply of enriched uranium, but, not surprisingly, in light of today's tight supply situation, that offer was rejected by the Brazilians. It also confirmed a long-held Brazilian suspicion that the United States really wants to keep underdeveloped nations technologically dependent, while itself growing rich on the immensely profitable sale of enriched uranium. The Brazilians refused to discuss the matter, and the large American delegation headed home after one day of talks. A terse communiqué mentioned the stalemate and only vaguely hinted at a future meeting.

A Heavy American Hand

Our achievements to date are: (1) We broke our word by not consulting the Brazilians, prior to the vice presidential trip to Germany, on a matter deemed vital to Brazil. Consequently, it is difficult to believe that the Brazilians will soon trust us again. It is equally doubtful that any prudent Mexican official, for example, will put much faith in his own country's special relationship with the United States. (2) We have succeeded in propelling the Brazilian nuclear program forward. Not only is the West German deal still intact, but a larger number of Brazilians are now convinced that the nuclear option is worth serious consideration. If by some slim chance we were able to cancel all or part of the Brazilian-West German nuclear accord, that would make the Brazilians even more determined to go ahead—by themselves if necessary, even though it would take them longer and cost more in real resources. That would have two additional unfortunate consequences: The new, independent program would not have to submit to any outside safeguards, unlike the present arrangement with Germany. And a nuclear and Gaullist Brazil would be much more inclined to develop a nuclear weapons system—something no responsible Brazilian official now espouses—because the heavy American hand in this affair has only strengthened the cause of those hardliners who promote an ultranationalist nuclear policy.

The militants' simple message is: America stands in the way of future Brazilian grandeza. *How? By keeping Brazil permanently dependent on, and inferior to, the United States, particularly in advanced technology. Recent developments confirm the worst suspicions and force others, who had given the United States the benefit of the doubt, into rethinking their own, more moderate, views.*

One curious fallout of the new U.S. policy is Argentina's public support for the Brazilian position, which may lead to cooperation in nuclear development. That these two natural rivals should forge an atomic entente is not only ironic, but also avoidable. The Argentine nuclear program is more advanced than Brazil's, and its sources of foreign assistance perfectly complement those of its larger neighbor. Between the two nations, they know everyone in the nuclear trade. Neither one is bound by the nonproliferation treaty, nor by Latin America's version of that agreement, the Tlatelolco treaty.

Three Bad Assumptions

Poor policy is usually rooted in bad assumptions. I detect three of them: Brazil's nuclear program is susceptible to modification, because it is the brain child of a few local politicos who suffer from premature delusions of grandeur. The United States has to act the way it does, because there are no available alternatives. Brazil is susceptible to our influence, in part because of its recent economic difficulties.

The first miscalculation is probably the biggest. Brazil's nuclear policy is not simply a matter of prestige, although there exists in Brazil a current of nationalist feeling that is both volatile and widespread, as well as easily underestimated—possibly because it is less *anti-American than that usually found south of the Río Bravo.*

But prestige accounts for only a small part of Brazil's current nuclear strategy. At the heart of the rationale is worry over the country's future well-being, which in turn depends on the development of massive new energy resources by the end of the century. Fossil fuel and hydroelectric power will not be enough, since planners believe Brazil's requirements will rival those of any nation immediately below the superpower slot. According to their time schedule, nuclear power is the only way to fill the gap by the year 2000.

This conviction is reinforced by the fading of the so-called Brazilian miracle after the revolution in oil prices beginning in 1973. Brazil now imports 80 per cent of its fuel requirements, and only strenuous efforts to increase exports will erase the massive trade deficits the country has incurred. High fuel bills have slowed growth, and nuclear energy is believed to be vital if Brazil is to escape the economic strangle hold of foreign oil-producers.

The second assumption, that the United States has no other choice, is also wrong, provided that policy-makers are willing to exercise patience and persistence in following a different policy. The German-Brazilian accord might have unraveled by itself. Until we blundered into the china shop, serious doubt was arising about the quality of the goods being offered. Furthermore, given Brazil's pinched budget, there might have been a stretch-out or even cancellation of some parts of the agreement; American alternatives, if presented at the proper moment, might have been listened to in Brasília.

Presenting Brazil and West Germany with a carefully developed list of extra safeguards (which we could have offered to pay for) could have made diversion of weapons-grade plutonium all but impossible. There is evidence that both countries would have welcomed suggestions, at least until we poisoned the atmosphere.

Now, of course, national pride is at stake; public positions are chiseled in granite, and any suggestions from Brazil's former friend will be treated with suspicion, if not outright hostility. Indeed, the current regime may even accelerate development, despite current budget restraints, in order to prove Brazilian independence. It is an indication of our lost opportunity to recall that the Geisel administration, in direct contrast to its predecessor, had been trimming back the grand projects begun in the euphoric early 1970s.

That raises the last mistaken assumption —that thanks to their economic problems, Brazilians are under our thumb. This requires a reminder that making foreign policy involves more art than science. It may well have seemed in early 1977 that Brazil was vulnerable to pressure. That calculation, based on the 1974-1975 slowdown, was quite wrong, because the Brazilians are lucky. They are now in the process of fashioning a second economic miracle. Admittedly, the first one, which featured high growth rates (around 10 per cent a year) between 1967 and 1973, was not literally a miracle, that is an inexplicable event according to the economic laws of nature. The second one, however, comes closer to the type found in the New Testament, particularly in the story involving loaves and fishes. Demonstrating a perfectly elastic supply curve, like the one in Matthew, the Brazilians seem to come up with abundant supplies of new exports at good prices when others happen to falter momentarily. Thus, coffee, soybeans, and orange juice are propelling Brazil toward the number two position in world export of agricultural products. Two years ago, it was cotton and sugar. Two years from now it may well be a different list, but the cornucopia seems unlikely to fail.

All of this naturally breeds a certain amount of self-confidence among Brazilians. That self-confidence also helps to explain their rude response to our other great cause of the moment, human rights. This prickly issue surfaced a week after the State Department mission returned, and it led to Brazil's cancellation of a quarter-century-old military agreement with the United States. It was not the most important military or security agreement the Brazilians could have revoked, but it was a warning that patience was wearing thin in Brasília. Moreover, no such step had been taken before, not even during the most difficult days of the Quadros and Goulart regimes.

Lofty Intentions, Pure Ideals

The cancellation came after the release of the State Department's report on the state of human rights around the world, mandated by Congress to cover all countries with which the United States has military assistance programs, including Brazil. To soften the blow, the State Department sent the report to Brazil's foreign ministry before transmitting it to Capitol Hill. The ministry rejected the report out of hand and returned it to Washington. The stated reason was the by now familiar cry over American intervention in the internal affairs of another country. Perhaps. More certain is the fact that such reports have a highly patronizing tone, which many human rights advocates would have us eschew, except in the case of regimes they don't like.

The United States meant to do "good" in Brazil, but good intentions are not enough. A foreign policy based solely on a few, simple moral precepts can get even the most virtuous into trouble. Though Don Quixote charged across La Mancha with the loftiest of intentions and the purest of ideals, he succeeded only in battling windmills and scattering sheep. This is not to suggest that morality in foreign policy is per se a quixotic adventure. But the American operating moral code had better be well grounded in a reality that includes a mature understanding of what is possible in a sinful world. Otherwise, we will end up wrecking windmills.

Somehow, the Brazilians have not appreciated our efforts to make them better. Even the opposition party finds it difficult to be scolded as if they were naughty boys. The real anger goes deeper than that. The Brazilians do not appreciate being lumped together with the likes of Idi Amin and the current robber band running Ethiopia. Moreover, they dislike seeing a policy of hostility toward them matched by friendly overtures to the police states headquartered in Hanoi and Havana. Quite aside from bruised feelings, the fact is that official public criticism invariably drives the criticized nation into protests over interference in its internal affairs. And that in turn makes impossible the small, but often worthwhile, gains achieved through quiet diplomacy. Official U.S. criticism also strengthens those in Brazil whose commitments to any definition of human rights are less than fervent. At the same time, it in no way encourages the present leadership to take any further risks on behalf of "decompression."

Making Repairs

What happens next? The administration may choose to go forward and place more pressure on Brazil. If it does, relations will come close to the breaking point; the Brazilians have already said as much. Alternatively, the United States could decide to do nothing for a while (the present course of action) and simply let the kettle cool off.

In the meantime, can the special relationship be patched up? Will Brazil resume its place as first among equals in Latin America—a kind of proto-partner of the United States? That seems doubtful, at least for now. The truth is that Brazilians are not merely angry, they are bitter. Bitterness lingers. As Brazilians see it, they did enjoy a particularly close relationship with the United States.

Favors were exchanged over the years and a bank account of good will had steadily accumulated. Then suddenly, this year, shocked Brazilians discovered that account was empty, their only comfort a bank president lecturing them on the virtues of thrift.

Recently, relations have improved slightly. The United States has backed off its previous hardline position on nuclear proliferation, and Brazilians are openly relieved at Germany's continued intransigence on the issue. Letters have been exchanged between the White House and the Palacio do Planalto, and Carter has eased the pressure on Bonn. Terence Todman, assistant secretary for inter-American affairs, hinted recently that even the memorandum of understanding would be maintained in principle (although the second consultative meeting called for by the memorandum is now three months overdue). Finally, Mrs. Carter in her June visit made only the vaguest public references to the nuclear and human rights issues, alluding to misperceptions on both sides.

But the United States needs to do more than refrain from doing additional damage; it also needs to make repairs. Meanwhile, there is the lingering question: Has Don Quixote given up knight-errantry or merely reined in Rocinante for a breather?

One further aspect of recent American actions toward Brazil is disturbing. It has to do with priorities in the hemisphere. If the new American design really does include the assumption that drawing up an agreement favorable to tiny Panama is a major feature, while erasing others with big Brazil is merely a detail, then I suggest that design needs radically new engineering, as well as a different engineer.

MEXICO'S OPPORTUNITY: THE OIL BOOM

by George W. Grayson

> You can divide the countries of the world into two types, the ones that have oil and the ones that do not. We have oil.—*José López Portillo*

As President José López Portillo completes his first year in office, he is witnessing the worst economic conditions in Mexico since the Great Depression. The post-World War II boom, which saw the country's Gross Domestic Product (GDP) shoot up 6 or 7 per cent annually, has ended. Population now grows faster than the economy. Mexico's 63 million inhabitants make it the world's tenth largest nation, and population is expected to double by 2000 when Mexico City—now third behind Tokyo and Shanghai—will be the planet's largest metropolis. This steep rise (3.2 per cent per year) means that half the country's inhabitants are under 15 years of age. Soon they will be elbowing their way into a labor force half of whose current number (17.5 million) already lacks work or is marginally employed. It also means that U.S. cities will continue to attract hundreds of thousands of "nondocumented" emigrants from Mexico, where 17 per cent of the people earn less than $75 a year and three out of 10 cannot afford a minimum balanced diet.

In an attempt to create jobs, boost incomes, and breathe life into the egalitarian goals of the 1910 revolution, Luis Echeverría, president from 1970 to 1976, encouraged public sector investment in everything from steel-making to skyscraper construction. He put particular emphasis on infrastructure projects requiring heavy capital goods imports. Because Mexico has one of the world's lowest taxation levels and because Mexican investors, alarmed by Echeverría's leftist rhetoric, spurned government securities, the development program was financed largely by an expansionary monetary policy and external borrowing.

"The oil companies delighted their American and European shareholders with fat dividend checks, but won few friends in Mexico."

The upshot was that the public debt rose fivefold to $20 billion under the mercurial Echeverría, while private sector indebtedness surpassed $7 billion. The burden of these loans, over half of them made by American financial institutions, becomes apparent when one remembers that the nation's GDP is only $79 billion. With the possible exception of Brazil, Mexico is the most debt-ridden country. A confluence of factors—the size of the debt, Mexico's propensity to import more than it exports, double-digit inflation, fear of political instability—brought massive capital flight, a halt to private investment, and two devaluations of the once-vaunted peso in late 1976.

Despite a recent surge in Mexican exports, a modest slowing of inflation, and a decrease in the capital flight, conditions remain grim. Nonetheless, López Portillo and his key advisers exude a quiet confidence that the floundering economy can be righted and the economic miracle of the 1950s and 1960s restored. This guarded optimism springs from the discovery of oil deposits as large as those in the Middle East, from which Mexico expects to earn nearly $20 billion by 1982.

Mexico's desperate need for foreign exchange and the United States' accelerating demand for foreign oil commend the exchange of U.S. dollars for Mexican petroleum. But four circumstances complicate this overtly sensible interchange: (1) a history of foreign exploitation of Mexican resources before the 1938 take-over of the major oil firms, (2) the constraints placed upon increased production by Mexico's national oil company and the union that dominates it, (3) Mexico's relations with the Organization of Petroleum Exporting Countries (OPEC) and pressures to ship refined products to a diversified market, and (4) the imperative of Washington's pursuing a policy that combines sensitivity to Mexico's sovereignty with an understanding of how Mexican oil can resolve problems confronting the two nations.

All's Well that Ends Well

With the price of natural gas having increased threefold in recent years, petroleum fourfold, and uranium sevenfold, the possession of energy reserves obviously enhances a nation's power. This was not the case 69 years ago, when entrepreneurs first discovered commercial quantities of oil in Mexico. Then, vital resources served as a magnet, attracting ruthless profit-seekers, avaricious transnational firms, and the diplomats and soldiers of major powers. Once these foreigners had wheedled, bribed, intimidated, and coerced local politicians and their praetorian guards, the resources fell under the sway of outsiders, offending Mexico's dignity and attenuating its sovereignty.

Such exploitation of Mexico occurred under the aegis of Porfirio Díaz, a venal dictator who ruled for 35 years after seizing power in 1876. Díaz believed in the inestimable value of technology, the advancement of his country through investment in mines, railroads, factories, and harbors, and the superiority of white men. (He showered himself with talcum to hide his Indian heritage.)

The vain strongman befriended two foreigners who pioneered the development of Mexico's petroleum. The first was Edward L. Doheny, a wily product of the rough-and-tumble American oil industry in which he had made a fortune. He began his quest for black gold near Tampico and in San Luis Potosí in 1892. Eight years later, he organized the Mexican Petroleum Company of California, explored widely, and spent about $3 million before drilling a gusher in the lake Santa Margarita in the Ebano region of San Luis Potosí.

The second entrepreneur was Weeman Pearson, whom Díaz lavishly paid to construct a drainage canal in Mexico City, a port in Vera Cruz, and a railroad in the Isthmus of Tehuantepec. The Yorkshire contractor found himself in Mexico in 1901, when the great Spindletop well sent a jet-black stream of oil 2,000 feet over Beaumont, Texas. Knowing that the geology in parts of Mexico was similar to that of Texas, Pearson invested nearly $25 million in exploration. In 1908, he founded the Mexican Eagle (Aguila) Company and shortly thereafter drilled the famous Dos Bocas well near Tampico, which initiated the first major stage in the production of Mexican petroleum.

Díaz encouraged both men's work, anxious to balance American against British interests, lest either become too strong. Fierce competition with Doheny notwithstanding, Pearson's Mexican Eagle Company—which boasted Díaz's son as a board member—became Mexico's pre-eminent producer. Winston Churchill contributed greatly to its success when in 1912, over strenuous opposition, he had the Royal Navy converted from coal- to oil-burning vessels. Thus the fleet glided into battle with the kaiser's *Kriegsflotte* propelled by American, Middle Eastern, and Mexican bunker oil.

Production soared from 10,000 barrels in 1901 to 3.9 million in 1908 to 193.4 million in 1921.

Output began declining in 1922. By this time, the productivity of the wells had diminished because of wasteful exploitation. The companies started to worry about their status under a viable government that might collect taxes and listen sympathetically to labor demands. The costs of production had begun to rise. And although the rate of well-drilling increased two-and-a-half times from 1921 to 1926, the majority of wells opened were dry as compared with a 62 per cent success rate before 1921.

The oil companies delighted their American and European shareholders with fat dividend checks, but won few friends in Mexico. They treated their holdings as foreign enclaves, sought the protection of their home governments, and arrogantly embroiled themselves in the host country's politics. These firms claimed not simply to hold 10- or 20-year concessions, but to own the mineral deposits that they exploited. The question of ownership constantly agitated relations between the corporations and the Mexican government.

While conditions improved somewhat in the 1930s, the petroleum workers endured physically exhausting work, squalid living conditions, low pay, and harsh discipline. The firms claimed that higher salaries and improved benefits were economically impossible to provide. Upon the election as president in 1933 of Lázaro Cárdenas, who promised to implement the social goals of the 1917 Constitution, the now unionized petroleum workers demanded better treatment by the oil companies. No doubt the companies could have made concessions, but they feared that demands would escalate and a dangerous precedent be set for their workers in other countries.

The ensuing conflict between the workers and the oil trusts is well known. It culminated at 10:00 PM on March 18, 1938, with a radio speech by the husky-voiced Cárdenas, who announced the expropriation of the 17 American and European corporations. While the labor conflict provided its catalyst and justification, the take-over was motivated by Cárdenas' desire to assert

Mexico's sovereignty after six decades in which the foreign firms had treated it as a fiefdom. President Franklin D. Roosevelt imposed a trade embargo on Mexico in retaliation for the expropriations.

How should the newly expropriated oil industy be run? For the Petroleum Workers Union (STPRM), the answer was simple: turn it over to the workers just as was done the year before with the nationalized railroads. Cárdenas rejected this approach because rail service had deteriorated under the union. Instead, he established a public corporation operated jointly by labor and government, with the latter boasting a majority of the appointments to its nine-member board of directors. Thus, on June 7, 1938, Petróleos Mexicanos (PEMEX) was formed.

The expropriation and related events shaped the development of Mexico's petroleum industry. First, PEMEX's Generation of '38—those dedicated engineers and managers who went to work for the newly formed public body—have consistently advocated conservation of Mexico's oil, lest production again plummet, as it did following the 1921 production peak. Second, despite the failure of Cárdenas to turn the industry over to the union, the *petroleros* (petroleum workers) enjoy excellent pay, generous benefits, and notable influence, especially in the hiring of PEMEX employees, as a result of their crucial role in keeping the oil industry operating immediately after expropriation. Third, because of resistance by the workers and the public at large, foreign capital has played a restricted role in Mexico's petroleum sector. Fourth, in accord with its original aims, PEMEX is expected to fulfill an important social mission: namely, supplying petroleum and related products at low prices to Mexican consumers.

"Sitting on a Sea of Oil"

The Aztecs discovered petroleum and used it before the Spaniards arrived in 1519. They burned it as incense to their gods, calked their boats with it, applied it to their bodies as a medicine, and utilized it as a dye and glue. But not until May 1901 did the commercial exploitation of petroleum begin when Pearson discovered crude at Ebano. By the time of nationalization, five major areas were under production.

In addition to the Ebano deposits, the so-called Golden Lane (*Faja de Oro*), though accounting for only 13 per cent of output in 1940, had given Mexico a worldwide reputation between 1908 and 1921; the rich Poza Rica fields, discovered 100 miles south of Tampico by the Mexican Eagle Company in 1930, contributed over one-half of the country's output at the time of Cárdenas' decree; and deposits in the Isthmus of Tehuantepec produced 25 per cent of national yield in 1938.

"The Aztecs discovered petroleum and used it before the Spaniards arrived in 1519."

After expropriation, PEMEX opened a new Golden Lane field southwest of the original *Faja de Oro*, the San Andrés deposit, and the national company also found oil in both the eastern and western parts of the state of Tabasco, as well as in the Altamira area north of Tampico, oil located in the central part of the state of Veracruz, and prolific gas reserves near Reynosa in the northeast state of Tamaulipas.

Extremely large reserves existed in the southeastern states of Tabasco and Chiapas. Frank M. Porter, president of the American Petroleum Institute, urged Director-General Pascual Gutiérrez Roldán to drill deep wells in this area. Gutiérrez Roldán heeded this advice in the early 1960s, and the investment paid handsome dividends when production began, six years ago, in the rich Reforma area.

Although production in the Reforma area amounted to only 0.4 million barrels in 1972, by December 1973, 14 producing wells in these fields yielded 71,000 barrels per day, equivalent to 13 per cent of total production. During 1976, output in Tabasco and Chiapas averaged 451,276 barrels daily, giving rise to one-half the nation's output of oil, condensates, and natural gas (894,219). By December 1976, the Reforma yield had climbed to 515,982 barrels per day. High quality crude and exceptional productivity characterize the wells in this area. While the average well outside Reforma furnishes approximately 120 barrels each day, those in the Reforma average over 5,500 barrels.

The Chiapas and Tabasco fields are also rich in natural gas. Most wells in Mexico yield an average of 1,000 cubic feet per barrel, but the amount of gas associated with each barrel of oil in this new area approaches 6,000 cubic feet. According to *The Economist*, reserves exceed 20 trillion cubic feet.

Mainly as a result of the Reforma output, Antonio Dovalí Jaime, director-general of PEMEX from 1970 to 1976, announced that as of December 31, 1975, Mexico's proven reserves totaled 6,338 million barrels—just over 1 billion barrels higher than the proven reserves a decade before. Curious as to how reserves had increased only 20 per cent while production had nearly doubled over a 10-year period, president-elect López Portillo named a task force to investigate the size of Mexico's holdings. This group of experts concluded that proven reserves actually stood at 11,160 million barrels, a figure which Jorge Díaz Serrano—the chairman of the task force and López Portillo's choice to head PEMEX—announced in December 1976. One year later, PEMEX stated that proven reserves total 17 billion barrels.

Why had such low reserves been reported before the task force study? The most cogent answer is that the Generation of '38, which held many important posts in the national oil company until Díaz Serrano made a number of new appointments, preferred a conservative figure lest Mexico once again become the focus of foreign aspirations. Many diplomats in Mexico City believe that not even Echeverría was informed of the large reserves because of his erratic behavior and flamboyant globe-trotting.

". . . the IMF . . . has limited Mexico's foreign borrowing to $3 billion in 1977."

PEMEX claims proven, probable, and possible reserves of 120 billion barrels. No doubt this puffing is designed to secure foreign investment, credit, and political support. Still, a number of foreign geologists and petroleum engineers consider 17 billion barrels to be an implausibly low figure and believe that reserves really exceed 60 billion barrels. Four factors bolster their optimism. To begin with, only about 10 per cent of Mexico's geologically promising structures have been explored; serious exploration is just beginning in Chihuahua, Baja California, Sonora, Durango, and Nuevo León. Second, *Excelsior* has reported the discovery of new fields in Tabasco State that will help double current production. Third, Díaz Serrano has described as "gigantic" recently found oil and gas deposits in Coahuila and Tamaulipas. Finally, the official figure excludes reserves in the continental shelf, where "Chac-1" and "Bacab-1"—two remarkably productive wells found at a depth of approximately 15,000 feet in the Campeche sound—indicate the presence of a new oil-producing province. The offshore petroleum fields consist of 60 structures, of which 24 have been selected for exploitation in the next two years. Of 70 exploration wells drilled in 1976, 25 proved productive, for an extremely encouraging 31.6 per cent success rate; during the same period, 200 of 257 development wells furnished commercial quantities of oil and gas.

Although PEMEX officials prefer to talk about the 17 billion barrels of proven reserves, they have announced a six-year development program that confirms Díaz Serrano's belief that "we are sitting on a sea of oil." As he has stated, "We intend to drill 3,476 wells, 1,324 of which will be for exploration and 2,152 to develop the already discovered fields." The goal of this program is to double the production of crude oil and gas liquids to 2,243 million barrels per day, and increase exports fivefold to 1,100 million barrels per day.

It is anticipated that natural gas output will increase the current level of 2 billion to 4 billion cubic feet per day by 1982. The program also calls for a 100 per cent increase in the output of basic petrochemicals to 18.6 million tons annually, with an increase in the number of plants from 60 to 115.

According to Díaz Serrano, the ambitious goals of the six-year plan will require $15 billion in foreign exchange. Sales of petroleum and petroleum products will generate about one-half of this amount; the rest will be obtained through foreign borrowing. In light of the abundant reserves, Mexican leaders feel they can secure the required loans. International bankers showed their interest in Mexican oil by oversubscribing PEMEX's last two loans, each for $300 million.

So Many Constraints

Although executives in PEMEX's headquarters are optimistic, there are a number of constraints on Mexico's ability to achieve its production goals. Even though foreign lenders are well disposed toward PEMEX, the International Monetary Fund (IMF), alarmed at the nation's incredibly high foreign debt, has limited Mexico's foreign borrowing to $3 billion in 1977. Unless this limit is removed or raised, it could hinder PEMEX's well-laid plans, because the Mexican government must borrow money for many things, including current debt-servicing, other than oil. Still, PEMEX will probably find ways to obtain international credits without their counting against the IMF-imposed limit.

Another problem facing PEMEX is expanding domestic demand for petroleum—a demand that could diminish the exports so vitally needed to earn foreign exchange. The six-year plan contemplates a 7 per cent annual increase in domestic consumption, but Mexico's population is growing faster than that of any other major country, and the nation's appetite for energy seems insatiable.

Of all the constraints, the most important is the inefficiency of PEMEX, which J. Paul Getty once barbed as "the only oil company I have known that lost money." Whether PEMEX has operated in the red is unclear because, along with some 400 other public firms, its income and expenditures flow through the national treasury. This makes it virtually impossible to ascertain an accurate profit and loss status.

"Well-connected politicians often own . . . the trucking companies that transport PEMEX products. . . ."

We do know that financial and personal connections between companies and PEMEX executives have strongly influenced the award of equipment and service contracts and concessions to operate gas stations. Well-connected politicians often own both the trucking companies that transport PEMEX products and the country's handful of private petrochemical plants.

Like all Mexican public corporations, PEMEX has a bloated bureaucracy. In 1938, the company's 17,600 employees produced 38,818,213 barrels of petroleum, while 81,042 workers rendered 238,270,853 barrels in 1974. Despite the enormous capital investment in the petroleum sector, the greater efficiency of technology with which to extract, process, and transport oil and related products, and the incredible quantities of petroleum found in the Reforma area, the annual per capita productivity of the *petroleros* only increased from 2,206 to 2,940 barrels during this 36-year period. In the same time span, per capita productivity in the United States rose from 3,186 to 15,124, and in Venezuela from 2,735 to 37,356.

Political cronyism and pressure to secure jobs for relatives and cohorts partially explains the large number of employees. More important is the role of the powerful Petroleum Workers Union, which makes the Teamsters look like a bunch of Little Lord Fauntleroys. Hero of the 1938 expropriation, the union has won high wages for its members and the best fringe benefits in Mexico. For example, in 1974 PEMEX spent $745 per *petrolero* on education, medical services, housing, recreation, and miscellaneous items. This outlay marked a 393 per cent increase since 1960. The union also looks after the employees' families. Over 50 per cent of the individuals hired by PEMEX in 1976 were related to current workers. The postexpropriation esprit de corps among workers has long since vanished as corruption suffuses their well-funded union. In many locals, large payments are required to obtain jobs and win promotions, and, as evidenced by the recent murder of the STPRM's secretary-general, violence is often used to settle disputes.

While vested interests succeeded in gutting President Carter's energy program, the Mexican chief executive, who wields much greater influence relative to other power contenders, has begun to reorganize PEMEX. He demanded that union leaders limit wage requests to a 10 per cent increase and endorsed foreign participation in the development of Mexico's petroleum resources. That López Portillo has spoken loudly will help to remove—or, at least, weaken—the constraints on achieving the goals of his six-year plan. As a matter of fact, exports, expected to be only 153,000 barrels per day in 1977, reached 240,000 barrels per day by August 1.

Assuming constraints on increased production can be overcome, the prospect of so much oil in Mexico raises three key policy questions. Will the nation's love-hate relationship with the United States and its desire for greater economic independence from its affluent neighbor lead to membership in OPEC? Irrespective of international affiliations, will Mexico make good on pledges to diversify its export market and sell a smaller percentage of its oil to the United States? Will Mexican exports consist mostly of crude or refined products?

No Go on OPEC

Despite Mexico's vocal commitment to Third World economic solidarity vis-à-vis capitalist nations, no major government official, political party, or interest group has endorsed membership in OPEC. As a high STPRM official stated in an interview on May 30, 1977: "Our nation thrives on charting its own course in international affairs." Apart from fraternal ties with other developing states, Mexico differs from most of the 13 cartel members. The majority of these countries export one principal item—oil—whereas Mexico also earns substantial foreign exchange from tourism, silver, coffee, and farm products. In comparison with the 80 or 90 per cent of hard currency which it ordinarily generates for most OPEC members, oil accounted for less than 8 per cent of the value of Mexico's exports in 1976.

Even more significant, the cartel sprang up in 1970 in reaction to price manipulation by multinational corporations on which OPEC nations depended for the exploitation, refining, transportation, and marketing of their oil. In contrast, Mexico freed itself from similar foreign influence four decades ago by expropriating the companies that dominated its industry. Unlike the OPEC countries, Mexico boasts a national oil firm that has gained invaluable experience and know-how since 1938. While all OPEC members have now created state companies, these tend to specialize in the lifting of crude as compared with the fully integrated structure of PEMEX. Further, the Mexican Petroleum Institute, a research center and think-tank, has a number of patents to its credit, and PEMEX performs a high percentage of its own engineering, design work, and equipment production.

". . . the powerful Petroleum Workers Union . . . makes the Teamsters look like a bunch of Little Lord Fauntleroys."

Joining OPEC would expose Mexico both to anticartel criticism and the loss of export preferences under the 1974 U.S. Trade Reform Act. Washington has already imposed this sanction on OPEC members, including two Latin-American states (Venezuela and Ecuador.) While the developed countries can cushion the impact of higher energy costs through their pricing of manufactured goods, most less-developed nations enjoy no such hedge, and the sharp rise in oil prices since 1973 has ravaged their economies. Mexico would do well to remain outside the body responsible for this increase, especially if it wants to gain influence at the expense of Venezuela in Central America and the Caribbean, where OPEC prices have exacerbated economic problems.

In addition, the cartel has had increasing difficulty arriving at a common price, as evidenced in December 1976, when Saudi Arabia and the United Arab Emirates agreed to only a 5 per cent increase while the 11 other members committed themselves to a 15 per cent rise in export rates. Although the members finally hammered out a compromise, such differences may emerge in the future and, though unlikely, OPEC could shift from coordinating prices to setting production quotas. This possibility makes the cartel even less attractive to a new producer such as Mexico, which, if a member, could play but a minor role in influencing the organization's policy.

As a result, Mexico has simply dispatched wide-eyed observers to OPEC sessions and charged prices somewhat higher than those of the cartel ($13.40 per barrel versus $12.70). Saudi Arabia and some other Arab members are reportedly opposed to Mexican membership, in view of its present modest export level (240,000 barrels per day) and its vigorous courting of Israel, which purchases 10 per cent of this output. An interest in attracting American Jews as tourists helps explain closer Mexican-Israeli ties.

A "Sell-America" Policy

Where will Mexico sell the bulk of its hydrocarbons? Every oil-related official document carries a de rigeur paragraph about the maximum diversification of purchasers and a key cabinet member has emphasized that "Mexico will not commit itself to supplying the United States with petroleum." Yet, several factors strongly favor a "sell-America" policy.

First, Mexico is used to doing business with the United States, which accounted for 62.4 per cent of its imports and 56.2 per cent of its exports in 1976. Second, financing from American banks, holders of over half of the Mexican government's foreign debt, is crucial to PEMEX's $15 billion six-year development program. Third, despite the bitter expropriation struggle four decades ago, American firms—often with Mexican partners—have provided invaluable exploration, geological, and engineering assistance to PEMEX. A U.S. company is expected to win a contract to build 10 drilling platforms, each sustaining 12 wells, to permit concerted development of the Campeche continental shelf. Fourth, because of high production costs and the absence of a deep-water port for supertankers, Mexico can most profitably sell oil and natural gas to the United States, which will continue to receive 80 to 90 per cent of its exports.

Strict conservation methods could limit U.S. oil imports to 8 mbd (millions of barrels per day) in the early 1980s. But the Central Intelligence Agency is probably more realistic when it projects that demand (22.2 to 25.6 mbd) will probably outstrip domestic supply (10 to 11 mbd) by at least 11.2 mbd by 1985. Secure sources such as Mexico (1.5 mbd), Canada (32,000 bd) and the North Sea (300,000 bd) should provide almost one-fifth of American imports at that time.

Díaz Serrano, an unabashed admirer of American petroleum technology, dispelled lingering doubts about Mexico's sales pattern on May 30, 1977, when he announced plans for a 800-mile, 48-inch gas-duct linking the Reforma fields with the U.S. border. From the pipeline terminal in McAllen, Texas, the gas will flow through existing lines across the sunbelt and southern states. Delivery would jump from 50 mcf (thousand cubic feet) per day (equivalent to 10,000 barrels of crude) in 1977 to 2,000 mcf per day (400,000 barrels) or 3 per cent of total American consumption when the $1.6 billion line is completed. In early August, Mexico signed a letter of intent to sell large quantities of gas to six American companies, including Texas Eastern Transmission Corporation and Tenneco, Inc.

López Portillo Calls the Shots

PEMEX will manage the construction of the system, compared by Mexicans to the trans-Alaskan pipeline. The company's lack of experience with such a major undertaking means that the project, scheduled for completion in two years, will probably not be finished until 1980 or 1981. The Export-Import Bank has agreed to supply $590 million in loans and loan guarantees: the six American firms have discussed putting up $800 million. Before work begins, Mexico and the United States must agree on a price. PEMEX wants to peg the gas price to BTU equivalents of OPEC oil entering the U.S. market ($2.60 per thousand cubic feet), an amount far above both the price of Canadian imported gas ($2.16) and that set in Carter's energy plan for domestic gas ($1.75). Negotiators are now working on a compromise.

Will Mexico sell mostly crude or refined products? Pressures are building for PEMEX to stimulate the economy and demonstrate its advanced status and technological *machismo* by exporting products. But López Portillo, who calls the shots, has emphasized the urgent need to move crude to galvanize his country's economic growth.

The imperative to earn hard currency springs from the current bleak economic conditions. In view of the huge investment required for refineries and the current worldwide surplus of refining capacity, more money can be made quickly by exporting crude. Consequently, PEMEX's recently published six-year investment program calls for a relative diminution in outlays for refining, while expenditures for drilling, production, and transportation rise.

Leftist politicians have attacked the government for selling Mexico's birthright to the United States. In fact, the current policy—staying out of OPEC, exporting to the United States, shipping crude—represents not capitulation to the Colossus of the North but a well-reasoned strategy to reduce Mexico's dependence on American and European banks and international lending agencies.[1]

What Next?

What policies will advance Mexico's economic interests, while satisfying U.S. security needs? In view of extreme sensitivity to outside interference in Mexican affairs, how can the United States and international financial agencies contribute to a rational policy?

---

[1] *For example, Francisco Ortiz Mendoza, leader of the Popular Socialist party's legislative faction, opposed the sale of natural gas to the United States, because it would "increase Mexican dependence."*

Immigration Control: The United States must act at once to stem the flow of illegal or "undocumented" Mexican immigrants to this country. At the very minimum, Carter's quasi-amnesty plan—permanent legal alien status for those who have lived in the United States since January 1, 1970, temporary legal alien status for those who entered between that date and January 1, 1977, and deportation of the rest—should be implemented.

At present the U.S.-Mexican border is the most traversed in the world and poses about as much of a barrier to illegal crossings as the Maginot Line. The Immigration and Naturalization Service has estimated that there are from 6 to 8 million people in the country illegally, 60 per cent of whom are from Mexico. Sharply reducing this flow is more a political than a technical problem.

"Leftist politicians have attacked the government for selling Mexico's birthright to the United States."

Many experts insist that a combination of methods—ubiquitous electronic sensing devices, spotlight-equipped helicopters, noncounterfeitable work cards, sturdy fencing, criminal penalties for employers knowingly hiring unlawful workers, expansion of the U.S. border patrol, etc.—will improve the situation. But Carter and Congress must grasp a nettle that is increasingly prickly—a resolute program could offend Hispanic-American voters who hold the political power balance in a half-dozen populous states.

Closing the border escape valve will force the Mexican government to confront difficult questions about Mexico's economic development. Action should be taken now because (1) future oil earnings can finance long overdue reforms, (2) postponing action will, in view of Mexico's population explosion, turn a flood into a tidal wave within a decade, and (3) López Portillo offers moderate, enlightened leadership that may not be offered by his successor. Restricting the border flow is not intended to sensitize the president to Mexico's needs. He is well aware of the Herculean problems facing his country. But many powerful constituencies—key industrialists, professionals, bureaucrats, labor leaders, businessmen, and political chieftains—must understand that only by promulgating structural changes can they avert massive social unrest and continue to enjoy a reasonably comfortable life.

With 7 per cent of the American work force unemployed and four out of 10 black teenagers without jobs, it makes no sense for millions of foreign workers to enter the economy. Many aliens do fill jobs that now seem too menial or demeaning for Americans. But the nation's welfare system is in shambles, and the Carter administration has voiced a determination to get people off welfare rolls and onto work rolls. While city youth may not flock at once to asparagus fields or apple orchards, there is a growing body of research that suggests incentives can be found to attract Americans to jobs currently held by aliens.[2] Labor and civil rights leaders who decry the presence of foreign workers must be prepared to recruit their unemployed constituents for the jobs that would open when the unlawful emigration declines.

Mexico is a valuable ally with which relations are improving as evidenced by the creation of three bilateral working groups in the aftermath of López Portillo's February 1977 visit to Washington. Sensitivity and flexibility must accompany a new border policy. During a five- to 10-year transition period, temporary migration visas could be issued for limited periods to vital-

[2] *Sociologist R. Wayne Kernodle of the College of William and Mary, who has conducted extensive research on migrant workers on the eastern shore of Virginia, is convinced that Americans will work in food-gathering if the pay is decent and employment conditions are humane.*

ly needed workers. The quota for legal immigrants from Mexico should be increased to its September 1976 level of 62,000 each year. (It is now 40,000.)

Population Growth: The United States, both through bilateral contacts and international financial institutions such as the World Bank, should provide all the assistance possible to Mexico's nascent family planning program. Efforts over the past several years have reduced population growth from 3.6 to 3.2 per cent. Future population growth is unclear because of the large number of women just now reaching childbearing age. Family planning, more successful in urban centers, has barely touched many small cities, much less the countryside where families average 5.7 children (compared with 4.4 in urban areas). Mexico's oil earnings can finance a comprehensive rural family planning program.

Labor-Intensive Industry: Over one-third of Mexico's work force is currently unemployed or underemployed. In good times, the Mexican economy generates 300,000 jobs each year; during the recent recession, the figure may have fallen below 200,000.

Under President Robert McNamara, the World Bank has insisted that developing countries undertake vigorous population control programs as a prerequisite of major assistance. A similar requirement should be applied with respect to labor-intensive industry. Here the World Bank, along with other multilateral lending institutions, might recommend: (1) credit policies that promote labor-intensive production, (2) tax benefits for employers who create jobs, (3) a tax on capital gains and a higher levy on imported capital goods, (4) improvement of vocational education opportunities, and (5) restraint on unreasonable social benefits for workers that make machines more attractive to employers than human beings.

Meanwhile, the U.S. Agency for International Development and the Department of Commerce should offer Mexicans assistance in marketing items in developing countries. An often heard complaint is that even if a country makes a commitment to labor-intensive methods, appropriate technology is difficult to find or is simply unavailable. For this reason, the United States should support the creation of a special institute, under the aegis of the United Nations, whose mission would be to catalog existing labor-intensive technology, help develop new applications of this technology, and disseminate this information to interested countries.

To encourage the creation of jobs in Mexico, the United States has proposed establishing a $2 billion joint industrial development fund, the purpose of which would be to provide Mexican entrepreneurs with low-interest, long-term loans to establish light industry and labor-intensive agricultural projects in northern and central states beset by high unemployment.

". . . American shoe and textile manufacturers cannot stand a flood of Mexican goods."

Among labor-intensive activities that might be emphasized are speciality farm crops in northern Mexico; irrigation, soil conservation, and road-building projects throughout the nation; and food-processing, furniture, clothing, shoes, and leather goods in Guanajuato, Chihuahua, Michoacan, Zacatecas, and Jalisco—states that have generated more than half of the illegal immigrants apprehended since 1969.

Trade Policy: If Mexico embarks upon a serious program of labor-intensive production, and if it is willing to reduce the extreme protectionism it practices, the United States should facilitate the entry of more items into its market. Any move in this direction will cause organized labor to read the riot act to a Democratic administration just as it did 13 years ago to halt the "Bracero" program and as it has done with respect to the border-industry plan. However, AFL-CIO leaders must realize that although Mexico has stepped up the sale of goods north of the Rio Grande, it ran a $2 billion trade deficit with the United States in 1976, and that this strategically important country must be allowed to send more products to the United States in return for exporting fewer bodies.

In addition to placing more Mexican imports on the duty-free list, vexing practices such as the "seasonal tariff" on tomatoes should be relaxed. Already under heavy pressure from Asian imports, American shoe and textile manufacturers cannot stand a flood of Mexican goods. It may be necessary, therefore, to negotiate further limitations on imports from Hong Kong, Taiwan, and South Korea to give Mexico greater opportunities in the U.S. market. While favored relationships are frowned upon by the Office of the Special Trade Representative, self-interest dictates that Washington give a preference to Mexican wares to help defuse a potentially explosive situation in a country with which a 1,946-mile border is shared. Mexico is simply more important to American security than certain Asian nations.

It is naive to think that significant quantities of new shoe and textile imports can enter the U.S. market. These industries, now plagued by severe unemployment, generate strong protectionist pressure. Thus Mexico must cease protecting many manufacturers by shifting from quotas to tariffs on imports and identify other products for export to the United States. Under the General System of Preferences (GSP), the United States offers reduced tariffs on approximately 3,000 items exported by less-developed countries. Mexico has failed to take full advantage of this program. Its exporters often neglect to request the preference to which they are entitled, and there are no fewer than 500 GSP items that Mexico did not even attempt to export to America in 1976. Most important in this category were paper goods, dried fruits, metal products and chemicals.

Mexico must also look elsewhere for markets. It has signed trade accords with the European Economic Community and Brazil. Perhaps the best potential market for Mexican goods is Japan, whose 113 million inhabitants boast an average income of $4,000. U.S. ability to influence Japanese-Mexican relations is obviously limited. But if Washington is willing to recognize that the Japanese should play a role in the development of Mexican oil, this might entice Tokyo to look more favorably on Mexican goods. Washington and Mexico City might also consider a joint study of the Japanese market to determine appropriate exports.

Tax Reform: While exports must be encouraged, trade will not provide the engine for Mexico's economic growth. As López Portillo has emphasized, "It is essential to stress that our development depends on the productive efforts of the Mexicans themselves. . . ." The impetus can only come from within the country, by bringing more people into the market economy. At a time when many Third World nations are narrowing the gap between the rich and poor, this social fissure is deepening in Mexico, despite the country's rich array of resources, its position as one of the most advanced developing states, and the rapid advancement it has boasted—except for the last two years—since World War II. Even though politicians consistently trumpet the populist goals of the 1910 revolution, the position of the country's poorest 40 per cent has not improved materially since the overthrow of dictator Porfirio Díaz 67 years ago. As for the well-to-do, economist David Felix points out that while in 1950 the average income of the top 5 per cent of households was 22 times greater than that of the poorest 40 per cent, two decades later the multiplier had risen to 34.

To stimulate demand for domestic goods, income must be redistributed toward the 20 million Mexicans who occupy the base of the country's social pyramid as spectators rather than participants in the market economy. Petroleum sales will generate some of these moneys. Major tax reform is also required. (At 11.2 per cent of GDP, Mexico has one of the world's lowest payment records.) Given the economic uncertainty and the 35 to 40 per cent increase in production costs since devaluation, a major tax increase would raise the hackles of businessmen, possibly spurring capital flight. The most prudent move, therefore, should be to boost the yield from present rates, inasmuch as an additional 60,000 million pesos could be generated each year if the collection machinery were streamlined. For technical guidance on fiscal matters, international lending agencies, the Internal Revenue Service, and American universities could help. But increasing the payment of taxes by the affluent will require resolute political action by López Portillo.

Energy Conservation: Although Mexico has a great deal of petroleum, attention must be given to husbanding these reserves. The government now sets low energy prices, thereby encouraging energy- or capital-intensive production. Conservation practices such as highway speed limits, automobile mileage standards, efficiency criteria for appliances, and prudent electricity pricing techniques, should be encouraged. Technical assistance might come both from the increasingly conservation-minded Canadian and American experts and through the U.S.-Mexican working groups responsible for economic questions.

Energy Diversification: Because oil will last only a few decades, diversification of Mexican energy sources should be emphasized. There are major deposits of commercial grade coal in Coahuila, which provide 11.1 per cent of the nation's energy needs. Mexico is one of the only countries with identified geothermal resources, located near Mexicali on the U.S. border, which can easily be developed. But next to petroleum, Mexico's greatest potential lies in solar energy, to which López Portillo has shown a strong commitment. As one of the first countries to take part in the Solar Energy Project of the Organization of American States under the Mar del Plata Resolution of 1974, Mexico has purchased solar water pumps for arid areas in Sonora, Durango, San Luis Potosí, and northern Baja California. Also under investigation is the widespread use of solar photovoltaic cells for hot water heating and heat generation.

Abundant, pollution-free, self-renewing —solar power offers many advantages for a sun-drenched country like Mexico. One of its often overlooked benefits is decentralized power generation. Mexico could become a world leader both in petroleum production and in the advancement of nonconventional energy sources. Solar energy could also be used to produce liquid and gaseous fuels, such as alcohol, methane, and hydrogen. Success with solar energy might induce Mexico City's policy-makers to reevaluate their fledgling nuclear program under which the first light-water reactor, Laguna Verde I in Vera Cruz State, will come on line around the end of the decade.

The United States and international agencies can provide modest assistance to Mexico. But Mexicans must manage their own development. Unless decisive political leadership is shown now, this ancient Aztec nation could find itself in the mid-twenty-first century with the same deformed economy, but it may have exhausted the abundant oil reserves with which to pursue the egalitarian ideals of the 1910 upheaval.

PANAMA TREATY TRAP

by Richard A. Falk

The new arrangements for the Panama Canal are regressive and unwise, if not utterly imperial. They make no genuine adjustment to changing international realities, and thus they are unlikely to remain acceptable to the Panamanian people for very long, nor should they.

In debating the new treaties, most American politicians presupposed the desirability of maximizing the U.S. role in running the canal for as long as possible and negotiable. Even supporters of the treaties rested their case on bedrock jingoism. The Senate Republican leader, Howard Baker of Tennessee, crowed that "building the Panama Canal was our 'moon shot' of the first decade of this century." And Senator Charles Percy (R.-Illinois), eager to dispel any illusion that he is an idealist, sought guidance by wondering aloud, in the midst of the treaty hearings, what Teddy Roosevelt would have wanted to do about the canal if he were still alive. Not to be outdone, Jimmy Carter ended his "fireside chat" about the canal in February with the astounding claim, undoubtedly correct, that a resurrected Teddy Roosevelt would have championed the new treaties; it is as if the imprimatur of the most ardently imperialist American president still remains an asset to persuade the country about what should be done in a controversial area of foreign policy.

The tone of advocacy was decisively set by spokesmen for the Carter administration, who argued, above all, that the United States can do everything under the 1977 treaties that it ever wanted to do under the 1903 arrangements.

These feelings about the Panama Canal demonstrate with unmistakable clarity that the United States has not yet outgrown imperialism. Indeed, the debate over the treaties was so narrow that it amounted to a conversation between rational imperialists who favor ratification and sentimental imperialists who oppose. Treaty rationalists argued that certain cosmetic adjustments were necessary to avoid anti-American turmoil in Panama, while the sentimentalists insisted that the symbols of the American presence in the canal were inseparable from substance. What is impressive, and depressing in its implications for other issues, is the consensus that framed the debate. Both sides believe in a perpetual American right to use force to uphold U.S. interests in the canal. All agree that this right includes the discretion to intervene in Panamanian internal affairs if Washington thinks that is necessary to assure the so-called neutrality of the canal.

". . . the United States has not yet outgrown imperialism."

The narrowness of the debate reveals some truths about American attitudes toward the world that liberals, in particular, are reluctant to acknowledge. It is apparent that neither the worldwide movement against colonialism, which has succeeded virtually everywhere in recent decades, nor the trauma of Vietnam has changed the mentality of the American people or their elected representatives. Here is the United States, in the late 1970s, about to stumble into an open-ended commitment to intervene in a shaky Third World country, without even considering proprieties or costs.

At the same time, the United States has forced the Panamanian government to accept a bad bargain. Panama's current leadership agreed to the 1977 treaties principally because it is faced with a deteriorating and desperate economic situation and badly needs the economic sweetener that was added to the treaties by the American negotiators.

Panama's canal revenues under the 1977 treaties will depend on the volume of tonnage that passes through the locks. The best estimates are that Panama will increase its annual revenue from about $2.5 million to as much as $60 million, when and if the new treaties go into effect and until they expire at the end of 1999. Panama is only assured $10 million unconditionally each year and another $10 million from the surplus accumulated from operating revenues; the additional revenue projected for Panama is based on a per ton annuity that assumes a certain level of canal tonnage. These payments are far less than the revenues Panama would receive if the tolls were fixed, (as are Suez Canal tolls) largely by market considerations, rather than reflecting a policy of partially subsidizing international shipping interests. It is also far less than the $200 million per year that Panama had been demanding in the negotiations until last year, when it abruptly cut back its demands, apparently as a result of a deepening financial crisis that created a desperate need for some kind of immediate economic relief. More assured than the canal revenues, however, and directly helpful in meeting Panama's short-term crisis of foreign indebtedness, is an economic package accompanying the new treaties. Panama is to receive $295 million in U.S. loans and investment guarantees over the first five years, as well as $50 million in connection with arms purchases spread out over 10 years. These financial inducements are less than Panama had sought, and do not significantly alter the country's bleak economic outlook.

As the distinguished historian Walter LaFeber, of Cornell University, concludes,[1] "Only large canal revenues could rescue the governmental debt" and avoid an anti-governmental uprising in Panama. LaFeber believes that "... the rapidly deteriorating Panamanian economy and [General Omar] Torrijos' increasing dependence on outside private investors set the stage for the climactic negotiations of a new treaty during the summer of 1977."

Frustrated Nationalism

The new agreements are not likely to quell Panamanian nationalist demands for long and will probably make the United States the target of a continuing worldwide anticolonialist campaign. Indeed, the only way the new treaty regime can succeed is if the Panamanian government becomes even more repressive than it already is. The 30 per cent opposition to the treaty plebiscite in Panama, together with intense opposition to ratification among Panamanian nationalists across a wide political spectrum, indicates the degree to which the new arrangements are already unacceptable in that country. Even Torrijos, the leader of the Panamanian revolution, indicated his own misgivings at the September ceremony in Washington where he and Jimmy Carter signed the treaties. He drew a distinction between "two types of truths—logical truth and pleasant truth." Torrijos signed the treaties "in the name of logical truth," indicating that it was not pleasant to accept an arrangement that "does not enjoy the support of all our people, because the 23 years agreed upon as a transition period are 8,395 days, because while this agreement is in effect there will be military bases that make my country a strategic reprisal target, and because we are agreeing to a treaty of neutrality that places us under the protective umbrella of the Pentagon."

Supporters of the new treaties sometimes concede their colonialist features, but argue that they are a definite improvement over the 1903 Hay-Bunau-Varilla Treaty, that they are as progressive as American public opinion will tolerate at this time. Furthermore, they claim that unless Panamanian aspirations are at least partially satisfied, there could be a serious wave of anti-American violence, including possible sabotage of the canal. The

[1] *Walter LeFeber,* The Panama Canal *(New York: Oxford University Press, 1978), p. 202.*

new agreements, then, are held up as an example of politics as the art of the possible. This view assumes that a delay of 23 years before American troops leave Panama will prove acceptable, or that a regime of permanent protective custody administered from Washington is preferable to the present arrangement.

But the evidence is that Panamanian nationalists are neither satisfied nor appeased by the 1977 treaties. It is one thing to struggle against a colonial heritage that arose at the beginning of the century, but quite another to legitimate the colonial character of the relationship late in the twentieth century.

"The new agreements are not likely to quell Panamanian nationalist demands for long. . . ."

To dramatize his own protest, Leopoldo Aragón, a former political prisoner who was expelled from Panama by Torrijos, burned himself to death in Stockholm outside the American Embassy last September. One of the most widely known and respected Panamanian political figures, Miguel Antonio Bernal, also living abroad in exile, denounced the new treaties as "far from fulfilling the aspirations of the Panamanian people." Bernal argued that the new arrangements replace the "perpetuity imposed by force" in 1903 with a "legalized perpetuity." In an interview published by *Intercontinental Press* last September, he indicted the Torrijos regime for conferring such legality on the American presence and for creating a permanent American right of intervention: "We consider this as the most aberrant, disgraceful, and unacceptable type of perpetuity, as a stigma that this generation and future ones will be forced to bear, for it legalizes the American presence on our soil." Bernal reminded "the Panamanian and American governments, which have been working hand in glove, that the disappointment and dissatisfaction of a people can only be followed by hatred and rebellion"; the treaties, he argued, represent "one of the worst concessions in Panamanian history, because they fly in the face of the struggle and sacrifices made by our people for 73 years."

These Panamanian reactions against the treaties gain additional credibility from the extent to which the 1977 agreements won support from individuals such as retired Admiral Elmo Zumwalt, former chief of naval operations, and William F. Buckley, the conservative commentator—that is, from individuals normally associated with an aggressive U.S. foreign policy that makes no sentimental or idealistic concessions to the Third World. It is clear that their support, as well as that of opposition figures like Gerald Ford or Henry Kissinger, is based on the conviction that, indeed, the new treaties effectively maintain—rather than transform—the American role with respect to the canal. That impression is also fostered by Deputy Secretary of State Warren Christopher's almost gleeful insistence that, "According to the joint chiefs, these treaties are not only as good as the existing arrangement in terms of our national security, they are far better."

One reason for confusion over the treaties is that Torrijos has successfully projected a leftist, nationalist image, especially in the United States. It is true that Torrijos built his political base by claiming nationalist and social reformist credentials. But these earlier features of his rule look largely opportunistic in retrospect, and his true political inclinations seem associated with personal power and wealth. Recently, he has drifted to the right, opening the country to promiscuous foreign investment, siphoning off a personal fortune for his family and coterie, compiling an abysmal human rights record, and alienating and repressing progressive elements in his own society.

As one Latin-American expert, Martin Needler, concluded months before the treaties were signed, the "odds are that Torrijos' leftism and nationalism will erode and the lineaments of a classic, personalistic Latin-American dictatorship not interfering with the social and economic status quo will emerge." Needler even suggested that Torrijos was following a path strikingly similar to that of the Cuban dictator Fulgencio Batista, who also started out as a populist reformer but moved rightward to satisfy personal greed and meet economic pressures. (It has often been theorized that given their similar historical and economic ties to the United States, whatever happens in Cuba will probably also happen eventually in Panama.)

To Intervene Or Not To Intervene

These concerns can be further clarified in relation to the issue of intervention, which people on all sides of the American debate concede to be the Achilles' heel of the 1977 agreements. On this point, the administration says one thing to reassure the Panamanians that their sovereignty is not being infringed upon, but quite another to reassure Americans that their rights will be preserved even after the removal of American troops in 1999. American senators insisted on being promised that the United States retain permanent, discretionary interventionary rights to uphold its interests in the canal. After the original negotiated text was agreed upon, various steps were taken to provide added reassurance for the American side, including the Carter-Torrijos "understanding" of October 14, 1977.

Torrijos has been much praised by American politicians for his flexibility in these respects. Of course, as the dictator of Panama, Torrijos need not obtain any genuine assent from Panamanian lawmakers to assure ratification. However, tilting the treaties even further in the American direction exposes their colonial features, thereby strengthening resentment in Panama.

As is well known, the nonintervention norm is practically synonymous for Latin Americans with sovereignty itself. To grant the United States a permanent, unilateral right to intervene in Panama on behalf of the canal's so-called neutrality is inconsistent with even moderate nationalist aspirations in Panama. Little wonder that Panamanian demonstrators against the treaty contended that Torrijos had accepted a colonial status for Panama, evidently renouncing the country's sovereign rights in exchange for a few Yankee dollars.

From the very beginning, administration spokesmen sought to quiet conservative critics of the treaties who complained that the right of intervention was ambiguous in the 1977 arrangements. They insisted that it was implicitly there. For instance, early in the hearings before the Senate Foreign Relations Committee, Secretary of Defense Harold Brown was asked by Senator Dick Stone (D.-Florida) whether the United States could intervene to deal with an internal situation in Panama that it believed might threaten the neutral operation of the canal. Brown replied that in his view, American officials would have "the right to take whatever action we considered necessary."

"Recently, [Torrijos] has drifted to the right, opening the country to promiscuous foreign investment. . . ."

The defense secretary added that this was what Torrijos had in mind at the signing ceremony when he said that Panama was placing itself "under the protective umbrella of the Pentagon." (Significantly, Torrijos went on to say that "this pact could, if not administered judiciously by future generations, become an instrument of permanent intervention.") Ambassador Sol Linowitz, one of the U.S. negotiators, also supported this view by telling the Foreign Relations Committee that there was "no limitation" on American rights; "there is nothing which says that that threat is to be limited to a particular type of threat."

Problems emerged when the Panamanian negotiators gave their own version of the U.S. role in Panama. Speaking before the National Assembly, Romulo Escobar, the chief Panamanian negotiator, claimed the American role did not extend to threats to the canal that arose out of problems of "internal order." Torrijos, also speaking in Panama, stated that the neutrality treaty meant that "if we are attacked by superior forces, the United States is obliged to come to our defense." Somewhat self-consciously, he explained that "a weak country like Panama needs the protection of a major power if we are attacked by superior forces." And he reassuringly added that nothing in the treaties gave the United States any right to take action on internal strife in Panama.

"The ambiguity of the canal treaties is vital to the bargain."

Although these two interpretations are contradictory in spirit, the treaty text is ambiguous enough to make them both plausible. Rational pro-treaty forces in the United States understood the necessity of the ambiguity. Buckley's *National Review* editorialized that its own pro-treaty position was premised on an unlimited, discretionary, American "right of intervention," but that it understood why such a right could not be spelled out. The U.S. intervention in the Dominican Republic in 1965, the conservative magazine pointed out, enabled American troops to quell a domestic threat of radicalism without Washington ever having to claim a formal right to intervene. On that occasion, the Organization of American States (OAS), under pressure, granted the United States an appropriate figleaf justification. In the Panama Canal context, *National Review* argued, future U.S. leaders must simply understand and act upon their right of intervention, whether the perceived threat is internal or external. Linowitz gave a revealing demonstration during a White House press briefing of how some future international lawyer might deal with the touchy issue of intervention if the occasion arose:

> *Under what conditions would we intervene in the canal to protect the neutrality?*
>
> Linowitz: I don't like the word intervene. Under what conditions would we be in a position to move? The answer is if the permanent neutrality of the canal were jeopardized.
>
> *Who would decide that?*
>
> Linowitz: We would. Then the United States would be in the position to take such steps as might be deemed necessary.

It is worth recalling that none other than Ellsworth Bunker, the other negotiator of the canal treaties, reassured an OAS meeting of ministers of foreign affairs in 1965 that in the Dominican Republic, "We are not talking about intruding in the domestic affairs of other countries; we are talking simply about the elementary duty to save lives in a situation where there is no authority able to accept responsibility for primary law and order." One can easily imagine the rationale for a future intervention in Panama: "We are certainly not seeking to intervene in Panama's internal affairs, but only to uphold the neutrality of the canal, a responsibility enshrined in a treaty and beneficial for all states."

The interventionary right is further endorsed in the Carter-Torrijos "understanding," which confers upon the United States an unrestricted right to defend the "neutrality" of the canal without securing the prior assent of the Panamanian government. Yet the understanding also retains an element of ambiguity, by expressly stating that the neutrality treaty shall not be "interpreted as a right of intervention in the internal affairs of Panama."

Given potential developments in Panama, including the prospect of a turn to the left in Panamanian politics, this ambiguity might place future American leaders in a difficult, dangerous situation. It is worth recalling that the ambiguity in the Geneva accords of 1954 encouraged Hanoi and Washington to proceed, each on reasonable grounds, in contradictory directions that culminated in the Vietnam war. The North Vietnamese regarded the Geneva accords as settling the future of all of Vietnam after a two-year interval enabling an honorable French withdrawal. The Americans, on the other hand, construed the agreements as partitioning Vietnam into two states, thereby giving South Vietnam full sovereign rights to make whatever arrangements it saw fit to defend itself against internal and external enemies.

The Vietnam analogy is instructive in another respect. The United States converted the ambiguity into a commitment (to the Saigon regime) that soon took on a life of its own. It was widely argued that any refusal to uphold this commitment, however foolish the commitment might be, would damage the reputation of the United States as an ally and an alliance leader. In Panama, the commitment to defend the "neutrality" of the canal is also likely to assume a symbolic significance that could induce American leaders to honor it even when they realize it is foolish and costly to do so.

The ambiguity of the canal treaties is vital to the bargain. If it is resolved in Panama's favor, then the arrangements become unacceptable to the United States. This is easy to understand, because the main threat to American interests in the canal comes from the possibility of internal developments in Panama. The prospect of an external invasion by some other power seems remote to the point of irrelevance; and besides, in that eventuality, Panama would almost certainly welcome any U.S. help it could get.

Is There A Better Way?

But the surfacing of this dilemma raises some deep questions that have thus far been kept off the public agenda. The main question is whether it is feasible or beneficial for the United States to insist upon a colonial role for itself into the next century. Such a role seems bound to entangle the American government on the reactionary side of Panamanian politics, as well as to risk U.S. involvement in a series of unpopular, violent struggles. The situation in Panama is very unstable: rapid population growth, a highly inequitable distribution of wealth, growing unemployment, heavy foreign indebtedness, an adverse trade balance, and a long tradition of militant opposition politics.

Would it not be better and cheaper for the United States to leave the canal to the Panamanians? Have not the British been fortunate to be free since 1956 from the burdens and prerogatives associated with the administration of the Suez Canal? The Panamanians need canal revenues so badly that it is difficult to imagine why they would want to interfere with transit rights; and in the unlikely event of such interference, action appropriate to the circumstances could be taken whether authorized by treaty or not.

The new canal arrangements, although intended as a positive contribution to international peace and security, are an anachronism. Their only justification is a continuing insistence that the United States must dominate the Caribbean and the Gulf of Mexico area as a "*mare nostrum* of the United States." (This was the argument recently advanced by Hanson Baldwin, formerly of *The New York Times*, in the *American Enterprise Institute Defense Review*.)

No less an authority on the American role in the world than George Kennan is sensitive to the drawbacks of going part way on the canal and proposes "turning the canal over entirely to the Panamanians."[2] Kennan is convinced that the canal is no longer militarily or commercially important enough for the United States to justify the burdens of joint administration and defense.

[2] *George F. Kennan,* The Cloud of Danger: Current Realities of American Foreign Policy *(Boston: Atlantic-Little, Brown, 1977).*

In light of this geopolitical reality, he argues, it places the United States in an exposed, risky, and unpopular position to maintain its role. It is sad that Kennan's view, which proceeds from a rather conservative assessment of U.S. interests, has not been seriously considered. One could take his argument further and point out that it would not only be advantageous for the United States to end its special role in the canal, but it would also be a positive contribution to the construction of a viable system of world order.

Another option would be to seek the partial internationalization of responsibility for the Panama Canal. Panama could be given administrative control and the economic benefits, while the international community could be entrusted with the mission of assuring transit rights and neutral management. This mission could be assigned to the OAS, the United Nations, or even a newly created international entity with the power to propose whatever measures might be necessary to keep the waterway open, including forcible occupation. There is no assurance that internationalism would work in a period of crisis, but this doubt exists with all options. At least under an international scheme the United States would not be insisting on discredited prerogatives to act unilaterally; nor would it find itself burdened by a commitment of uncertain scope and application. Furthermore, the arrangement would uphold the principle that international waterways like the Panama Canal belong to the entire world community.

". . . the foreign policy consensus [is] set by the Pentagon and the political right."

There is a precedent of sorts for such a step. After World War II, the United States proposed the internationalization of the waterways of Europe, including the Kiel Canal. Harry Truman, making this proposal in a radio report to the nation on his return from the Berlin Conference in August 1945, said "we think this is important to the future peace and security of the world." This at least suggests that at one time the internationalization of other countries' canals and waterways was not alien to American official sensibilities. The only option, short of turning the canal over to the Panamanians or internationalizing it, that genuinely serves true American and world interests would be to modify the 1977 treaties by shortening the transition period, by renouncing any unilateral U.S. right to use force, and by giving Panama an option after U.S. withdrawal to terminate any arrangements of joint defense. It is evident from Torrijos' remarks on various occasions that he would much prefer a resolution that went further in according Panama full sovereign rights.

In a search for a Panama Canal arrangement that would be politically and morally palatable, both domestically and internationally, the United States has pressured the current Panamanian regime to assent to arrangements that create new problems without solving the old ones. But it is poor politics, and even worse morality, for those who consider themselves anti-imperialists to find their refuge, however tacitly, in the cause of rational imperialism.

In the end, the real question is whether the Carter administration could have done better. Was it truly trapped by the nostalgic affinity of the American people for the canal and by the political imperative of winning the support of the joint chiefs of staff? If so constrained that nothing more than the new arrangements could have been achieved, was it an exercise in benevolent statecraft to push ahead anyway at this time? These are difficult questions for which no convincing answers can be given. To some extent, we must await the judgment of history.

From the outset, the Carter administration seemed convinced that it had to build a center-right coalition to win support for the treaties, and that more liberal outlooks could be ignored. The constraints imposed by such a coalition induced an unstable and anachronistic arrangement for the canal. But the canal is probably not as much of a special case as some pretend, and a similar coalition-building process is at work across the whole spectrum of American foreign policy, including the international economic area, although with different sectors of society and bureaucracy playing the role that the joint chiefs played in the Panama context.

If this assessment is correct, it suggests that an American president is locked into the status quo to such an extent that it is virtually impossible to implement progressive reforms. This rigidity critically limits the capacity of even the most enlightened political leadership in this country to adjust to a changing world situation. It also suggests the need for fracturing the foreign policy consensus, whose terms of reference are set by the Pentagon and the political right.

LATIN AMERICA: A NOT-SO-SPECIAL RELATIONSHIP

by Abraham F. Lowenthal

Not since the heady days of John F. Kennedy and the Alliance for Progress has Washington lavished so much attention on Latin America. The president and his wife, the vice president, the secretary of state and his deputy, the secretary of the treasury, and the U.S. ambassador to the United Nations all visited the region during the Carter administration's first 18 months, traveling to a total of 17 different countries, many of them more than once. Terence A. Todman, Carter's original assistant secretary of state for inter-American affairs, managed to tour all the countries of the hemisphere before he became ambassador to Spain last July. The Panama Canal issue absorbed more high-level official energies than any other single foreign policy question during Carter's first year-and-a-half in office.

Will this vigorous initial concern with Latin America endure and eventually produce lasting positive results? Or will a familiar cycle be repeated—a burst of interest in Latin America complete with visits, speeches, and proclamations of new policies, followed by concrete decisions (or failures to decide) that weaken or even contradict the very policies just announced? Will basic problems go unaddressed, as has been the case so often in the past? The answers lie primarily in the economic realm. How the United States deals with fundamental economic issues will influence inter-American relations much more than any initiatives the Carter administration has taken so far.

It took former Secretary of State Henry Kissinger years to discover Latin America. The Carter administration, by contrast, began with an expressed concern for the region, stressed often by the president himself. His second major foreign policy address as president was to the Organization of American States, whose headquarters in Washington he has already visited three times (more than any previous president). The first visit by a chief of state to Washington after Carter took office was from Mexico's president, José López Portillo. President Carlos Andrés Pérez of Venezuela followed soon thereafter. In September 1977, 17 Latin American heads of state converged on Washington to witness the signing of the Panama Canal treaties. Each visiting chief executive met individually with Carter, who devoted the better part of a week to his visitors. Neglect, benign or otherwise, is no longer Washington's official approach to the nations of the Western Hemisphere.

Fewer Promises

The Carter administration has begun to reform the rhetoric and concepts of inter-American relations. Shopworn phrases like "Pan-American community" and "special relationship" are being largely abandoned, as Washington concedes that its treatment of Latin America and the Caribbean has often been discriminatory and one-sided. The United States is not again promising preferential treatment for Latin America. Instead, this administration has focused on the growing significance of key Latin American countries in dealing with a global agenda of issues equally important to North and South America. The Carter administration on the whole has been treating the countries of the Western Hemisphere as they wish to be treated—as individual, sovereign nations, each with interests of its own.

Under Carter, the U.S. government has also mustered the courage to tackle two thorny problems that previous administrations had avoided: Panama and Cuba. Even after Kissinger and his colleagues turned their attention to these issues in 1974, they deliberately stopped short of measures that would have risked major domestic criticism. Candidate Jimmy Carter, too, was notably cautious on these matters during the 1976 presidential campaign. From the moment he took office, however, Carter committed himself to revising the troubled U.S. relationship with Panama by recognizing that country's sovereignty over the Canal Zone, and to moving, on a measured and reciprocal basis, toward renewed relations with President Fidel Castro's Cuba. By the time of his first National Security Council meeting, Carter had accorded the Panama Canal issue top billing. He rejected advice from inside

"It took . . . Henry Kissinger years to discover Latin America."

his administration and out to leave U.S.-Cuban relations alone until the Panama problem could be resolved. Instead, Washington began to press forward on both issues and even linked them to others—such as the recognition of Vietnam and initiatives to improve relations with Jamaica and Guyana—to demonstrate its acceptance of ideological diversity and its intention to deal with all nations, regardless of size or political bent, on the basis of mutual respect.

By negotiating new treaties with Panama and by successfully, if not always gracefully, pushing them through the arduous process of Senate ratification, President Carter accomplished a necessary task. And by establishing direct and public diplomatic contact with Cuba and expressing interest in an eventual resumption of full bilateral relations, the Carter administration ended an outmoded and self-defeating U.S. policy. Cuba's African involvements and the White House's somewhat irascible reaction to them have obviously complicated the process of eventual rapprochement between Washington and Havana. Whatever the course of

U.S.-Cuban relations, however, the United States has improved its own capacity for dealing with the challenges Cuba presents by abandoning its ossified stance of the 1960s and early 1970s.

Additionally, the Carter administration has moved away from broad, undifferentiated regional policies toward more carefully tailored bilateral and subregional approaches. This process of refining U.S. policy in the Western Hemisphere (to an extent, a return to the historical pattern disrupted by the sweeping generalities of the Alliance for Progress) had already made headway in previous years. For instance, the memorandum signed in 1976 by Kissinger and Brazilian Minister of Foreign Affairs Antonio Francisco Azeredo da Silveira set up special mechanisms for handling U.S.-Brazilian relations. The Carter administration has concentrated not only on Brazil, but also on Mexico, Venezuela, and the Caribbean. Brazil and Mexico account for one-fourth of all U.S. trade with less developed countries outside the Organization of Petroleum Exporting Countries; these two countries plus Venezuela account for almost 70 per cent of all U.S. trade with Latin America and well over half of U.S. investment in the hemisphere. All three countries warrant more high-level attention than they previously received, not only because of expanded U.S. investment and trade but also because of the enlarged international role they will play as middle-rank powers.

The Carter administration has also recognized the potential significance for the United States of improved relations with the countries and territories of the Caribbean, America's third border. Spurred by the impact of burgeoning immigration from the Caribbean, Washington is paying attention to the region's economic problems for the first time in years. Study missions and task forces have been created within the U.S. government to deal with Caribbean issues, and a multilateral consultative group has been convened under World Bank auspices to coordinate external development assistance. Caribbean development is finally being considered on its own merits, rather than solely within the narrowly defined terms of military security that dominated U.S. perceptions of the region—between periodic Marine landings—for generations.

No Carter administration policy affecting Latin America is as dramatically new as its stand on human rights. Kissinger seemed mostly indifferent, if not hostile, to this issue; this administration gives it pride of place. Despite contrary congressional instructions, the Ford administration generally supported loans by international financial institutions to nations that flagrantly violated human rights; the Carter administration has already opposed more than 25 such loans, mostly in Latin America. The United States was not previously a party to the Inter-American Convention on Human Rights;

"Carter has altered the U.S. reputation for automatically identifying with authoritarian regimes."

under Carter, Washington not only signed the agreement, but also persuaded several other countries to do so after years of delay. The United States has recently spearheaded efforts to strengthen substantially the budget, staff, and authority of the Inter-American Commission on Human Rights. And this administration has also found ways—through formal and informal meetings and other expressions of interest and sympathy—to build new links with democratic opposition groups throughout South and Central America and the Caribbean.

To an impressive degree, Carter has altered the U.S. reputation for automatically identifying with authoritarian regimes. Fundamental American values—particularly respect for human rights and a preference for constitutional democracy—have been forcefully reasserted. The lives of hundreds of people in several countries have improved, at least in part as a result of pressures from Washington. Significant numbers of political prisoners have been released in Chile and Haiti and some have been let go in several other countries, and lists of political prisoners have been made available in Argentina and Chile. Commissions to investigate human rights conditions have gained entry to several countries. Reports of the use of torture have decreased. Most important, perhaps, a mood of cautious hope has begun to grow that brutal repression is no longer being legitimated. And although the Carter administration's role in precipitating this year's outbreak of elections throughout Latin America and the Caribbean should not be exaggerated, it is fair to say that the United States has been consciously and effectively reinforcing this trend, particularly in Peru and the Dominican Republic.

The increased attention paid to the countries of Latin America and the Caribbean, the abandonment of paternalism, the recognition of Latin America's potential role in dealing with a broad global agenda, the priority given to key bilateral relationships, and the reassertion of fundamental national values as a guide for policy are all commendable changes. The administration also deserves praise for so far resisting the impulse toward military intervention that has so often marked Washington's approach to the region. The previous four American presidents all launched major interventions in Latin America within their first two years in office—the Guatemalan invasion of 1954, the Bay of Pigs fiasco of 1961, the Dominican intervention of 1965, and the massive efforts in 1970 to destabilize the Allende government in Chile. It is highly unlikely that any similar adventure is being carried out or contemplated by the Carter administration.

An Orgy of Attention

It is too soon, however, to conclude that the improvements Jimmy Carter and his team have introduced in U.S.-Latin American relations will be of lasting importance. Many of the toughest problems affecting the region—particularly items on the economic agenda—have yet to be seriously faced. Whether the administration's impressive start will ultimately amount to much depends critically on decisions and actions yet to be taken, as well as on trends and developments beyond any president's control.

The burst of high-level activity expended on Panama and Cuba, for example, may turn out to be insignificant, or even counterproductive, as a way to improve inter-American relations over the longer term. The orgy of official attention to Panama, in particular, may make it much harder to get high-level attention for economic issues. The administration's initiatives on the Panama and Cuba issues were unquestionably courageous efforts to remove troublesome political problems of the past. But as bridges to a "new era of inter-American cooperation," as President Carter and others have heralded them, they appear in danger of being left hanging, precisely because the underlying economic issues in hemispheric relations remain unresolved.

Despite its talk about the individuality of the respective countries of Latin America and the Caribbean, the Carter administration has been remarkably insensitive in several specific areas. U.S.-Brazilian relations deteriorated seriously in 1977 as a result of objective clashes of interest (some of them long-standing) and of early mistakes by the Carter team. Particularly damaging was Vice President Walter F. Mondale's highly publicized direct approach to West Germany concerning its sale of nuclear reprocessing technology to Brazil, an approach made prior to any direct U.S. discussion of the matter with the government of Brazil.

After a brief honeymoon between incoming administrations in the United States and in Mexico, U.S.-Mexican relations were also strained in 1977. The principal reason was the somewhat peremptory proposals by the United States for dealing with massive

Mexican immigration. A Carter plan calling for strict measures to control the flow of "undocumented immigrants" from Mexico was sent to Congress last August with little prior consultation with Mexican authorities—or, for that matter, with Mexican-Americans. It should have been obvious that a genuine jointly devised approach to this problem would be far more likely to succeed than a unilateral one. Moreover, it could have helped assure Mexican cooperation on other matters of shared concern, such as guaranteeing U.S. access to Mexico's huge reserves of natural gas and its projected reserves of petroleum.

Many Latin American and Carribbean countries have been hurt by individual U.S. decisions: to raise tariffs on imported sugar; to sell surplus tin from the government stockpile in order to lower the price; to grant or deny certain airline routes; and to tighten tax regulations on business exemptions for conventions abroad. The gap between announced policy and actual decisions is nowhere more notable than in U.S.-Caribbean relations. The administration's Caribbean initiative seems to be fizzling as specific choices have to be made. State Department and Agency for International Development recommendations for doubling U.S. government support for Caribbean development were turned down, first by the Office of Management and Budget and then, on appeal, by the president himself. Caribbean development has been officially accorded high priority, but an administration that has established so many priorities is unable to make such a commitment very meaningful.

Ghosts of Paternalism

Washington's new human rights policy is difficult to evaluate, because it is unclear how much emphasis is being placed on the policy's several distinct, and not always compatible, objectives. The policy is supposed to win renewed domestic trust in the government and its foreign policies, retake the ideological advantage from the Communist parties of Eastern and Western Europe, provide a legitimate basis for sustained U.S. government communication with those in opposition to authoritarian government, disassociate the United States from repressive regimes and their acts, and actually influence the treatment of individuals abroad. Contradictory signals abound, reflecting intra- and interdepartmental disputes within the U.S. government about ends and means, as well as different evaluations of external circumstances and trends. In the relatively uncharted domain of human rights, broad policy guidelines are necessarily abstract and often unenlightening. In practice, policy is defined case by case, country by country, loan by loan, and speech by speech through an iterative process in which the personal styles and ambitions of individual participants in the policy-making process are probably more influential than any other factor.

"Carter's record to date on North-South issues . . . has been mixed at best."

As the human rights policy takes shape, several problems are emerging. Excessive expectations can easily be aroused, as in Nicaragua, risking eventual disillusionment. Heavy-handedness from abroad, no matter how noble the cause, can actually strengthen the domestic hold of repressive regimes, at least temporarily; this may have happened, for a time, in Chile. Policies fashioned to deal with one set of important problems—to fight inflation and stabilize economies, for instance—may contradict and even undermine efforts to promote civil and political liberties, as in Peru. Conversely, policies designed to protect individual rights may not only constrain the development of the countries denied credit by international financial institutions, but may also severely damage the institutions themselves. Vigorous implementation by Washington of the human rights policy in the Western Hemisphere can conjure up ghosts of the paternalist past. And, finally, the whole policy may be used perversely by a strange right-left alliance in Congress and U.S. society as a means of avoiding the resource transfers sought by Latin American and other Third World countries. These difficulties do not argue against a major U.S. concern for human rights, nor should they obscure what the policy has already accomplished. The policy's lasting impact, however, will depend to a considerable extent on how carefully this concern is calibrated. The danger is growing that exuberant and single-minded pursuit of human rights objectives may eventually produce its own backlash, turning officials away from the concern that these issues should always evoke.

But economic issues present the most vexing questions about the administration's policies toward Latin America. Unfortunately, Washington's desire to win Latin American cooperation on global problems is tangible only with regard to the issues the United States itself deems to be urgent: energy, monetary policy, and nonproliferation.

The issues that most deeply concern the majority of Latin American countries—improving access for middle-income countries to the markets, capital, and technology of the industrialized nations; increasing the amount and availability of concessional aid to the poorest countries; making the terms of international trade in commodities more predictable and more favorable to producers; and making multinational corporations more responsive to the interests of host countries—are accorded much lower priority. Unless these and similar North-South problems are confronted, the Carter administration's embrace of a so-called global approach may turn out to be an empty shell, addressing Latin America's principal concerns even less adequately than the old regional approaches.

Carter's record to date on North-South issues—admittedly restricted by recession and adverse public opinion—has been mixed at best. The administration has sometimes succeeded in resisting strong protectionist pressures. But access to the markets of the United States and other industrialized countries is certainly not being significantly expanded, as it must be if Third World aspirations are to be accommodated. To many Latin Americans, the Multilateral Trade Negotiations under way in Geneva seem thus far largely unresponsive to their needs; industrialized countries are likely to secure greater benefits from trade liberalization than are less developed countries, at least in the short run. Even more troubling is the scheduled expiration in January 1979 of the waiver provisions of the Trade Act of 1974, which allow the secretary of the treasury to delay the application of countervailing duties to goods benefiting from favorable tax treatment in exporting countries. Unless agreement can be reached by January, any Latin American export to the United States currently receiving a government incentive will be subject to countervailing duties within 12 months of a U.S. manufacturer's complaint.

Developments on other North-South issues are not much more encouraging. Obtaining U.S. capital is becoming more difficult, not less, for most of the countries of Latin America and the Caribbean. Concessional aid is relevant only for a few poor countries in the hemisphere, but even they are getting little help from the United States. The administration's request for a 28 per cent increase in worldwide U.S. aid has been whittled down in the authorization and appropriation processes; even if the increase had been appropriated in full, it would still have been quite small in absolute terms and would have left the United States far below the U.N. objective that aid be equal to .7 per cent of a country's Gross National Product. Of course, much more credit is available to Latin American and Caribbean countries from international financial institutions, and this will continue to be the case if the U.S. Congress approves the necessary appropriations. But the debt service paid by nations in the Western Hemisphere on earlier loans now consumes 93 cents out of every dollar borrowed from the United States and the international lending institutions. Moreover, credit from private sources is rapidly drying up for precisely those countries that are in greatest financial difficulty—Peru and Guyana, for instance. The short time-horizon of commercial banks practically assures a perverse cycle of ever-deepening debt.[1]

Despite the Carter administration's rhetorical receptiveness to international commodity agreements, the main difference in this field between this government and its predecessors is that now many more officials are tied down either negotiating or preparing to do so.

Concrete results are sparse. The International Sugar Agreement has been concluded (though Senate ratification is uncertain); and a rubber agreement is being hammered out, but this commodity is of little interest in Latin America. Other negotiations—including those on copper—seem painfully slow and unpromising.

Aside from a few scattered statements, there is scant evidence that the U.S. government will pressure multinational corporations (MNCs) toward greater responsiveness to the needs of developing countries. Richard N. Cooper, under secretary of state for economic affairs, told a group of business executives that the U.S. government would henceforth remain neutral in disagreements between American companies and host countries rather than automatically taking the side of U.S. corporations. But the actual behavior of American embassies has not changed perceptibly. Indeed, the administration has not yet done anything to repeal two pieces of legislation—the Hickenlooper Amendment first adopted in 1962 and the 1972 Gonzalez Amendment—which still threaten developing countries with U.S. government coercion on behalf of MNCs in cases of nationalization or expropriation.

Finally, little is being done, despite rhetoric to the contrary, to improve the terms governing technology transfers. President Carter's proposal, announced in Caracas last March, to establish a "new United States foundation for technological collaboration" was notable mainly for its complete omission of any further details.

The Carter administration's accomplishments in Latin American policy, then, are so far more style than substance. Attention is being paid to the region, but few problems have been resolved and several have not been tackled. The issues granted priority in Washington are the same as in the past. Rhetoric and tone have changed more than choices and actions. Emphasis has been placed on setting goals, more than on elaborating strategies to achieve them. The major innovations in U.S. policy have been in the most intangible arena, human rights. On matters of dollars and cents the Carter administration has so far produced only small change.

Initial skepticism may still be overcome as trade and tariff negotiations evolve, as specific commodity agreements are worked out, as actual investment disputes arise and are dealt with, as projects demanding increased resource transfers for the Caribbean and elsewhere are considered, and as the president's proposal to establish a foundation for technology is elaborated. No one who favors positive change should help make it unlikely by expressing too much pessimism.

It must be noted, however, that Carter has thus far repeated a familiar pattern.[2] Whether calling its approach a "Good

[1] *See Albert Fishlow, et al, "The Third World: Public Debt, Private Profit,"* FOREIGN POLICY 30 *(Spring 1978).*

[2] *For a more complete discussion of these issues, see Abraham F. Lowenthal and Gregory F. Treverton, "The Making of U.S. Policies Toward Latin America,"* Working Paper #5 *(Washington, D.C.: Latin American Program, The Woodrow Wilson International Center for Scholars).*

Neighbor Policy," an "Alliance for Progress," a "Mature Partnership," or a "New Dialogue," or pointedly eschewing rhetoric and labels, as Carter has done, one administration after another has promised to improve U.S.-Latin American relations. Always goaded by a period of tension in hemispheric relations, successive governments have inevitably announced reforms, pledged greater attention to the needs of the area, and vowed their support for Latin America's social and economic development. In earlier days the United States sometimes promised to help secure democracy in the region. "Human rights," rather than "democracy," is now the slogan, but the point is the same.

Rhetoric or Results

The next phase in this historic cycle, which the Carter administration may now be entering, has generally seen the newly expressed policy toward Latin America vitiated, or even contradicted, by U.S. government actions. Despite the promises that they will receive enhanced consideration, Latin American interests are slighted or contravened. Despite the pretense of consultation and negotiation, Latin Americans are the victims of unilateral decisions made in Washington or New York. Whatever the official rhetoric of cooperation, Latin Americans learn that private interests in the United States can use public instruments to achieve their will. Although Washington promises to help Latin American development, generous resource transfers from the United States often wind up tied to political concessions or special commercial privileges. Events of the past few months—the sugar tariff increases; Washington's decision to sell surplus tin despite the adverse impact on Bolivia; the threat to impose countervailing duties; the decision to curtail sharply the proposed Caribbean initiative; the unilateral proposals to deal with the problem of undocumented aliens—fit the classic mode.

What explains this persistent gap between each new administration's proclaimed Latin American policy and the pattern of decisions, actions, and omissions that ultimately comprise the real policy? Why does the resolve of new administrations to improve inter-American relations so often come to naught, or to only a bit more?

Many of the U.S. government's decisions and actions affecting Latin America and inter-American relations result from initiatives in other policy arenas—foreign or domestic—with limited consideration, if any, given to their likely impact in the hemisphere. The many examples include the sugar and tin decisions; the policies regarding nuclear proliferation, arms transfers, and human rights; many provisions of tax law and its implementation; and a number of trade policy decisions. Actions of this sort are often not significantly influenced by regional considerations or by the U.S. government personnel working on inter-American affairs. Those within the administration primarily concerned with inter-American relations may push hard for alternate policies. That they so often fail reflects the relative lack of priority accorded to the region.

"It is much easier for the [U.S.] government to manage its relations with the Soviet Union or China than with Chile or Peru."

A second point, often ignored, is that a multiplicity of nongovernmental entities and processes, which no administration can easily control, influence the shape of inter-American relations. These entities—multinational corporations, private banks, and labor unions, for example—operate within a structure strongly affected by past and present U.S. government decisions. Official policy can influence or constrain private actions, for U.S. citizens, individual or corporate, are rarely entirely oblivious to Washington's preference. Still, what the U.S. government decides to do, or not to do, in

Latin America cannot by itself alter the main impact of the United States. In a curious sense, it is much easier for the government to manage its relations with the Soviet Union or China than with Chile or Peru. Latin American and Caribbean countries are very strongly influenced by decisions taken by Exxon, the American Smelting and Refining Co. (ASARCO), United Brands, Citibank, Manufacturers Hanover Trust, or Chase Manhattan, to name just a few examples. And some of the main problems in inter-American relations—especially access to capital and technology—are issues over which the U.S. government has considerably less influence than nongovernmental actors.

A third reason for the contrast between announced intentions and subsequent actions has to do with the policy-making process itself. Each new administration brings to Washington a fresh cadre of officials determined to do better than their predecessors. They often bring with them concepts and policies forged by task forces and study groups. The new recruits draw on this background to draft policy directives and presidential speeches. In time, however, their influence is attenuated by the persistent pressures of special interests and sometimes by the passive resistance of the career bureaucracy.

Because private U.S. interest groups can pursue their particular objectives through many different channels in the executive branch and Congress, broad and consistent reforms of U.S. policy are hard to achieve. Any reform that penalizes a well-organized group—copper companies, sugar or citrus growers, shoe manufacturers, labor unions, or church groups—can usually be shelved or defeated by a coalition assembled within the highly fragmented structure of U.S. foreign policy-making. Even when the proposed reform promises to benefit U.S. society as a whole, the group likely to be injured can often prevent the reform's adoption. And even when a new policy is formally adopted, an administration must then ensure its full implementation at all levels of sharply divergent bureaucracies. The Treasury Department is often decisive in shaping and implementing U.S. policies on commercial and monetary matters; on export subsidies, countervailing duties, and other elements of trade policy; on the negotiation of commodity agreements and buffer stocks; on the behavior of international financial institutions; in short, on most of the substantive issues in contemporary inter-American relations. The Departments of Agriculture, Energy, Justice, and Commerce; the Export-Import Bank; the Civil Aeronautics Board—not to mention the Pentagon and the Central Intelligence Agency—all have direct influence on U.S. policies affecting Latin America. To ensure that all segments of the U.S. government will cooperate to pursue a new policy, an administration must be willing to give that policy significant priority. Constant monitoring, innovative coordination, and energetic implementation are required. That kind of priority is, and must be, rare.

New administrations also find it hard to follow through on proclaimed intentions because of the often underestimated and still growing role of Congress. Trade policy, human rights, arms transfer policy, agriculture policy, foreign aid, and other matters important in the hemisphere are today strongly influenced by Congress. Almost any new policy initiative must first run the gauntlet of congressional scrutiny, influenced by constituent pressures of all sorts, before it can be fully implemented. Few proposals survive this ordeal unscathed.

Constant Tension

Lasting improvements in U.S.-Latin American relations are difficult to achieve for three reasons that are more basic: the reality of declining but still remembered U.S. hegemony in the hemisphere, the emergence of sharp clashes of interests between the United States and the countries of Latin America and the Caribbean, and the absence of a coherent and widely accepted vision in Washington of how inter-American relations should be restructured to respond to these two changing facts of hemispheric life.

An overwhelming imbalance between the United States and the countries of Latin America and the Caribbean has long conditioned the realities of inter-American relations. Because the United States is so much bigger, richer, stronger, and more extensively involved around the world than any other country in the hemisphere, what is crucial for a Latin American nation may be of marginal significance in Washington. Moreover, what may appear to be mutually advantageous from Washington's perspective seems exploitative from a Latin American standpoint. Because so many in the United States still think of Latin America as a U.S. sphere of influence, an intolerable affront to sovereignty—like the reservation to the Panama Canal treaties introduced by Senator Dennis DeConcini (D.-Arizona), providing the United States with the permanent right to send its troops into Panama to protect the canal—can be approved with few qualms in the United States. The inevitable result of this continuing imbalance of power, real and perceived, is constant tension rooted in ambition, fear, jealousy, and resentment. As the bases for America's hegemonic presumption erode, tensions will probably not be relaxed but rather increased.[3]

During the next few years, a new Latin American assertiveness resulting from enhanced power and from changes in the composition of the area's leadership will exacerbate the tension. Traditional pro-American elites are being replaced all over the hemisphere by civilian and military technocrats, often of a nationalist bent. These new leaders, many of them trained in U.S. graduate schools, tend to identify their countries' interests independently of, and even in confrontation with, the United States. But another important source of increased inter-American disagreement is the change in the focus of Latin American economies from inward-turned import substitution to outward-oriented export promotion. Most Latin American countries, except for the smallest, no longer care about obtaining bilateral concessional assistance from the United States. They, like other Third World countries, primarily seek new rules and practices that will improve their access to markets, capital, and technology in the industrialized world.

As Latin American and other Third World economies expand and as their export potential and their thirst for capital and technology grow, conflicts will inevitably arise between them and the industrialized countries. The specific issues will include commodities, tariffs, countervailing duties, debt management, technology transfers, the conservation and management of resources, the terms of capital and labor migration, and the formulation and management of international rules to govern these and other problems. As Brazil, Mexico, Venezuela, Argentina, and other Latin American countries strive to fulfill their potential, they will encounter a growing tendency of industrialized countries to defend the status quo through protectionism, preservation of existing international monetary arrangements, nonproliferation policies, and the like.

Consequently, to achieve a major and lasting improvement in its relations with Latin America, the United States will have to help establish a new international economic and political order within which the claims of Latin American and other aspiring powers are more fully accommodated.[4] A reformed international order would reconcile U.S. interests with those of Latin American and other Third World countries in

[3]*See Abraham F. Lowenthal, "The United States and Latin America: Ending the Hegemonic Presumption,"* Foreign Affairs, *October 1976.*

[4]*For an outline of such an order, see Albert Fishlow, "A New International Economic Order: What Kind?" in Fishlow, et al,* Rich and Poor Nations in the World Economy *(New York: McGraw-Hill, 1978).*

ways ultimately more favorable to Third World interests than under the existing order. More of the world's manufacturing would take place in the South, and painful adjustments would have to be accepted by the North. Increased benefits from international trade in raw materials and other primary products would accrue to the less industrialized countries. The advantages derived by the rich countries from prior accumulations of capital and technology would decrease. The present and prospective benefits from the world's commons—especially from the seabed and outer space—would be distributed in a more equitable manner. The rules and regimes affecting these and other international issues would be made in fora where the interests of the countries of Latin America, among others, would be protected. To a large extent market forces can be used to make the new international order work, but substantial structural change will be required to assure that markets operate in a world where leverage, influence, and rewards are not so unevenly distributed.

No administration to date has seriously attempted to change the structure of the international order, which has so overwhelmingly favored the United States. Economic concessions granted by Washington to Latin American countries and others have always been provided grudgingly in exchange for cooperation on specific political or strategic matters. Never has the United States sought to transform the very nature of its relationship with the rest of the hemisphere. If Jimmy Carter wants to inaugurate a truly new era in U.S.-Latin American relations, that is the challenge his administration must face.

PUERTO RICO: OUT OF THE COLONIAL CLOSET

by José A. Cabranes

The problem of Puerto Rico is colonialism, and decolonization stands at the front and center of the island's politics and its relations with the United States, now and for the foreseeable future.

Colonialism in Puerto Rico has been unique—"colonialism with the consent of the governed," it has often been called. So it is not surprising that the decolonization process there may have few counterparts or precedents elsewhere in the world. But that process may prove to be as difficult, confusing, and painful for all concerned—including U.S. policy makers—as any experienced by the European powers in Africa and Asia. The universal Puerto Rican longing for political change today presents the United States with a major domestic political dilemma and a serious foreign policy problem.

There is not yet a clear consensus among Puerto Ricans about the island's political future. There is, however, a very definite consensus about its present status as a "commonwealth": Things cannot remain as they are. Puerto Ricans must work toward a relationship with the mainland that will lift the enormous psychological burden of decades of dependency and political inferiority, enabling the island's 3.2 million people to live in peace under a permanent form of government.

None of Puerto Rico's political parties is happy with the commonwealth arrangement as it now stands. Advocates of both statehood and independence regard it as essentially colonial. As Oreste Ramos, a fervently pro-American conservative senator and leader of the dominant prostatehood New Progressive Party (NPP), recently told the U.N. Decolonization Committee, "the political inferiority inherent in Puerto Rico's present status is an insult to the national decorum of the United States and to the dignity of the people of Puerto Rico." Advocates of independence put the matter in less genteel terms.

Even the defenders of Puerto Rico's present status, formally adopted in 1952, now call for "a new dimension of sovereignty" that will give the island "the maximum plenitude of autonomy." A generation ago, the Popular Democratic Party (PDP) pronounced colonialism dead, proclaiming the birth of the *Estado Libre Asociado de Puerto Rico* (deliberately translated as "Commonwealth of Puerto Rico" rather than as "Free Associated State of Puerto Rico"). But at the United Nations, it recently joined unlikely companions—Cuba and its Socialist and Third World allies—to draw attention to its frustrated petitions to the United States for greater autonomy.

Puerto Rico's three historic political movements—supporting statehood, commonwealth status, and independence—are now all firmly committed to the vigorous pursuit of political change. A referendum on the island's status has been set for 1981 by the prostatehood administration of Governor Carlos Romero Barceló. Romero rejects the widespread belief that a statehood petition must be supported by an overwhelming majority of the voters in order to be taken seriously by Congress. He has an uncomplicated faith in the principle of majority rule and believes that statehood requires no greater mandate than a simple majority. Nevertheless, Romero's followers expect a surge of support for statehood, and possibly even a prostatehood majority in the 60-70 per cent range, especially if PDP traditionalists begin to fear that their leaders are heading toward something akin to independence. Romero is convinced that a Puerto Rican statehood petition would be accepted by the required majority of each house of Congress, but he unequivocally states that its rejection would compel him to support independence rather than see Puerto Rico endure indefinitely what he regards as the inequality and powerlessness of commonwealth status.

The proponents of a more viable commonwealth status, on the other hand, hope to stem the rising statehood tide and move the island toward a new and permanent relationship of "free association" with the United States. Meanwhile, the independence forces, confident that both of these political drives are pipe dreams that will be frustrated by Washington, expect eventually to be able to pick up the pieces and mobilize a disappointed people toward national sovereignty.

The collapse of support for the status quo, even among many original proponents of the island's commonwealth status, has polarized Puerto Rican society. Many of the island's citizens believe that an imminent political showdown will settle whether Puerto Rico, after 80 years under the American flag, will join the federal union or move toward significantly greater (or complete) freedom.

The Forbidden Word

Except among Puerto Rico's *independentistas*, the word "colonialism" has been absent from the political lexicon of U.S.-Puerto Rican relations for a generation. Determined to prove themselves trustworthy fellow citizens—Americans with a colorful heritage and language, but surely as American as apple pie—proponents of statehood and commonwealth status focused their campaigns for political change exclusively on Washington, avoided references to "colonialism," eschewed political identification with Third World peoples, and left the anticolonial arena of the United Nations to the small minority of independence advocates. Yet no word other than "colonialism" adequately describes the relationship between a powerful metropolitan state and an impoverished overseas dependency, disenfranchised from the formal lawmaking processes that shape its people's daily lives.

In 1978 the statehood forces and those seeking modification of the commonwealth arrangement came out of the colonial closet. Inspired in part by the directness of expression and the political achievements of blacks, chicanos, and even Puerto Ricans in the mainland United States, Puerto Ricans on the island have become more assertive and less deferential in expressing their political aspirations. Romero has unabashedly spoken of the "vestiges of colonialism" that exist in the current relationship, and the frustrated proponents of reformed commonwealth status have shown themselves less reluctant to use that forbidden word in speaking of Washington's failure to heed their pleas for a greater measure of self-government.

The statehood movement originally took root among the island's blacks and poor whites.

In a climactic two-week period in late August and early September, Puerto Rican leaders of every political stripe—including even Maurice A. Ferré, the Puerto Rican-born mayor of Miami—appeared before the U.N. Special Committee on Decolonization, dramatizing the widespread dissatisfaction with the status quo. In doing so, they effectively recognized the existence of an alternative forum for efforts to resolve the prolonged Puerto Rican identity crisis. They also shattered the delusion of a generation of U.S. policy makers that the question of Puerto Rico's political future is strictly an American domestic issue, a quaint political notion that is reminiscent of similar claims asserted by European colonial powers during U.N. anticolonial hearings in the 1950s.

Even Romero, who faithfully stated the traditional U.S. position "that intervention by [the U.N. committee] is neither necessary nor appropriate nor acceptable to the people of Puerto Rico," took the occasion of his appearance at the U.N. to observe that the principle of self-determination enshrined in the U.N. Charter "includes the right to pass from the status of free associated state [or commonwealth] to statehood as well as the right to pass from the status of free associated state to independence." Although he admitted that "vestiges of colonialism" endure in Puerto Rico, Romero nevertheless testified, as the State Department wished, that the U.N. had no business intervening as long as the Puerto Ricans had the capacity to initiate steps to change their political status.

Because the United States is not a member of the Decolonization Committee, the State Department had to work through sympathetic official participants, notably Australia. But for the first time it could not persuade the committee to put off formal action on the issue. On September 12, 1978, after the failure of compromise efforts by India and others, a resolution proposed by Cuba was adopted by a plurality composed of Socialist and Third World states but, significantly, without a single dissenting vote. In relatively muted terms, it criticized alleged U.S. violations of the Puerto Rican people's "national rights," endorsing independence and any form of "free association" between Puerto Rico and the United States based on "political equality" and a recognition of "the sovereignty of the people of Puerto Rico" under international law. It went on to note the widespread dissatisfaction on the island with the current political status. Importantly, the resolution omitted any direct reference to political integration or statehood as an acceptable political fate for the island.

Although officially ignored by the U.S. and Puerto Rican governments, the adoption of the resolution was a setback for American diplomacy. For decades, the matter of Puerto Rican political status was defined out of existence as a foreign policy concern, and a reexamination of U.S. policy at the U.N. was avoided, despite the evident pressures on the island for political change. Consequently, the willingness of so many mainstream Puerto

Rican leaders to appear before the Decolonization Committee this time around took U.S. diplomats by surprise. They were alarmed to find the leaders of the procommonwealth PDP openly supporting a Cuban draft resolution in an effort to embarrass the United States and the prostatehood forces.

The traditional U.S. hard-line position—that nothing but deferral of U.N. consideration was acceptable, that nothing but the status quo was tolerable—frustrated the efforts of representatives of all the Puerto Rican factions to negotiate a consensus resolution defining a projected process of "self-determination" for Puerto Rico. Accordingly, each of the political groups, except the statehooders, scrambled to consolidate committee support for its ideological position. The PDP's collaboration with the Cubans and the resulting adoption of the Cuban-drafted resolution unnecessarily discredited the United Nations in the eyes of the statehooders, perhaps precluding any conciliating role the organization might have been able to play in the island's future. It also made possible the labeling of Puerto Rican political parties as either pro-American or anti-American, severely aggravating political tensions and, by all accounts, greatly strengthening the hand of "pro-American" Romero in a political dogfight with his predecessor and rival, "anti-American" Rafael Hernández Colón.

Blessings of Civilization

If all this proves to be as much of a surprise to the American public as to the befuddled U.S. diplomats at the United Nations, it is only because, as Gloria Emerson aptly observed in writing about Vietnam, "We have always been a people who dropped the past and then could not remember where it had been put." The contemporary Puerto Rican political imbroglio is the legacy of what President William McKinley's secretary of state, John Hay, called the "splendid little war" against Spain in 1898 and the subsequent U.S. colonial experiment. The controversy accompanying U.S. intervention in the Cuban civil war of that year led Congress to adopt a resolution offered by Colorado Senator Henry M. Teller disclaiming "any disposition or intention to exercise sovereignty" over Cuba and asserting the determination of the United States eventually to "leave the government and control of the island to its people." However, this self-denying resolution clearly did not apply to Spain's other colonies, including Puerto Rico.

The invasion and trouble-free occupation of Puerto Rico on July 25, 1898, were followed by a proclamation to the Puerto Rican people suggesting that the island would have a more direct and lasting link to the mainland American political system than that envisaged for Cuba. The proclamation, issued by the commander of U.S. forces in Puerto Rico, Major General Nelson A. Miles, asserted that the Americans, "bearing the banner of freedom" would "bestow upon [the Puerto Rican people] the immunities and blessings of the liberal institutions of our government . . . [and] the advantages and blessings of enlightened civilization."

That Puerto Rico would become part of a new empire was confirmed by the terms of the 1898 Paris peace treaty, under which Spain merely abandoned "all claim of sovereignty over and title to Cuba," but ceded Puerto Rico, Guam, and the Philippines to the United States. For the first time in American history, as American historian Julius W. Pratt wrote, "in a treaty acquiring territory for the United States, there was no promise of citizenship, . . .there was no promise, actual or implied, of statehood. The United States thereby acquired not 'territories' but possessions or 'dependencies' and became, in that sense, an 'imperial' power."

Political resistance to colonialism was widespread in the United States from the outset. The nonpartisan Anti-Imperialist League, organized even before the Treaty of Paris was signed, drew to its standard a wide variety of national leaders opposed to the annexation of territories that were given no hope of statehood in the American union.

Its opposition to government without the consent of the governed was echoed in Congress in 1900 when the Democratic minority of the House Ways and Means Committee asserted that U.S. policy toward Puerto Rico was "pure and simple imperialism.... It does not matter in which form territory is acquired, it is to be held under our Constitution with the object of finally being admitted into the Union as a State."

If you scratch the skin of any Puerto Rican . . . you will find an *independentista.*

Imperialism was described by Democratic candidate William Jennings Byran as the "paramount issue" of the 1900 presidential campaign, and with the electoral victory of McKinley and Theodore Roosevelt, the United States effectively joined the major European powers in the rush to empire. The following year, the Supreme Court blessed the colonial experiment in the celebrated Insular cases, in which the new territories were held not to be "foreign territory," but nevertheless not "a part of the United States" for all constitutional purposes. In the Court's view, Congress was empowered "to locally govern at discretion."

"Discretion" soon came to mean moving the Filipinos toward independence even as the Puerto Ricans were drawn increasingly into the U.S. fold. As early as 1900, congressional reports drew a distinction between Puerto Rico's "law-abiding and industrious" people, who were believed to be overwhelmingly white, and the oriental people of the Philippines, who had vigorously and "ungratefully" resisted American rule from the beginning by claiming the right to national independence. Characteristically, Representative Thomas Spight (D.-Mississippi), compared the Philippines and Puerto Rico by invoking geographical proximity, the alleged racial similarity of Puerto Ricans to white Americans, and the injunctions of the Monroe Doctrine. Puerto Rico could become part of the United States, and its people American citizens, he told the House in 1900, because Puerto Rico was located within a traditional American sphere of influence:

> Its people are, in the main, of Caucasian blood, knowing and appreciating the benefits of civilization, and are desirous of casting their lot with us.... Its proximity to our mainland, the character of its inhabitants, and the willingness with which they accept our sovereignty, together with the advantages—commercial, sanitary and strategic—all unite to enable us to make her an integral part of our domain.

Their collective naturalization by Congress in 1917 (the year after the Philippines was first promised its eventual independence) cemented a relationship under which the Puerto Ricans have endured the mixed blessings of colonial rule by a nation convinced of its decent intentions and embarrassed by the very notion of colonialism.

First under the "organic acts" passed by Congress in 1900 and 1917, and now under the 1952 commonwealth constitution adopted by its people, the form of Puerto Rico's local government has been patterned on those of mainland state governments. The current structure extends to the island all congressional legislation unless Congress chooses to make it "locally inapplicable." Although Puerto Ricans are exempt from paying federal income tax (enabling the island to attract mainland investments in recent years), local taxes there are as high as the combined federal and state levies in many states. Similarly, because the island's economy is wholly dependent on trade with the mainland, its cost of living is comparable to that of New York City. Yet Puerto Rico's people do not vote in presidential elections or elect any voting representatives to Congress. These circumstances once drove former Governor Luis A. Ferré to dub Puerto Rico "a one-armed state."

During the half century before Puerto

Ricans were first permitted to elect their own governor in 1948, the islanders benefited enormously from improvements in sanitation, public health, education, and public works. The price for this, acceptable to many in a land of frightful poverty, was political subordination, effective economic domination by mainland U.S. interests, and a deep, abiding sense of dependency and powerlessness.

Calling the American Bluff

From the beginning of the century, the island's politics have been shaped by the struggle of political parties advocating one of three basic options for political status: statehood, independence, or some intermediate objective ("self-government," "commonwealth," or, now, "free association").

The statehood movement originally took root among the island's blacks and poor whites, who sought rapid economic improvement and the protection of American democratic institutions from the island's creole elite. It is no coincidence that the founder of the statehood movement was a black physician and populist, Dr. José Celso Barbosa, who had studied medicine in Michigan during Reconstruction and was inspired by American institutions. The island's original labor and socialist movements were staunchly pro-American and allied to Barbosa's statehood party as well as Samuel Gompers's American Federation of Labor.

From the 1930s through the mid-1960s, the statehood movement fell under the control of some of the island's wealthiest and most conservative families. Its revival in the 1960s and 1970s is due not only to the growing identification with the mainland (resulting largely from migration and travel between the two places and the modernization of the island's society) but also to Romero's evocation of the Barbosa vision of statehood as an instrument for social and economic justice. In his 1973 book, *La estadidad es para los pobres*, Romero argues that only the relatively well-to-do need worry about paying federal taxes under statehood, while the great majority of Puerto Ricans would benefit from full participation in all federal aid programs. His NPP followers see no conflict between libertarian and egalitarian goals; in U.S. citizenship they find an implied promise of political equality in an American system liberal and pluralistic enough to incorporate a racially mixed, Spanish-speaking people who by and large have embraced American institutions and believe in U.S. national self-advertisements.

If the American rhetoric of eight decades has been a bluff, the statehood drive will call that bluff. Its goal is nothing more and nothing less than Puerto Rican power within the American system—the sort of power that comes from having two senators and seven or eight representatives in the U.S. Congress.

The boom built on cheap labor may be over forever.

The independence movement, on the other hand, has always been strongest in the middle and upper classes, especially in the bar, the universities, and related elites. Originally a conservative (and sometimes, at the margins, a cryptofascist) force, it is now largely a movement of the Left. Despite its electoral failures in recent years, the independence movement is far from dead. It was once a major political force on the island, and its appeals to Puerto Rican values and sense of national identity should not be underestimated.

Divided today between the democratic socialist Puerto Rico Independence Party (PIP) and the much smaller, Cuba-oriented Puerto Rican Socialist Party (PSP), the independence movement faces seemingly insurmountable obstacles. Decades of economic integration with the United States, coupled with a growing dependence on federal funds, impede separation. Moreover, profound popular faith in the social and economic merits of the U.S. political connection is compounded by an equally profound fear that a small, poor, and overpopulated island with few natural resources cannot hope to prosper on its own. Perhaps the greatest obstacle to the appeal of independence has been the absence since the 1940s of heavy-handed colonial administrators who could be readily blamed for the island's troubles.

Nevertheless, leaders of the independence movement believe they have an effective veto over any efforts to admit Puerto Rico into the union. Their confidence is based on the conviction that Congress will not admit a territory in which a significant proindependence minority, supported by an unknown number of antistatehood PDP members, would tenaciously resist "assimilation." Their strenuous resistance is their trump card, for, as civil libertarian Roger Baldwin once observed, if you scratch the skin of any Puerto Rican, no matter how enthusiastic an American citizen he may be, you will find an *independentista*. It is the hope of PIP and PSP leaders that in time U.S. rejection of other options will indeed abrade the skin of their compatriots.

Frustrated in elections at home, the *independentistas* have pressed their case in recent years before the U.N. Decolonization Committee, in an effort to embarrass the United States into moving the island toward independence. Urging that the General Assembly restore Puerto Rico to its list of "Non-Self-Governing Territories," they argue that Puerto Rico's removal from that list in 1953 by a plurality vote of the General Assembly merely reflected U.S. domination of the world body. Citing international law, they maintain that a colony cannot consent to the perpetuation of its colonial status; therefore, the U.N. should not accredit a form of government that does not meet its contemporary criteria for determining whether a territory has achieved what its Charter calls "a full measure of self-government."

The difficult-to-define middle ground between statehood and independence has invariably been the terrain of a broad coalition of pragmatists who place political power and economic problem solving above ideological preoccupation with abstract notions such as equality or freedom. The political base of the procommonwealth PDP, which held power virtually without interruption between 1940 and 1976, was in the Puerto Rican countryside. Its leadership, however, was composed largely of technocrats and middle-class professionals who have been joined in recent years by a new class of conservative industrialists and merchants spawned by Operation Bootstrap, the much-touted PDP economic development program.

Bread, Land, and Liberty

During the anticolonial period following World War II, the Philippines achieved its long-promised independence, and Puerto Rico moved toward commonwealth status. This ambiguous and little-understood political formula was devised by Luis Muñoz Marín, a brilliant, charismatic, bilingual nationalist whose reform-minded PDP originally won control of the island's legislature in 1940 with a commitment to "Bread, Land, and Liberty." Fearing the possible economic consequences of independence, Muñoz Marín steered his political movement toward a form of decolonization that would involve neither independence nor statehood—a "third road to freedom" granting Puerto Rico an island government organized under a locally adopted constitution. As far as Congress was concerned, the change from colony to commonwealth was more form than substance. The House report of June 19, 1950, flatly stated that the legislation launching the commonwealth arrangement "would not change Puerto Rico's fundamental political, social, and economic relationship to the United States."

The *Estado Libre Asociado de Puerto Rico* was neither a member of the union nor an independent nation. Nor did its inventors regard it as a way station to either status. A political arrangement based upon the principle of the consent of the governed (and therefore not "colonial"), it was expected to permit a desperately poor people to retain mutually advantageous economic ties with the United States without losing its national identity. Muñoz Marín acknowledged that commonwealth status was an "imperfect" solution to the island's colonial condition. To those who yearned for greater self-government, Muñoz Marín touted the flexibility of American constitutional formulas and indicated that the 1952 "compact" between Puerto Rico and the U.S. Congress could and would be amended in order to complete the job left undone by compromise.

The commonwealth idea was an authentic expression of the postwar American liberal worldview: a poor and racially mixed Third World community undergoing modernization as a result of the inventive application of American capital and American liberal ideology. Chief Justice Earl Warren euphorically proclaimed the commonwealth "perhaps the most notable of American political experiments in our lifetime."

The relationship was not without its benefits for the United States. By 1977 Puerto Rico's annual purchases from the mainland had soared to more than $3.9 billion; on a per capita basis, Puerto Rico ranked second to none as a purchaser of U.S. goods. Under Operation Bootstrap, American manufacturers alone had invested about $5 billion in Puerto Rico by 1976. Puerto Rican soldiers have served in every U.S. military engagement since the beginning of the century.

To some extent and for a time, the commonwealth idea worked. Between 1940 and 1977, the per capita annual personal income of Puerto Ricans increased from $118 to $2,472 (the highest in Spanish America), with the result that the island came to be touted as a "showcase of democracy" and an alternative to "Castroism."[1] It was only natural that when John F. Kennedy organized the Alliance for Progress, largely in response to the hemispheric challenge of Castro's revolution, he tapped as its first director Teodoro Moscoso, the technocrat who had managed Operation Bootstrap.

If it had ever seemed a problem for American foreign policy, by the early 1960s Puerto Rico seemed so no longer. Like the Filipinos, the Puerto Ricans had apparently exercised their right to self-determination: They had obtained the political status they requested, they were prospering, and they seemed politically content.

But even as the United States eliminated Puerto Rico as a foreign policy concern, Cuba and Third World and Communist allies began in the mid-1960s to take up the cause of the independence movement. At the time, the strength of the commonwealth idea was beginning to erode. Yet the beneficiary of that erosion was not the independence movement, but rather the movement for statehood and political equality within the American system. The results of the island's quadrennial elections tell the story and reveal one source of the current confusion.

Puerto Rican General Election Results Since Commonwealth Began

	Party(ies) Favoring Commonwealth	Party(ies) Favoring Statehood	Party(ies) Favoring Independence
1952	67.0%	12.9%	18.9%
1956	62.5	25.0	12.5
1960	58.2	32.1	3.1
1964	59.4	34.7	2.7
1968	52.1	45.1	2.8
1972	51.4	44.0	4.5
1976	45.3	48.3	6.4

Note: *The political status question was not necessarily the chief campaign issue in these general elections. Percentages may not total 100 due to electoral participation of independent voters and parties not advocating a political status alternative.*

A 1967 plebiscite on political status gave 60.41 per cent of the vote to proponents of a reformed or "perfected" form of commonwealth status and 38.98 per cent to the statehood movement. The *independentistas* denounced the plebiscite as a nefarious political maneuver to win from Puerto Ricans an endorsement of their political impotence.

[1] *A classic example may be found in "Why Puerto Rico Thrives as Cuba Crumbles,"* U.S. News and World Report, *March 28, 1960.*

Complaining of persecution and poor phrasing of the ballot, they boycotted the polls: The independence option drew a mere .6 per cent of the vote.

In the 1976 general elections, the combined votes of the statehood and independence parties constituted a clear majority of the electorate, for the first time since the commonwealth came into being in 1952.

Although conventional wisdom has it that commonwealth status made possible Puerto Rico's economic miracle of the past quarter century, in fact the reverse is probably true. Puerto Rico's economic expansion made possible the islanders' toleration of a political relationship with the United States that was not fundamentally different from the overtly colonial status that preceded it. Freedom from federal taxation, an elected governor, local self-government, tax incentives for American industry, and the possibility of participating in federal aid programs all antedated the commonwealth.

As long as economic expansion and optimism lasted, the commonwealth idea prospered. But it has apparently failed to survive the economic contraction of recent years and the realization that the boom built on cheap labor may be over forever. The island, dependent on trade for its livelihood and on U.S. capital for its development, has been largely absorbed into the high-cost American economy and finds it increasingly difficult to hold its own against mainland and foreign competitors. In the mid-1970s the island's official unemployment rate reached over 22 per cent, the highest since Operation Bootstrap. Declining private investment coupled with rising public spending and a rapidly growing social welfare system brought the island close to financial collapse in 1975-1976. The magnitude of the crisis was overshadowed only by the more spectacular financial trauma of New York City.

A Welfare State, Made in the U.S.A.

The Puerto Rican sense of powerlessness and dissatisfaction has been deepened in recent years by the fiscal austerity resulting from these massive financial difficulties and the increasing reliance on federal funds. As a result of efforts by procommonwealth and prostatehood administrations alike, the island has come to be included in a growing number of federal aid programs. Invoking the U.S. citizenship of the island's people and insisting upon treatment equal to that of citizens on the mainland, successive commonwealth governments have managed to increase total federal outlays to Puerto Rico from $767 million in 1970 to $3 billion in 1976. Oblivious to the long-term impact of the wholesale extension of federal programs to the island, the executive and legislative branches of the U.S. government—not the Puerto Ricans—have turned Puerto Rico into a veritable welfare state. Official Washington was largely unaware in 1974, for example, that extension of the food stamp program to the island would cost the U.S. Treasury nearly $600 million a year by 1976, about two-thirds of Puerto Rico's people being eligible to participate.

Recognizing shortcomings in the present political arrangement, the PDP has pledged to work to reform, "perfect," or "refine" the island's commonwealth status. For a generation it has talked of rewriting the 1952 compact with Congress to transfer to Puerto Rico many of the powers now exercised on the island by the federal government, including some or all jurisdiction over communications, labor relations, trade regulation, immigration, and environmental matters. Autonomists also argue for independent Puerto Rican membership in international technical and cultural institutions. A more wide-ranging proposed reform would grant Puerto Rico effective veto power over congressional legislation applicable to the island. These proposals were designed to strengthen Puerto Rican self-confidence and meet the criticism that commonwealth status sanctions virtually unlimited congressional government of Puerto Rico without the islanders' concurrence.

A number of these reforms were embodied in the "Compact of Permanent Union Between the United States and Puerto Rico," fashioned in 1975 by a joint commission appointed by Hernández Colón and Richard Nixon and designed partly to redeem the PDP's long-standing pledge to expand the island's self-government. The two most notable proposals for reform would have given Puerto Rico virtually complete control over minimum wages (to establish lower rates than on the mainland) and environmental regulation (to avoid mainland timetables for reaching various standards).

The compact was introduced in Congress in 1975 by the PDP's resident commissioner. But its passage was stalled by the Ford administration's indifference, objections by mainland labor and environmental lobbies, and the strenuous opposition of many vocal Puerto Ricans. The latter included the statehood movement, dissident autonomists who felt the compact was too moderate, and the independence movement.

The statehood movement broke new ground in the November 1976 general elections by sweeping the PDP from every major political office on the island and winning the resident commissionership in Washington. The NPP victory effectively killed the proposed compact, ending years of efforts to revive and fortify the commonwealth idea.

Perhaps more important, the coincident victories of the statehooders in Puerto Rico and Jimmy Carter in the United States led to the removal of the procommonwealth forces from national political party affairs. Prostatehood Democrats, members of the local chapter of Americans for Democratic Action, led by a young politician with the emblematic name of Franklin Delano López, were early allies of Carter, while the PDP-affiliated Democrats backed Senator Henry M. Jackson (D.-Washington). After the 1976 election, the NPP quickly moved to take over the official Democratic party of Puerto Rico. Statehooders have been affiliated with the mainland Republican party since the turn of the century, when the GOP was the home of the U.S. progressive movement and the party of America's black people. Although it was also the party of imperialism, it was the only U.S. political party that did not question the permanence of Puerto Rico's position in the American system. The local branch of the Democratic party had been identified with the PDP ever since Muñoz Marín asserted his control in mid-century. However, with the newly democratized Democratic primary rules, statehood advocates have now been able to take control of the Puerto Rican affiliates of both major parties, and they can be expected to seek commitments to statehood in both national party platforms in 1980.

Responding to demands by the López group, the Democratic National Committee unanimously decided in mid-1978 to hold a primary in Puerto Rico to determine control of the local Democratic organization. The prostatehood Democrats promised that, if victorious, they would hold a presidential primary in 1980 for the island's 22-delegate national convention slate. Now tentatively set for the same week in February 1980 as that of New Hampshire, the presidential primary promises to introduce the island's political status issue into national presidential politics. Because national party primaries are regarded by orthodox autonomists as a step toward eventual statehood, the PDP boycotted the 1978 party primary and all but abandoned its traditional informal ties to the national Democratic party. It then apparently accelerated its search for political arenas other than Washington for the assertion of its political claims.

A Bombshell and a Milestone

The U.S. response to Puerto Rican initiatives at the United Nations was ambiguous. Moving adroitly in July to pre-empt a possible international embarrassment, Carter issued a proclamation to the Puerto Rican people solemnly affirming the U.S. commitment to the principle of self-determination and pledging to "support, and urge the Congress to support, whatever decision the people of Puerto Rico reach" in the 1981 political status referendum. There was no suggestion that presidential support was conditioned in any way upon the size of the majority in the 1981 referendum.

To the few people in the United States who paid attention to Carter's proclamation, it was nothing more than a restatement of traditional American political values. To the Puerto Ricans, it was a political bombshell and a milestone of considerable significance. Carter had acknowledged that political change was possible and would have his personal support. He had thus deftly begun to move away from the policy of his predecessors, which was carefully limited to extolling the status quo. Dwight D. Eisenhower had stated his willingness to support independence if the Puerto Ricans opted for it, but only Gerald Ford, as a vacationing lame duck president, had ever expressed support for the statehood movement.

Another sign of subtle but tentative change in American policy appeared last August, when U.N. Ambassador Andrew Young issued a carefully worded statement saying that "the United States would do nothing to stand in the way of a decision by the Puerto Rican people to extend an invitation to the United Nations, the Organization of American States, or other appropriate international bodies to observe a referendum."

By now some of the major Puerto Rican groups that appeared before the United Nations regarded it as the only authoritative and disinterested body capable of guaranteeing the integrity and fairness of any process for political change. This fact was ignored by the officials charged with implementing U.S. policy. Their actions suggested that the Carter and Young statements had no substance beneath them, that American policy on the issue would follow the usual lines. Middle-level officials from the State Department and the National Security Council staff defined the short-range U.S. policy objective as little more than avoiding the appearance of being soft on Cuba at the United Nations. The longer-range policy objective was to safeguard the congressional appropriation for international organizations from the kind of backlash that followed the U.N. resolution condemning Zionism.

In their zeal not to appear soft on Cuba, U.S. diplomats failed to take the high ground at the United Nations. They discouraged the efforts of several Puerto Rican liberals to build a multiparty consensus on a framework for the projected decolonization process and on the advisability of requesting U.N. observers for the proposed referendum. Indeed, U.S. diplomats approached various Puerto Rican leaders who planned to appear at the United Nations, expressing the hope that they would go home. The tactic failed.

As the Decolonization Committee hearing progressed, it became apparent that the United States did not have the votes to obtain a postponement of action. At that stage the United States urged its surrogates on the committee to work toward a consensus resolution in order to prevent the possibility of a Cuban resolution and a U.S. defeat. But it was already too late, because the various Puerto Rican factions, particularly Hernández Colón's PDP, were openly irritated with U.S. tactics. The Cubans, seeking to avoid a major confrontation with the United States and yet wanting to satisfy their traditional friends in Puerto Rico, scaled down their original resolution and accommodated the interests of the procommonwealth forces, thereby assuring the tacit support or abstention of a number of states. As a result, the Cuban resolution was adopted by a vote of 10 states in favor and none against, with 12 abstentions and two states absent or not participating.[2]

[2] *Voting in favor of the Cuban resolution: Afghanistan, Bulgaria, Czechoslovakia, China, Ethiopia, Cuba, Iraq, Syria, Tanzania, and the USSR. Voting against the Cuban resolution: none. Abstaining: Australia, Chile, Fiji, India, Indonesia, Iran, Mali, Sierra Leone, Trinidad, Tunisia, Sweden, and Yugoslavia. Not participating: Congo (Brazzaville). Absent: Ivory Coast.*

If Washington won a victory by preventing a majority vote for the Cuban-sponsored resolution, it was surely a Pyrrhic victory. For by failing to promote discussion about a consensus resolution among Puerto Rican political parties, U.S. diplomats severely aggravated tensions and hostilities among them and possibly set the course for continuing difficulties at the United Nations. During the hectic caucusing at the U.N. meeting, the PDP forces feared that unless they directly and actively defended their plans for the commonwealth, the field would be left to the statehooders and *independentistas,* who might tacitly agree to discredit the commonwealth idea by placing Puerto Rico on the U.N. list of non-self-governing territories. That would have left only statehood or independence as acceptable results of the self-determination process. Thus, the PDP moved to pre-empt any such anticolonial alliance by establishing, instead, an "anti-annexationist" front with the proindependence PSP and its Cuban patrons.

The days when Washington could treat Puerto Rico with benign neglect are over.

At the United Nations it should have been possible to avoid what India's delegate called "the twilight zone of controversial legality" (the question of whether Puerto Rico should be put back on the U.N. list) by building a consensus around the three important new elements in the case: the call by the governor of Puerto Rico for a referendum in 1981; Carter's statement that he would support whatever status the Puerto Ricans might choose in that referendum; and Young's statement that the United States would not object to U.N. observation of the referendum.

Unfortunately, U.S. diplomats were simply unwilling to face the fact that the substance of the controversy is political change—decolonization—in Puerto Rico. Like previous administrations, they regarded the suggestion of decolonization as a stigma to be avoided rather than the key to a major political problem. The State Department preferred to stand behind the precedent of the 1953 U.N. General Assembly decision that eliminated Puerto Rico from its list of non-self-governing territories, despite the fact that U.N. practice has never honored precedent in such an obviously political matter.

American diplomats were unprepared to consider that Carter's pledge to support the outcome of the 1981 plebiscite offered an opportunity to develop an authoritative process for Puerto Ricans to exercise their acknowledged right to self-determination.

A Colonial Office?

U.S. inertia and political misconceptions have been reinforced by the unwillingness of successive administrations to place responsibility for a Puerto Rico policy in any particular federal department, whether concerned with domestic or foreign affairs. The establishment or designation of any such central office might imply the existence of significant problems in Puerto Rico or evoke memories of the old Division of Territories in the Interior Department (the American "colonial office"). As a result, it is difficult, if not impossible, for the U.S. government to react quickly and intelligently to fast-breaking political developments in Puerto Rico or to shape the direction of U.S. relations with the island.

Until now, any government expression of untraditional views on the subject of Puerto Rico's political status has been regarded as a form of U.S. pressure on the Puerto Ricans and therefore a deviation from the principle of self-determination—a principle apparently interpreted only to mean that the United States will be bound in advance to do whatever the Puerto Ricans decide. But whatever the conclusion of Puerto Rico's prolonged identity crisis, it will invariably affect the United States and its relations with the world community.

By defining the question of Puerto Rico's relations with the United States as an entirely Puerto Rican matter, Washington is largely giving up any chance of affecting the outcome in Puerto Rico. More important, the United States is missing an opportunity to help steer the decolonization process in a way that would reassure all political groups that the process is fair to all and valid in the eyes of the world community. Because neither the United Nations nor the United States is now in a position to advise the Puerto Ricans on how to conduct their decolonization process, the rules of the game will be determined by whatever political party holds the reins of power when it takes place. The results of this curious definition of self-determination may be internecine conflict among Puerto Rico's bitterly divided political groups, with unknown domestic and international political repercussions.

That there will be repercussions cannot be doubted. Approximately 2 million Puerto Ricans now live in the northern industrial cities of the United States. As U.S. citizens, they move freely between the island and the mainland, carrying with them the political anxieties of their compatriots at home. Moreover, the February 1980 Democratic presidential primary in Puerto Rico will draw national attention to the island's politics.

The absence of a U.S. political backlash against the Cuban victory at the United Nations was due only to happenstance. The New York City newspaper strike resulted in a virtual blackout of news about the proceedings of the U.N. Decolonization Committee meeting. Next time, there will be no such luck. The Puerto Ricans will be back at the United Nations in August 1979, and probably for every session of the committee until the island's political future is settled.

Jimmy Carter has recognized the possibility of political change in Puerto Rico and, for better or for worse, he has stimulated the forces of change there. Andrew Young has carefully avoided heavy-handed pronouncements that the matter falls exclusively within U.S. domestic jurisdiction and has left the door open to a fruitful U.N. role in the determination of Puerto Rico's future. Washington must now deal on a continuing basis with the major domestic and foreign policy problems raised by the need for political change in Puerto Rico. The first order of business is to identify the relevant players in the drama. All of the principals (including the *independentistas*) should be invited to describe the constitutional processes that would meet their individual expectations and to state their concerns about pending proposals. Even if the expectations of some groups seem unreasonable or foolish, it is vital that U.S. policy makers learn directly what these expectations are, if only to be able to comprehend future political maneuvers in Congress or the United Nations.

This straightforward approach would allay the suspicions of some Puerto Rican leaders, especially in the opposition, that only an incumbent Puerto Rican government can hope to have direct official contact with the federal government and that their own chances of being heard are limited to mysterious or clandestine contacts in Washington or to public disruptions there and at home.

In a quite different decolonization context, the British held constitutional conferences in London with representatives of all significant groups in a colony to discuss the process by which the colonial relationship would come to an end. Two basic ground rules governed the British practice: acceptance of the metropolitan state's authority and an effective agreement that the inevitable outcome would be independence. Neither of these applies to the current Puerto Rican situation. Nevertheless, the British experience and common sense recommend that the metropolitan state be well informed and in direct contact with all political groups in the territory.

At the very least, a new central coordinating office in Washington responsible for Puerto Rico could serve as a point of contact and a source of up-to-date information for the federal bureaucracy. But its larger objective should be to meet periodically with Puerto Rico's political leaders and to keep in close enough touch with the Puerto Rican political scene to make informed contingency plans for the decolonization process. The office could sponsor informal discussions about what it will take to make Puerto Rico a state, an independent republic, or an autonomous entity freely associated with the United States. It could also help chart a useful, if limited, role for the United Nations in Puerto Rico.

The United States and Puerto Rico would benefit from the common recognition that political change on the island is inevitable, that it is possible only through electoral processes, and that those processes will be devoid of legitimacy if significant groups repudiate or boycott them. The United States may not be able to point the Puerto Ricans in any particular direction, but it should be ready to identify and reinforce the elements of any consensus that may emerge in Puerto Rico. In the absence of a consensus on the process for decolonization, the possibility for violence in Puerto Rico and on the mainland looms ever larger. Many wary Puerto Ricans—fearing that mainland officials, preoccupied with their other problems, will ineptly handle Puerto Rican policy—have begun to invoke the specter of Belfast.

The days when Washington could treat Puerto Rico with benign neglect are over. U.S. policy makers must now give serious thought to the future of an 80-year-old relationship. If and when they organize to deal with political change on the island, they can expect to receive the blessings of the president, who expressed his sympathy with Puerto Rico's political isolation and powerlessness by telling Puerto Rican friends in 1976 that he understood their concerns because "I am from the deep South, and you are from the deep, deep South."

DATELINE NICARAGUA: THE END OF THE AFFAIR

by Richard R. Fagen

"We will win," said the middle-aged woman standing on a street corner in Managua, "and they," she said, shifting her eyes toward a National Guardsman standing across the street, "will lose." The guardsman, Israeli automatic rifle at the ready, was patrolling a *barrio* (neighborhood) that a few days earlier had been under the control of the Sandinistas and now had been retaken by the National Guard. The modest rows of wood and concrete homes and small stores were pockmarked with bullets. Several had been completely destroyed by the aerial bombardment that preceded the ground attack. Spent 57mm shell casings marked "Made in U.S.A." lay in the gutters—along with discarded U.S. Army combat rations, half-eaten tins of peanut butter and beans and frankfurters. At the next intersection, a pile of corpses still smoldered. As the breeze shifted, people moved to avoid the downwind stench.

It was the middle of June 1979, and what the Sandinista National Liberation Front (FSLN) called the final offensive against the Somoza dynasty and the National Guard had already been under way for several weeks. As the Sandinistas and their supporters were careful to point out, what was happening in Nicaragua was a national insurrection, not a civil war. Fed up with more than four decades of tyrannical and brutal rule, the citizenry had revolted. Inspired but not necessarily directly led by the Sandinistas, thousands of young men and women had taken up whatever arms were at hand. Hundreds of thousands of other Nicaraguans helped in what way they could: by closing their shops and businesses during the general strike of June; by sheltering and supplying the multitude of *muchachos heróicos* (brave boys and girls), as the Sandinista militias are known; or simply by passing information or aiding in the myriad of other tasks necessary to keep the struggle going.

This national insurrection was not, of course, the first expression of the outrage of the Nicaraguan people and of the military and political capabilities of the FSLN. The uprising of September 1978, almost a national mutiny, was in some sense a dress rehearsal for 1979. Then, for three weeks Sandinista regular troops and militias battled the Guard in the provinces. They seized but were not able to hold four important, middle-sized cities. If nothing else, September proved that Somoza and the Guard were more than willing to launch air attacks against the civilian population, drag young men and women out of their homes and shoot them in the street, and torture and murder persons suspected of belonging to or simply supporting the Sandinista movement. September also demonstrated to the FSLN that to succeed, an insurrection against Anastasio Somoza Debayle and the Guard would have to be countrywide, better armed and equipped, and tactically more sophisticated. Both the dynasty and the Sandinistas realized that the next round would be even bloodier, longer, and more definitive. History has borne them out.

"Bullets for breakfast, bullets for lunch, bullets for dinner, and bullets before going to bed."

History has also reaffirmed the seemingly infinite capacity of the U.S. government to misread and mismanage the situation. In the aftermath of September, this took the form of an ill-conceived and unsuccessful mediation between Somoza and the more pro-American sectors of the opposition under the auspices of the Organization of American States (OAS). In June 1979 it took the form of Secretary of State Cyrus Vance's roundly rejected call in the OAS for a peace-keeping force, followed by an extended and byzantine series of attempts to pressure and manipulate the five-person Sandinista-backed provisional government into a regime more compatible with U.S. interests.

Plunder, Exploitation, and Brutality

If the autumn of 1978 and the summer of 1979 were the dress rehearsal and the staging of the final offensive against Somoza, the scripting of the drama goes back to the beginning of this century. In 1912, after three years of unsuccessful attempts by Washington to stabilize Nicaragua by political and diplomatic means after the flight of dictator José Santos Zelaya, the U.S. Marines were landed. At stake were the outstanding loans of U.S. and European creditors, and also the possibility of canal-building rights through southern Nicaragua. The Marines stayed for 13 years, withdrawing only temporarily to return again in 1926 for seven more years. Only in 1933 did the occupying troops finally depart, leaving in their stead the U.S.-created National Guard headed by General Anastasio Somoza García. For the next 46 years the Somoza family never relinquished direct command of the Guard, and seldom gave up the presidency—and then only to hand-picked subordinates. Meanwhile, the Somozas and a close coterie of associates empowered and enriched themselves to an extent considered exceptional even in an area noted for plunder, exploitation, and brutality.

Although the Marines fought for years against nationalist General César Augusto Sandino—after whom today's Sandinistas are named—they were never able fully to defeat his guerrilla army. But with the Marines gone, Somoza García struck an uneasy truce with the insurgent general in 1933. Shortly thereafter, Sandino was assassinated after a dinner of reconciliation with Somoza. For the next 22 years, the senior Somoza ruled Nicaragua as a personal fiefdom, with the Guard as his private army and enforcer and with the continuing support and approval of the United States.

The dynasty expanded. When Somoza García's second son, Anastasio Somoza Debayle (Tacho), graduated from West Point in 1946 as a 20-year-old, he was given an important post in the Guard. Somoza García was assassinated in 1956, and his eldest son Luís moved immediately into the presidency while Tacho stayed on as commander of the Guard. By 1967 Tacho had added president of the republic to his list of offices. Shortly thereafter, Luis died of natural causes. In best family fashion, Tacho subsequently appointed his son, Anastasio Somoza Portocarrero, commander of the Guard's elite training facility and assault brigade.

From the outset, the dynasty was welcomed in Washington as a solid pillar of pro-American and anticommunist strength in an otherwise troubled area. In 1954 Nicaragua was the main staging ground for the Central Intelligence Agency-sponsored invasion that overthrew the left-Nationalist government of President Jacobo Arbenz Guzmán in Guatemala. In 1961 the Somozas played a similar role in the staging of the CIA-organized Bay of Pigs invasion of Cuba. Nicaraguan troops participated in the U.S. occupation of the Dominican Republic in 1965, and the Somozas even offered to send the Guard to fight communism in the Far East, first in Korea and later in Vietnam. (Their offers were declined.)

Until the early 1970s, through Republican and Democratic administrations alike, the Washington-Managua alliance seemed unshakable. But cracks were opened after the earthquake that leveled much of central Managua in 1972. The Somoza family turned the nation's disaster to its own advantage by siphoning off relief funds and speculating in land and commercial properties, thus eroding much of its legitimacy with the Nicaraguan middle class and private sector. Although this was not yet evident to Washington, the domestic bases of support for the dynasty were beginning to crumble just as surely as the foundations of Managua's buildings had crumbled when the earthquake's first tremors hit.

So close was the identification of Washington's interests with the continued rule of the Somozas, however, that little actually changed in the U.S. posture toward Nicaragua until the Carter administration took office. Aware that support for the dictator had been eroding among the Nicaraguan middle class and private sector, and hoist on Carter's campaign pledges to introduce human rights considerations into foreign policy decisions, Democratic policy makers acknowledged that some changes in the Nicaraguan situation were inevitable. On the other hand, the new administration also feared any alternative to Somoza that would not be firmly controlled by the most conservative of the anti-Somoza forces. Meanwhile, Somoza's powerful friends in the U.S. Congress and elsewhere were doing everything in their power—in the name of anticommunism and hemispheric stability—to insure that the four-decades-old policy of U.S. support for the dynasty continued. The now familiar confrontation between human rights rhetoric and the ideology and geopolitics of the Cold War entered early into the late 1970s debate on Nicaragua.

State of Siege

What gave bite to Washington's Cold War fears, of course, was the increasing importance of the Sandinista movement in the anti-Somoza struggle. Founded in 1962 as an anti-imperialist, revolutionary organization dedicated to overthrowing Somoza, the FSLN had only limited popular support and won no significant military victories during the first five years of its existence. It then turned its activities more to political work and the rural sector. It was not until 1974 that the FSLN again made headlines outside of Nicaragua when it took 12 members of Somoza's inner circle hostage at a Christmas party and exchanged them for 14 political prisoners. A state of siege was imposed by Somoza, repression increased, and the battle was joined in both city and countryside, although still only intermittently.

Even after the audacious Christmas assault, the Sandinistas still did not have widespread popular support. In fact, in 1975, in an acerbic internal debate over tactics, the FSLN split into two tendencies: The "Prolonged Popular War" tendency believed in the necessity of extensive political work, especially in rural areas; the "Proletarian Tendency" emphasized linkages to the urban working class. By 1976, a third tendency, known as *"Insurreccionistas"* or simply as *Terceristas* ("the third ones"), had emerged. The Insurrectionists were instrumental in forging links between the FSLN and middle class and business groups, and their leadership and statements tended to reflect social democratic ideas as opposed to the more Marxist orientations of the other two.

Only in 1977 did the situation begin to change. A group known as the Twelve was formed. Composed of influential businessmen, clergy, and intellectuals, it called openly for Nicaraguans to join the armed struggle to force Somoza's resignation. In October, responding in part to pressure from the United States, Somoza lifted martial law and censorship for the first time in three years. There was an immediate response: labor unrest, student demonstrations, a wave of disclosures in the local press, and armed attacks by the FSLN against several provincial towns.

Clearly alarmed by the escalation of armed activity in Nicaragua, the Carter administration redoubled its efforts to find a political solution dominated by persons it considered to be acceptable moderates. Key to this hope was Pedro Joaquín Chamorro, the editor and publisher of the opposition newspaper *La Prensa* and a long-time power in the Conservative party (the legal opposition party to Somoza's captive Liberal party). As founder of the Union for Democratic Liberation (UDEL), a political group encompassing a relatively wide spectrum of Nicaraguan opinion, Chamorro was firmly committed to a political strategy for getting rid of Somoza. In January 1978, however, Chamorro was assassinated. Tens of thousands of Nicaraguans took to the streets to protest his murder, and within days a general strike and lock-out called by UDEL largely paralyzed the capital and other major cities. Again the Sandinistas struck, attacking National Guard garrisons, and again the dynasty's repression was fierce.

In May 1978 a centrist umbrella organization known as the Broad Opposition Front (FAO) was formed. Initially it included UDEL, the Twelve, business groups, various labor organizations, and traditional opposition parties. But yet again these Washington-backed sectors of the opposition lost the initiative when, on August 22, the Insurrectionists attacked and captured the National Palace while Somoza's rubber-stamp congress was in session. Exchanging their hostages for 59 colleagues in Somoza's jails, the Sandinistas staged a triumphal march to the airport through streets lined by thousands of cheering Nicaraguans. Another general strike ensued, and on September 9 the Sandinistas launched new attacks on National Guard garrisons in five provincial cities.

The events and the aftermath of that bloody September are well known: Thousands of young people, armed with pistols, small caliber rifles, and shotguns joined the regular Sandinista troops. The rebels captured four cities. The counterattacks by the Guard were swift, brutal, and eventually successful—at least militarily. Cities were bombed, civilians killed by the thousands, and young people executed by the hundreds. In Nicaragua, and in much of the rest of the hemisphere as well, there was an upwelling of revulsion against Somoza and the Guard.

The Carter administration's dilemmas were increased rather than diminished by the events of September. Overt support for Somoza was no longer a viable policy, especially after the Inter-American Commission on Human Rights published a strong condemnatory report on the actions of the Guard and the Somoza regime. As more and more sectors of the Nicaraguan opposition turned pro-Sandinista in the context of profound hatred of Somoza, the centrist, electoral, non-Sandinista solution so favored by the Carter administration became more difficult to find.

But this was not for lack of trying. Under the auspices of the OAS, a team composed of representatives from the Dominican Republic and Guatemala as well as William Bowdler, director of the State Department Bureau of Intelligence and Research, met for many weeks at the end of 1978 and the beginning of 1979 with Somoza and the opposition, represented by the FAO. The U.S. goal was to stitch together a solution to the Nicaraguan crisis that for all practical purposes excluded the Sandinistas. But Somoza ultimately rejected the national plebiscite that was proposed. The United States then tried to lever the FAO into accepting a compromise solution more acceptable to Somoza. Thoroughly disgusted, some of the FAO representatives walked out in protest.

The White House and intelligence agencies conducted a desperate search for a Cuba-Sandinista connection.

The failure of the mediation was the overture to the June insurrection. Even while the mediation was in progress, the Sandinista-supported United People's Movement (MPU), composed of more than 20 student, labor, and neighborhood organizations, announced a decidedly conciliatory 12-point program for a post-Somoza Nicaragua. It included provisions for a substantial private sector in a reformed economy and guarantees of individual and political liberties. Then, during the first week in March, the three Sandinista tendencies—all of which had endorsed the MPU program—announced that they had agreed on a unified military command and strategy. By April there was fighting in the northern city of Estelí and elsewhere. During May, clashes between the Guard and the Sandinistas were everyday occurrences. On June 4 the the general strike began.

Practically all commercial and professional activity in the country ground to a halt. Within days, *barrios* from one end of Managua to the other were in arms, sometimes fully under the control of the *muchachos*, at other times left in smoking ruins by the ground and air attacks of the National Guard. "We've had weeks of bullets," said an old man in Managua. "Bullets for breakfast, bullets for lunch, bullets for dinner, and bullets before going to bed. But after they bomb you, bullets mean nothing."

Yet under this rain of bullets and bombs, beginning in September of 1978 and continuing through the summer of 1979, an unprecedented alliance had been forged: Well-armed and well-trained Sandinista regulars, perhaps numbering no more than 2,000, had been joined by thousands of young men and women loosely organized into militias. These combatants were backed by hundreds of thousands of ordinary citizens in the cities and countryside and supported at least rhetorically by every important opposition group in the country. There had been nothing like it in the history of Nicaragua and few similar events in the entire history of the continent. The national insurrection against *Somocismo* (Somozaism) was a reality. Within a few weeks León, the largest city after Managua, was fully in Sandinista hands, as were a number of other important provincial towns. A well-equipped Sandinista column had entered southern Nicaragua from neighboring Costa Rica, and for the first time the possibility of a Sandinista military victory was being mentioned by otherwise cautious observers.

Crude Stratagems

It was in this context of massive insurrectional activity, significant military achievement by the Sandinistas, and brutal attacks by the National Guard that the OAS met in Washington during the third week in June. The almost unanimous rejection of Vance's proposals for a cease-fire and a peace-keeping force suggested how out of touch Washington was with Latin American positions on Nicaragua. Meanwhile, in an attempt to placate conservative opinion at home and to justify diplomatic and perhaps even military intervention, the White House and intelligence agencies conducted a desperate search for a Cuba-Sandinista connection. Hardliners in the Carter administration, particularly on the National Security Council staff, harbored the hope that if other sectors of U.S. and international opinion could be convinced that Cuba was supplying the Sandinistas with both arms and advisers—perhaps even combat troops—they would come to support much tougher measures against the Sandinistas.

But all of these maneuverings failed, and Washington was faced with the reality of a Sandinista-backed provisional government that to most other observers appeared quite moderate in both membership and program. Composed of Violeta Chamorro of the Conservative party (widow of the martyred *La Prensa* publisher), Alfonso Robelo of the FAO, Sergio Ramírez of the Twelve, Moisés Hassán of the MPU, and Daniel Ortega of the Insurrectionist tendency of the Sandinistas, the provisional government immediately received the stamp of approval from all important opposition forces in Nicaragua and increasingly won support from anti-Somoza governments in the hemisphere and elsewhere. However, three of its members were quickly labeled radicals or Marxists by the Carter administration, and a frenzied effort followed in late June and July to undercut the five-person junta. At first this was attempted by proposing negotiations between an interim government named by the Nicaraguan Congress and the already-named provisional group. When all sectors of the opposition rejected that plan, the United States tried to modify the provisional government directly through the addition of several more conservative members. This too was unanimously rejected by the Nicaraguan opposition.

As each crude strategem was revealed and then abandoned, impatience and hostility toward the United States mounted both inside and outside Nicaragua. In June the question on everyone's lips in Managua was, "Why doesn't the Carter administration break relations with Somoza now that it has admitted he has to go?" In July, when the administration tried—with some success—to enlist the aid of Venezuela, Costa Rica, and Panama in its machinations and then threatened to withhold support for reconstruction unless certain conditions were met, Reverend Miguel D'Escoto, the provisional government's foreign minister-designate, exploded in anger: "The only way to characterize this is blackmail. . . . They're trying to bargain with the blood of our people."

Twisted Perceptions

Explanations of the unerring capacity of the U.S. government to be months and even years late in recognizing Nicaraguan realities—and Washington's consistently applied pressure for the most conservative and ultimately unworkable solutions—seem at first glance rather obvious: Cold War perspectives coupled with the presence of Marxists in the Sandinista movement congealed into a pervasive fear of an other-than-pro-U.S. post-Somoza regime—a "second Cuba," in the words of the more intemperate. A beleaguered and unpopular president, despite often expressed concerns about human rights in foreign policy, was not about to take risks that might lead to further accusations of weakness in the face of communism, of losing Nicaragua. Geostrategic fears of Central American dominoes—or at least substantially increased pressure on neighboring dictatorships should Somoza fall—worried national security planners.

Forty-five years of official support for the Guard and the dynasty left deeply worn grooves in military and diplomatic bureaucracies and perspectives. A powerful web of congressional friends and right-wingers outside the Congress gave Somoza a Washington lobby enjoyed by few other tyrants. When all of these feelings and forces are interrelated and set against the background of more than a century of U.S. hegemony, intervention, and gunboat diplomacy in the Caribbean basin, the American actions seem understandable and predictable, if not forgivable.

But there is an additional, less obvious explanation for the Carter administration's inability to see the handwriting on the wall in Nicaragua—and elsewhere. Washington seems incapable of understanding the nature and implications of a popular insurrection against tyranny, its partly spontaneous, organic, and nonelitist character. Even after Iran, whenever rebellion breaks out anywhere, Washington sees disorder, chaos, and uncertainty—opportunities for the Communists. What is neither perceived nor understood is the logic of the insurrection, its mass character, its essential legitimacy, its order and architecture expressed in the willingness of tens of thousands to persevere, suffer, and die if necessary.

This failure to understand is total. At the height of the June insurrection, a high White House official said that the National Guard had to be retained in order to "preserve order," to "prevent anarchy." At the very moment he was speaking, the Guard was looting shops and businesses, bombing civilians, and executing unarmed young men and women in the streets. A national security bureaucracy that could still claim in the summer of 1979 that the Guard was essential to order in Nicaragua was not simply stupid or ill-informed. On the contrary, it was and remains an apparatus so twisted in its perceptions of reality as to be incapable of understanding the nature of the tyranny; the fusion of Sandinistas, ordinary Nicaraguans, and even the business and commercial sectors; and the massive insurrection that had resulted.

To have opposed and tried to disrupt this process of fusion—as the Carter administration did—must therefore be seen as a profoundly interventionist and self-defeating policy. Wisdom, real concern for the people of Nicaragua, and even self-interest would have dictated an acknowledgment not only of the necessity to end Somoza's rule, but also of the need to accept and work with the political alliance created by the insurrection process itself. One of the most grotesque aspects of the U.S. reaction was that it took the televised execution of an American newsman, Bill Stewart of ABC, to jolt the White House into a new attitude.

The Sandinista movement—the provisional government, its program, its cabinet, the popular support one senses in the *barrios* —are all legitimate and representative expressions of the revolt of the Nicaraguan people

Washington seems incapable of understanding the nature and implications of a popular insurrection against tyranny.

against the dynasty. Washington talked the language of representation and democracy but was unwilling to accept as legitimate the politics that were springing from the still-smoking ruins of decades of dictatorship.

In setting itself against these political forces and forms, the administration only succeeded in tarnishing its own less-than-sparkling reputation among democrats in Latin America, angering vast sectors of the Nicaraguan population, prolonging the bloodshed, possibly moving the center of political gravity in post-Somoza Nicaragua to the left, raising the costs of reconstruction, and further confirming suspicions that it—like all of its predecessors—is not ready to allow Latin Americans to solve their own problems.

Now that Somoza and a significant portion of his most culpable friends, collaborators, and relations are safely ensconced in the United States with their plundered millions, one hopes that Washington has learned at least a modest lesson: A people that fought for two decades against the Marines, and then for 46 years against the Somozas will not easily allow its future to be stamped "Made in U.S.A." Of course, the meddling can continue. American power makes that possible, as does Washington's continuing arrogance. But it is to be hoped that the power will now be otherwise used and the arrogance substantially checked.

More specifically, what does it mean to be both supportive and noninterventionist in post-Somoza Nicaragua? At a minimum, it means continuing and extending the nascent policy of correct diplomatic and political relations with the Nicaraguan Government of National Reconstruction. In the last few moments of Somoza's rule, when Washington realized that the FSLN was only weeks or perhaps days away from a military victory, the negotiated departure of Somoza and the peaceful installation of the provisional government suddenly became official policy. This path had clearly become, in the administration's eyes, the lesser of two evils.

Now it is crucial to transform the grudging and dearly won acceptance of the new government into something more substantial. Aid for reconstruction, in all of its forms, will be the short-run litmus test of this acceptance—not only emergency and humanitarian aid to help feed, shelter, and care for refugees and others, but also generosity of intent and action in lending institutions and political forums both at home and abroad. Ironically, the Sandinista victory has given the United States yet another chance in Nicaragua. Can this kind of support be given without imposing political and economic conditions that violate Nicaraguan sovereignty? Can the decades-old attempts to shape Nicaraguan outcomes be contained? If the old ways continue, there is little to be gained and much to lose. Not the least of the victims will be the last shreds of the administration's credibility as the defender of human rights and democracy in Latin America. More important will be the continuing victimization of more than 2 million Nicaraguans who now need peace, time, resources, and understanding as they strive to rebuild their shattered country.

DATELINE PERU: A SAGGING REVOLUTION

by Abraham F. Lowenthal

Revolutions are more often proclaimed than carried out, especially in Latin America. While profound transformations are taking place in countries as different as Iran, Nicaragua, Angola, and Zimbabwe, what has happened to Peru's once heralded revolution of 1968? Although the Peruvian experiment has suffered major disappointments, some fascinating shifts have occurred—shifts that may open the way to more substantial changes in the 1980s.

Almost 12 years—three presidential terms in Washington—have passed since Peru's armed forces surrounded the National Palace in Lima with tanks and ushered President Fernando Belaúnde Terry to the airport. Army General Juan Velasco Alvarado and his colleagues in khaki announced their intent then to transform Peru's basic economic and social structures, to end external domination (especially by the United States), to seek a third path to development that was neither capitalist nor communist, and even to change national values. They would create a "new Peruvian man," one dedicated to "solidarity, not individualism."

Skeptics who considered the Peruvian military's earnest rhetoric as just another empty pronouncement were soon jolted. Within a week Peru had expropriated the International Petroleum Co. (IPC), an Exxon subsidiary long prominent in the country's politics, whose legal status was high on the agenda of U.S.-Peruvian relations. Within a year the regime had decreed a sweeping agrarian reform, which redistributed not only the small amount of land held by the peasants but also the rich sugar and cotton estates along the coast and the vast *latifundia* of the highlands.

With a burst of laws and regulations, the Peruvian military undertook to reform production and distribution, labor-management relations, the role of foreign enterprise in Peru's economy, the state's role in the economy and the media, and the nation's international relationships. Special emphasis was given to moving the economy steadily away from capitalist principles toward a quasi-socialist model. A new "social property" sector of worker-managed firms was intended to become the predominant mode of economic organization. An "industrial community" was created in privately owned firms, a reform that would give workers an increased stake in corporate profits and a say in management. An ambitious educational reform promised to attack class and ethnic divisions in a country where more than half the population in six highland provinces still did not speak Spanish when the 1961 census was taken.

The educational reform and the state-controlled media would promote the country's new social values: cooperation, not competition; social conscience, not selfishness; and renewed national pride. The military government launched a new agency—the National System to Support Social Mobilization (SINAMOS)—with full fanfare to mobilize the previously nonparticipant sectors of Peru's fragmented society, to raise popular consciousness, and to channel the resulting energies into the national political process. And Peru became a major participant in various international forums, taking the leading role particularly on new international economic order issues.

Not surprisingly, the new Peruvian man is nowhere to be found in Lima today. The military regime will more likely be remembered in a generation for having extended the superhighway from Lima all the way to the beach, thus facilitating its use by the middle class, than for profoundly reshaping Peru's values. *Limeños* from the upper class still enjoy the bullfights at Acho, and those from the lower classes still trudge along in the colorful procession of the Señor de los Milagros. All are much more moved by such old traditions than by the new social relationships or concepts of property Peru's military and civilian ideologues tried vigorously but vainly to introduce. The social property sector has all but disappeared. The industrial community reform has been eviscerated. SINAMOS has been scuttled with little more than a whisper of protest. Lima's upper-crust private schools have survived the educational reform almost intact. The traditional parties that dominated Peru's politics before 1968 persist today, with their leadership and their programs mainly unchanged. New parties, new leaders, and new concepts are hard to discover. And Peru's international profile has receded almost to invisibility.

Discredited and Disdained

As should have been expected, 12 years of military rule have done little to alter Peru's underlying realities. The country remains largely unintegrated ethnically and even geographically, its terrain dramatically punctuated by the Andes and the Amazon. Its economy continues to depend largely on the export of mineral and agricultural products. Income distribution has not been radically affected: Studies show that almost all the redistribution has occurred within the wealthiest quarter of the population.

Peru is still an overwhelmingly poor country, although a few families are impressively rich. As one intellectual pointed out after the devastating 1970 earthquake, which took some 70,000 lives, many highland Peruvians live every day the realities outsiders seem to notice only after a natural disaster: makeshift housing, inadequate food, no schools, no potable water, no access to medical care, and utter isolation. The revolution has not much changed any of these grim facts. Indeed, Lima seems poorer than it was 10 years ago. Beggars and pitiful street merchants are now a much more common sight. Visual impressions are supported by evidence that tuberculosis and other diseases are on the increase, that infant mortality is climbing, and that the overall rate of per capita economic growth in the past decade has been negative.

External debt and inflation expanded much faster than production or exports, and Peru found its economy in a shambles by the late 1970s. The steps taken by the military to restore economic health—drastic efforts to reduce government spending, incentives to increase the export of products in sectors where Peru has a comparative advantage, attempts to curb inflation and to cut down on external borrowing—have led not only to the pains of retrenchment but also to the reinforcement of the historic structure of Peru's economy.

What has changed in Peru, and remarkably so, is the structure and distribution of power. The traditional landed families and their financial institutions have lost almost all their influence. Individuals who have had the agility to retain wealth and prominence are rare. Most of Peru's former oligarchs have fallen from unquestioned authority to oblivion or even ignominy. Precisely those Peruvians whom every foreign reporter necessarily contacted 15 years ago are now out of touch.

The major newspapers—*La Prensa* and *El Comercio*—that set the agenda and established the limits of debate in Peru for years have been destroyed by a combination of government expropriation, intimidation, and intervention. No major newspaper has replaced them. Radio and television, also taken over by the state, contribute precious little to public information. Rags, tabloids, and weekly news magazines have sprouted, but periodic government crackdowns prevent them from printing anything controversial. No publication successfully defines issues for discussion in Peru today.

The Catholic church, once very influential in Peru, is now barely visible. Its early identification with the military government and the emergence of militant liberation theology priests, sympathetic to the revolutionary left but distrusted by the church hierarchy and many of the faithful, have hurt its reputation and unity. As a result, the church in Peru today is quiet, careful, and without much force.

The presence and influence of the United States—both of the American embassy and of U.S. corporations and other institutions—are sharply reduced from the levels of 1968. Marcona, Cerro de Pasco, Grace, and International Telephone and Telegraph have all more or less gone the way of IPC. Other corporations, such as Chrysler, have been driven out by tough competition. The Ford Foundation, once influential in Peruvian university circles, has seen its office shrink and its budget dwindle. Few of the major development projects in the country involve the U.S. Agency for International Development; the Soviets, the West Germans, the Japanese, and even the Spanish, the Swiss, and the Swedes are more visible. The Soviet, West German, and Cuban embassies are more active in cultural affairs than the U.S. International Communication Agency. Cuban and Soviet airlines now serve Lima's splendid but desultory airport.

More important, the USSR is now Peru's major source for tanks and other weapons. From the 1940s through the 1960s, the United States enjoyed overwhelming influence in all aspects of Peru's politics and economy; by now it is an important but not exclusive external actor in Peru, much as it was before World War II. In a recent year, Peruvian trade with both the European Economic Community countries and with those of the Council for Mutual Economic Assistance was as large as that with the United States. This represented a striking change from the days when the United States dominated Peru's commerce. This relative drop of American influence is part of a general region-wide (if not universal) decline of U.S. political and economic hegemony, but Peru's rulers no doubt consciously speeded the process.

The Peruvian armed forces are the source

of governmental authority at the national and provincial levels. But the military is now discredited, widely disdained, and audibly accused of corruption and incompetence. Peru's officer corps is generally on the defensive, apparently eager to use the scheduled 1980 elections to escape from office and return to the barracks. Peruvians of all stripes who used to predict that the military would rule for a generation now expect a civilian government within a year.

The traditional political parties have survived, but they lack dynamism and authority. No party appears to be able to project a vision of Peru in the 1980s that excites the country's imagination as Belaúnde's did in the early 1960s. It used to be said by the party faithful that only the American Popular Revolutionary Alliance (APRA)—Peru's oldest and largest party, founded in the 1920s by Victor Raúl Haya de la Torre—could save Peru. Others, no doubt, thought that only the army could muster the clout to reform Peru or that only the revolutionary left could force real change. Now it seems that no party or institution has the confidence to reshape the country. It is plagued by a vacuum of legitimacy and authority, if not of power. Ironically, the chief electoral beneficiaries of the past 12 years of military rule appear to be APRA, Belaúnde and his supporters, and some guerrilla leaders of the early 1960s—the principal targets of the army's hostility in 1968.

Repositories of Power

Where has all the power gone? In part, it has gone to a new group of entrepreneurs who have made a great deal of money during the past 10 years, mainly in import substitution industries and in mining. Whole new fortunes have been created from the sharp rise in the price of silver, for example. New "first families"—nationally oriented, aggressive, and conspicuous—have emerged in Lima. These families lack the social prestige and the political connections of the traditional upper class, but they are beginning to express themselves politically through the media and special interest associations.

In part, power has gravitated to the extensive technocracy that has emerged as a result of the explosion of the state's role in Peru's economy. Hundreds of technocrats—military and civilian—now play a crucial role in managing the economy. Before 1968 the state's share of national investment was probably lower in Peru than in any comparable South American country. Taxes were collected by private banks that actually charged the government for the use of its own revenue. Planning was anathema, and state enterprises were avoided. All that has changed. Not only do investment and production figures reflect the state's importance, but the vast Peruvian public bureaucracy occupies building after building in Lima: Petroperu, Pescaperu, Mineroperu, Centromin-Peru, Electroperu, the sugar cooperatives, and so on. The reach of the state into various parts of daily life is now much more insistent and effective, if sometimes disruptive and often ineffectual.

However Peru's politics evolves in the next decade, the requirements of the national and the international economy will probably cause the new technocracy to retain and even expand its influence. An interesting question is whether APRA, the perennial party out of power for the last 40 years, would be willing and able, if it finally won power, to engage the loyalties and skills of the technocrats, or whether it would insist on parceling out government jobs to the party faithful.

A third source of power—and one of expanding significance—is the increasingly mobilized populace. Trade unions, although still heavily influenced by the parties, are far stronger than they were in the 1960s, despite efforts by the regime to weaken them. *Campesinos* lack a well-articulated structure, but their participation in and influence upon the national political process is greater than ever before in Peru's history. Industrial unions have been gaining sharply in membership, political strength, and militancy. The teachers' union almost brought the country to a standstill in 1978. Major strikes, demonstrations, and outbursts of violence have occurred frequently since February 1975. Many of these begin in the outlying provinces, some of them apparently quite spontaneously, suggesting that there is an antiestablishment constituency ready to be more fully mobilized.

Part of this potential, at least, made itself felt in the 1978 elections for the constituent assembly in which five leftist parties received over 31 per cent of the vote. This was an astonishing gain over the 6 per cent the various leftist parties registered in 1962 and the trivial backing they appeared to have before the election scheduled for 1969. Hugo Blanco, an almost legendary radical peasant leader, alone accounted for over a third of the leftist tally, a display less of personal charisma than of widespread disaffection with the established parties. Class tensions have heightened considerably in Peru during the past few years; even the aborted reforms have contributed to radicalizing important elements of Peru's society by raising consciousness and expectations.

The fourth significant repository of power in Peru, not new at all, is external to the country—the private and official international financial community. The disappearance for a time of the anchovy; the thwarted hopes of discovering large amounts of petroleum; the international recession; and misjudgments of various kinds—such as the decision to build a major pipeline across the Andes before determining how much oil it would actually carry—conspired severely to upset Peru's foreign exchange balance during the 1970s.

By the end of the decade most of the country's export receipts were being used to service the debt. The result—pressure on Peru from the private commercial banks and from the International Monetary Fund to introduce austerity and to balance the accounts—has sharply reduced Peru's room to maneuver. Ironically, a regime that began with a serious determination to reduce Peru's dependence on foreign countries and institutions, now presides over a country apparently further than ever from autonomy. If the prices of copper, cotton, iron, and sugar climb, Peru's economy will boom in the 1980s. If a large expansion occurs in the first years after civilian politicians return to power, democratic politics will surely be reinforced. If, on the other hand, prices for Peru's exports fall, painful austerity measures and sharp political repression can be expected. How Peru's economy and politics evolve depends more than ever on matters beyond Lima's control.

Despite America's declining presence in Peru, U.S. government policies can still influence the country's future. Whether or not the United States and Peru's other creditors are flexible about rescheduling the Peruvian debt will ease or exacerbate its adjustment pains. How the United States reacts to a wide range of international economic order issues will help determine the country's prospects for economic development. The same applies to American domestic economic policies, which will significantly affect the level of demand for Peru's exports in Western industrialized countries. Finally, the extent to which Washington continues to pursue its human rights policies will have a strong impact on the country's political future, particularly as the 1980 elections approach.

The ultimate result of Peru's experiment will not be known for several years. The combination of an increasingly mobilized populace, burgeoning leftist parties, severely weakened sources of established power and legitimacy, external obstacles—both real and imaginary—to national development, and the now much stronger central government is bound to be volatile in the years to come. What will result in the 1980s cannot be predicted, but it can be said that the chances for violent swings to the left or to the right are much greater than they were a decade ago. Peru's generals and colonels may not have achieved a successful revolution, but it may yet turn out that they have made one possible.

CENTRAL AMERICAN PARALYSIS

by Richard Millett

U.S. efforts to respond to revolutionary change in Central America resemble those of a fire brigade during the London blitz. American officials rush frantically from place to place, trying to contain the damage and save what they can of existing structures. But they seem unable to deal with the basic sources of their troubles. Problems abound: an incipient civil war in El Salvador, a flailing economy and a Marxist-influenced government in Nicaragua, increased political violence in Guatemala, and lagging economic and political development in Honduras and Costa Rica. To forge a policy capable of dealing with Central America, the United States must drastically revise its approach to the region.

When Jimmy Carter took office, any suggestion that Central American affairs would emerge as the primary U.S. policy concern in Latin America would have seemed absurd. Since the 1954 Central Intelligence Agency-sponsored overthrow of Guatemala's left-leaning government, the United States has largely ignored Central America. The important canal treaty negotiations with Panama received some attention, but Panama has few historic ties with Central America, and the State Department does not group Panamanian relations with Central American affairs.

The Office of Inter-American Affairs was in fact a State Department backwater, usually manned by undistinguished individuals with little, if any, experience in the area. Political upheavals, such as the 1969 Honduran-Salvadorian war, or natural disasters, such as the Nicaraguan and Guatemalan earthquakes, invoked occasional flurries of activity. But for the most part, U.S.-Central American relations were simple and controlled. If any region could have been safely ignored by the United States in early 1977, it was probably Central America.

Both economic and political realities supported this assumption. With underdeveloped, basically agricultural economies, the five small countries and their 20 million inhabitants hardly threatened U.S. interests. The total area of Central America is just over 163,000 square miles; the republics range in size from Nicaragua (57,200 square miles, about the size of Iowa) to El Salvador (8,100 square miles, just larger than New Jersey). Guatemala has the largest population (6.9 million), followed by El Salvador (4.5 million), Honduras (3.6 million), Nicaragua (2.6 million), and Costa Rica (2.2 million).

The republics are poor relative to the United States: Costa Rica, the most prosperous of the Central American states, had a gross domestic product (GDP) per capita estimated at only $1,540 in 1978; Honduras, with a 1978 GDP of $480 per capita, was the poorest. The prime exports of Central America—cotton, coffee, bananas, and meat—could be easily obtained elsewhere. The Panama Canal's declining importance to U.S. policy and scheduled transfer to Panama diminish the area's strategic significance.

Central American politics were equally unobtrusive. In the three northern republics—Honduras, Guatemala, and El Salvador—pro-Western military dominated the governments; in Nicaragua a 40-year-old family dynasty seemed firmly entrenched; and in Costa Rica, which had no army, democracy seemed to be flourishing. All five nations usually supported the United States in international forums. None had formal relations with Cuba or China. Only Costa Rica, after long debate, had established diplomatic relations with the Soviet Union.

The American Proconsul

While the United States gave low priority to Central American affairs, Central American leaders devoted much of their energy to predicting, interpreting, and adapting to U.S. goals and interests. This subordination placed American ambassadors in the region in a very special and, at times, awkward position. Their traditional role was described in a 1927 State Department memorandum by then Under Secretary of State Robert Olds:

> Our ministers accredited to the five little republics, stretching from the Mexican border to Panama . . . have been advisers whose advice has been accepted virtually as law in the capitals where they respectively reside. . . . We do control the destinies of Central America and we do so for the simple reason that the national interest absolutely dictates such a course. . . . Until now Central America has always understood that governments which we recognize and support stay in power, while those we do not recognize and support fall.

Dr. Mauricio Solaun, U.S. ambassador to Nicaragua from 1977 to 1979, found that Nicaraguans, at least, partially retained this perspective, with the army even "saluting the American ambassador as if he were a proconsul." Ironically, it was in Nicaragua that the U.S. loss of power in Central America first became evident.

Shortly after taking office, Carter pressured the regime of Nicaraguan dictator Anastasio Somoza Debayle and the military governments of El Salvador and Guatemala for improvements in human rights and expansion of political freedoms. In El Salvador and Guatemala, the most visible result was the angry cancellation of military assistance pacts with the United States. Somoza responded with cosmetic changes that elicited a complimentary letter from Carter in summer 1978; but when revolution broke out, Somoza abandoned all pretence of reform and returned to brute force to maintain his dictatorship.

To the surprise of virtually every politician and military officer in Central America, Somoza defied subsequent U.S. pressure to give up the presidency. Unwilling to resort to force, U.S. policy drifted for several months while Venezuela, Panama, and Costa Rica increased their support for the revolutionary Sandinistas.

The extent to which the United States had lost control over Central America became evident when the Sandinistas began their final offensive in late spring 1979. Not a single Central American nation supported the Carter administration's proposal for sending an inter-American peace force to Nicaragua. When the United States then approved an Organization of American States resolution calling for the replacement of Somoza with a totally new government, only Costa Rica, among the Central American republics, voted with the United States.

Many Central American moderates feel that the United States takes their problems seriously only when they begin killing one another in the streets.

By mid-July 1979, when Somoza fled to Miami and control of the nation passed to the Marxist-influenced Sandinista Liberation Front, old patterns of U.S.-Nicaraguan relations—and therefore U.S.-Central American relations—were destroyed. The heritage of U.S. supremacy collapsed with Somoza.

Nicaragua—once a kingpin of American operations in Central America—was now warmly disposed toward Cuba, deeply suspicious of the United States, and committed to radical change at home and a nonaligned position abroad. Within Central America, the Sandinista triumph frightened conservatives, who in turn directed sharp expressions of anger at the Carter administration. Facing growing, increasingly violent opposition from the left, military governments in El Salvador and Guatemala feared that Nicaragua would provide inspiration and arms to revolutionary groups at home. Honduras, where thousands of Somoza's troops had fled for refuge, faced the possibility of serious clashes along its long, poorly defended border with Nicaragua. Increased conflict seemed certain in Central America. The State Department was forced to begin developing a new policy in the midst of spreading turmoil.

Lost Credibility

At this point, U.S. influence in Central America was at its lowest level in this century. Carter's human rights policy and his refusal to intervene to prevent a Sandinista victory confused and alienated much of the right, including the military, but failed to diminish the suspicions and hostility of the left. Moderate reformists, such as Christian Democratic and Social Democratic parties, appeared to be losing ground as forces became increasingly polarized. Decimation of their leadership by ultrarightist hit squads further compounded their problems.

Inability to control violence and contain Marxist influence in a region only two hours flying time from Miami contributed to an image of U.S. weakness in dealing with Central America in particular and the Third World in general. While most U.S. officials involved with Latin America policy recognized the urgency of formulating an effective program for Central America, their ability to do so had been consistently constrained by domestic and foreign political realities. There was no quick or cheap way to overcome 25 years of neglect or to restore the credibility lost during the Nicaraguan crisis. High-level administrative attention to the region was easily diverted by problems in areas of greater strategic significance, such as the Persian Gulf; and the willingness of Congress to appropriate significant funds for any effort in Central America was questionable at best.

In formulating a response to Central America's new political environment, the Carter administration had three basic options. It could decide that the costs of attempting to reverse the revolutionary process so outweighed the region's actual worth that the United States should withdraw and, at least for the present, allow events to run their course. Fear of domestic political consequences should a second or third Cuba emerge mitigated strongly against this option. Or, the United States could help prop up existing governments with military assistance and support. This would mean abandoning the human rights content of Latin America policy and would require isolating and perhaps even trying to reverse the revolutionary process in Nicaragua. A possible upshot would be U.S. military intervention.

The final option was to promote and identify with the process of basic change within the region, hoping at the same time to preserve a fair degree of political and economic pluralism. While discarding the traditional client-state approach to Central America, this option would actively seek to restore a modicum of U.S. influence and insure that none of the republics became dependent upon nations hostile to U.S. interests.

With little public debate, the Carter administration apparently chose the last option. Then Assistant Secretary of State for Inter-American Affairs Viron P. Vaky summarized this approach in September 1979 testimony before the House Foreign Affairs Committee:

> . . . Defense of the status quo will not avoid change; it will only radicalize it. . . . Failure on our part to identify with the legitimate aspiration of the people in these countries, and with those democratic elements who seek peaceful, constructive change, respect for human rights and basic equity will put us on the wrong side of history.
>
> Our task therefore is how to work with our friends to guide and influence change, how to use our influence to promote justice, freedom and equity to mutual benefit—and thereby avoid insurgency and Communism. Nowhere will this task be more crucial than in Nicaragua.

Unfortunately, attempts to implement this approach have thus far failed. Administration efforts to restore credibility to U.S. policies and stability to Central America have been consistently overtaken by events or undermined by congressional budget cuts. This has been most notable in El Salvador, Central America's smallest nation.

Assaults and Kidnappings

Since the early 1930s, the armed forces have dominated Salvadorian politics. As the population density of this agricultural nation increased, pressures for basic social and economic reforms mounted. Urged on by the handful of powerful families that controlled the economy, the military responded by using massive fraud to deny the moderate Christian Democrats victory in the 1972 elections. Throughout the 1970s the government encouraged the rise of right-wing, paramilitary groups that terrorized peasant and labor organizations, destroyed the Christian Democratic party's infrastructure in the countryside, and even murdered socially active priests. These events, in turn, led to the steady growth of armed, radical forces on the left that financed their efforts through spectacular assaults and kidnappings. By fall 1979 the nation seemed on the verge of civil war.

Encouraged by the United States, younger army officers ousted the hard-line military government in October 1979 and replaced it with a military-civilian junta. Their proclaimed advocacy of democratic reforms attracted strong U.S. support. Caught between violence from both right and left the new regime never gained full control of internal politics. The first junta collapsed in January 1980 when its civilian members quit in protest of military opposition to basic reforms.

Christian Democratic participation in a second junta led to a split within that party. Nationalization of banks, adoption of a new labor code, and promulgation of a far-sweeping agrarian reform law have failed to appease left-wing opposition and have infuriated powerful forces on the right. Only strong, direct pressure from the United States prevented a February 1980 countercoup by angry conservatives. By spring 1980 El Salvador was clearly in danger of drifting into civil war, a process accelerated by the brutal murder of Archbishop Oscar Arnulfo Romero, a heroic spokesman for justice for most Salvadorians.

While not as dramatic, events in the rest of the isthmus have been almost as frustrating for American policy makers. Guatemala, where internal violence has escalated considerably in the past few months, is a case in point. For well over a decade, bloody conflicts between left-wing guerrillas and government troops—supplemented by private far-right terrorist organizations such as the Mano Blanca—have been a recurrent facet of Guatemalan life. By 1979 murders of moderate and leftist political leaders had become so common that even Vice President Francisco Villagrán Kramer declared that "death or exile is the fate of those who struggle for justice in Guatemala."

Three factors have helped the right maintain control of Guatemala. While the population is the largest in Central America, nearly half of Guatemala's citizens are Indians, traditionally outside of active politics and impervious to appeals from the left. Furthermore, Guatemala's Central American neighbors, El Salvador and Honduras, also were under firm military control, insulating Guatemala from external subversion. Finally, high coffee prices and conservative economic policies produced a strong economy that reduced middle-class discontent. The recent growth in domestic petroleum production, which could enable Guatemala to reach self-sufficiency in a few years, contributes to the financial well-being of the country.

In the past year, the first two factors have changed considerably, thereby threatening economic stability. For the first time, substantial elements of the Indian population have shown signs of supporting and even joining the guerrillas. In March 1980 a confrontation between stone-throwing Indian women and army troops resulted in the machine-gunning of several women and the bitter condemnation of the army by the normally conservative bishop of El Quiché. Growing opposition has undermined control of two heavily populated highlands departments, Huehuetenango and El Quiché, and has produced a sharp drop in army morale.

The turmoil in El Salvador has created

acute anxiety over regional stability, leading many Guatemalan officers to talk openly about staving off subversion at home by fighting revolution in El Salvador. Also, the dispute between Guatemala and Great Britain over governing rights of the small Central American territory of Belize has increased regional tension. To date, mounting problems in Guatemala have precluded any intervention, but right-wing groups have funneled aid to their Salvadorian counterparts.

Frustrated and angered, the Guatemalan right has purchased full-page advertisements in local newspapers to denounce what they view as a weak U.S. policy that encourages left-wing uprisings and to charge members of the Salvadorian junta with membership in the Communist party. Rumors of a possible coup by the far right within the military have begun to circulate. But nothing is likely to happen before the U.S. presidential elections in November: Many right-wing Guatemalan politicians and military officers fervently hope for a victory by Republican candidate Ronald Reagan, believing this would remove U.S. opposition to their continuing or even escalating violent repression of the left.

Corruption is most visible in Honduras, where every area commander recently received a Rolex watch and a Mercedes Benz.

Honduras and Costa Rica have escaped the violence and polarization found in the other nations, but both are plagued by accelerating inflation, mounting labor troubles, and weak political leadership. Prospects for stability in Honduras, Central America's least-developed nation, are further clouded by strong public resentment of the flagrant corruption in the higher military ranks. This outlook is somewhat offset by the surprisingly honest results of the April 1980 Constituent Assembly elections. Although left-wing parties were excluded, the Liberal party defeated the military's traditional ally, the National party, and initiated a return to civilian rule. Overall, the mixture of reform and corruption makes difficult a balanced U.S. response.

Costa Rica's democratic traditions and its relatively advanced social programs help insulate it from the region's violence, but the consumerist orientation of its increasingly middle-class society makes it especially vulnerable to mounting economic problems. Those problems could reverse the usually cordial U.S.-Costa Rican relations.

Frenetic Search

Events beyond Central America also hamper efforts to forge an effective policy. Historically, the United States has not given consistent attention to the problems of small, poor nations. Many Costa Ricans saw the U.S. actions in the controversy over tuna-fishing rights as demonstration that the United States is more concerned with the interests of a few Californian fishermen than it is with the well-being and dignity of a small, democratic ally.

Crises in more vital areas divert American attention and resources and diminish any sense of urgency. Currently, Iran and Afghanistan overshadow Central America; they also reduce U.S. tolerance of foreign attacks on past American policies and promote domestic acceptance of possible U.S. military intervention. The priority given to issues in the 1980 U.S. elections further obscures efforts to develop a consistent Central American policy.

Establishing a responsive American policy is complicated by the administration's frequent inability to deliver promised aid. Nicaragua is a case in point. Despite efforts by Ambassador Lawrence A. Pezzullo and his staff, attempts to moderate the course of Nicaragua's revolution have enjoyed only limited success. A key element of the American approach was to be the demonstration that the United States could not only tolerate but also could actually support basic social and economic changes in Nicaragua. This required combining verbal assurances of support with significant amounts of reconstruction assistance. Other nations, notably Venezuela, Panama, and Costa Rica, were counted upon to promote political pluralism and reduce potential Cuban influence.

The initial scenario was optimistic. Congress quickly approved the reprogramming of over $8 million in emergency aid for Nicaragua. Other nations offered substantial credits, and multilateral agencies, such as the Inter-American Development Bank (IDB), began processing major new loans.

The recent situation is less hopeful. Rebuffed in initial efforts to moderate the revolution, Costa Rica, Panama, and to a lesser extent, Venezuela have reduced involvement in Nicaragua. The processing of IDB and other multilateral loans has slowed dramatically. U.S. government efforts to provide a $75 million aid package have been cramped by a seemingly endless series of congressional roadblocks. Originally projected for late 1979, this package has been the subject of sharp debate; amendments, highly objectionable to Nicaragua, have been added to the authorization bill. Finally, the entire appropriation has been further delayed by the congressional mood of budget slashing.

These setbacks contributed to growing demoralization within Nicaragua's private sector and increased suspicion among the Sandinista leadership that the United States will never really support a revolutionary regime in Central America. As a U.S. diplomat in Managua recently observed, "We could have done so much with that money just a few months ago, but we've wasted our best opportunities in this country."

Costa Rican political leader Rodrigo Madrigal Nieto suggests the creation of a mini-Marshall Plan for Central America. Current U.S. aid to the region now totals just over $100 million annually. Nieto's proposal would cost about $1 billion more a year. Given the high level of U.S. expenditures abroad, that increase is relatively modest. American election-year politics, however, preclude any move in this direction before 1981. Instead, the Carter administration promotes the newly founded Caribbean-Central American Action, a program headed by Governor Bob Graham of Florida and designed to enlist private support for the region. While the Action program might produce limited benefits for Costa Rica and perhaps Honduras, it is unlikely that private investors will respond generously to the current, unstable conditions in the other three republics. In the absence of any joint executive-congressional commitment, the confusion and resentment generated by U.S. efforts in Central America will likely continue.

The result is a chaotic American policy. U.S. programs in Central America are inconsistent, confused, and indecisive. Statements of policy and expressions of concern lack credibility. The repeated visits by Assistant Secretary of State for Inter-American Affairs William Bowdler are perceived more as frenetic searches for a way out of crises than as any indication of serious, long-range interest in the area's problems. Many Central American moderates feel that the United States takes their problems seriously only when they begin killing one another in the streets.

Washington's Dilemma

Recent events raise the critical but uncomfortable question of what the United States should do if a moderate response becomes impossible. That point was reached in Nicaragua in June 1979, but the State Department continued to advocate a moderate compromise until Somoza fled to Miami. The approach only exacerbated the problem of diminishing American credibility. A similar point may be rapidly approaching in El Salvador. By supporting the current junta as the only alternative to violent civil conflict, the Carter administration is identifying with social and economic policies well to the left of any previously espoused by the United States in that part of the world. Yet the Salvadorian far left continues to denounce U.S. policy.

Part of the American dilemma stems from lack of experience in mediating between moderate regimes and radical opposition. Whereas the United States has successfully resolved disputes between moderates and conservatives, as in the Dominican Republic in 1978, American intervention in conflicts such as the current one in El Salvador demands a new kind of diplomacy. Furthermore, as many Salvadorians repeatedly point out, foreign intervention in such conflicts usually accelerates the polarization process and ultimately drives both the home government and the outside power toward the right. Despite these difficulties, standing aside and letting events run their course is politically unacceptable to the Carter administration—especially given the possibility that the result might be an anti-American, Marxist regime.

In the past, the United States counted on Central American armies to defend American interests in that region. The history of U.S. military influence in Central America is long, and the ties are intimate. Paradoxically, in every Central American country except Costa Rica, which abolished its army over 30 years ago, the military has become a major problem for American policy making.

No army in Latin America had more officers and men trained in U.S. military schools, and none had a closer relationship with the United States than did Nicaragua's National Guard. Yet the guard became the corrupt instrument of the Somoza family. Its brutality drove thousands of Nicaraguans to join the Sandinistas, and its internal weaknesses ultimately led to its total destruction. Such an outcome surely challenges the rationale for American training and support of other nations' armed forces, especially now that El Salvador's security troops—once again, groomed by the United States—are threatened with a similar fate.

The U.S. government's proposals for supporting the Salvadorian junta include a request for increased military assistance, notably a $5.7 million package for improvements in training, transportation, and communications. This proposal invoked considerable criticism, including a letter to Carter from the late Archbishop Romero, who claimed that such assistance "instead of favoring greater justice and peace in El Salvador, undoubtedly will sharpen . . . the repression."

In Guatemala and Honduras, conditions within the armed forces pose similar challenges for U.S. policy makers. In both countries, hopes for peaceful reforms in human rights and political freedoms require the acquiescence, if not the active support, of the military. In each nation significant segments of the officer corps, especially at junior levels, are sympathetic to such changes. But the higher ranking officers seem allied with the oligarchy and, in Guatemala, committed to a policy of brutal repression that ultimately alienates the armed forces from the general population. Corruption is most visible in Honduras, where every area commander recently received a Rolex watch and a Mercedes Benz. Again, it is difficult to see how efforts by an external power can deal effectively with such problems.

U.S.-sponsored training programs could educate officers on how corruption and popular alienation eventually destroyed the pre-1959 Cuban army and the Nicaraguan National Guard, but in the immediate future there is little the United States can do beyond encouraging these forces to reform themselves. Until this happens, American support for these armies only associates the United States with repression and brutality.

"We have frequently mistaken the support of governments for the friendship of populations. . . ."

From the standpoint of American policy, the essential question in Central America is whether the United States can live with and perhaps even support revolution in its own back yard. Although the United States accommodated nations such as Mexico, the traditional answer in Central America has been a firm no. The Carter administration indicates a willingness to change this response, but with qualifications: only if Cuban influence is limited; only if an unspecified amount of pluralism is allowed; and only if each Central American country refrains from involvement in its neighbor's politics.

An Avenue of Escape

Remaining unspecified is what the American response could or should be if those guidelines are ignored and if revolution—particularly revolution directed against unpopular, repressive, military regimes—spreads throughout the region. Being forced to choose between acceptance of control over much of Central America by hostile forces and open intervention by American troops is the ultimate nightmare of American policy makers. While either option entails disastrous political consequences, current international and domestic political trends may tip the balance toward intervention. It might be impossible to find any effective option between doing nothing and sending in the Marines.

A concerned State Department recently tried to defuse the issue. In his April 8, 1980, speech on Central America, Bowdler pointedly remarked that "we will not use military force in situations where only domestic groups are in contention." This, however, leaves open the possibility of U.S. military intervention in response to perceived involvement by Cuba or any other outside power.

One possible avenue of escape from this dilemma would be to seek major involvement by others, such as Venezuela, Mexico, Western Europe, and even Japan, in efforts to stabilize and develop Central America. The U.S. government has already moved in this direction. Testifying before the Senate Foreign Relations Committee last December, Deputy Secretary of State Warren Christopher declared: "We need to try to find out how the Latin Americans think we should address the problems of Central America and their own problems. We don't approach it on a U.S.-dominated or know-it-all basis. I think that is a fundamental change in our attitude toward Central and South America."

Unfortunately, U.S. consultations with other countries on Central American problems are no more credible than direct U.S. relations with that region. Seeing little evidence of long-range planning or of a meaningful financial commitment and having no interest in overt association with frantic U.S. efforts at crisis management, most nations avoid direct involvement in the face of Central America's mounting turmoil.

Mexico has joined with its northern neighbor in support of the new Nicaraguan government but has criticized the U.S. position in El Salvador, where Mexican sympathies seem to lie with the left. Venezuela has been more directly involved with Central America, but U.S. efforts to coordinate policies with the administration of President Luis Herrera Campins are complicated by Herrera's close ties with the area's Christian Democratic parties. The United States is already suspected of favoring small parties of this type and cannot afford any closer links with a single minority political faction.

In Congress there is widespread consensus on the bankruptcy of traditional policies toward Central America. Senator Edward Zorinsky (D.-Nebraska), chairman of the Subcommittee on Western Hemisphere Affairs of the Senate Foreign Relations Committee declared that in dealing with the area, "the fundamental mistake we make . . . is to back governments or regimes which enjoy little or no popular support."

A similar stand was taken by Senator David Durenberger (R.-Minnesota), who told the Senate Foreign Relations Committee that U.S. policy in Central America had "too long been characterized by inattention, ignorance, a lack of concern, and a blind acceptance of the status quo." Durenberger added that "we have frequently mistaken the support of governments for the friendship of populations while many people in these regions have labored under the twin burdens of repression and poverty."

It is easier to recognize past mistakes than to correct them. A turnaround in U.S. policy requires positive commitment rather than continual obsession with fears of domestic political embarrassment and expanded Cuban influence. The current attitude produces a policy that is perceived as a holding action, designed to slow the rate of change but incapable of affecting the nature of that change. This type of policy generates little enthusiasm and attracts few capable followers.

A Failure to be Responsive

A recurrent fear expressed in discussions of contemporary Central America is a new variation of the old domino theory. Many observers argue that failure to limit Cuban influence in Nicaragua, to prevent radical victories in El Salvador and Guatemala, and to deal effectively with the economic problems of Honduras and Costa Rica, would deal an irreparable blow to U.S. prestige throughout the hemisphere. Capital flight would increase, moderate political factions would collapse, and hard-liners on the right would resort to all-out repression to maintain their power.

Although exaggerated, such scenarios contain an element of truth. Central America is a small community, and events in any one nation often affect developments in another. Thus, the governments of Honduras, El Salvador, and Costa Rica are already concerned about the impact on their populations of radio broadcasts originating from Nicaragua.

Such interdependence works both ways. The key challenge for U.S. policy is to offer a viable, pluralistic alternative to radical violence as a means of altering existing social and political structures and promoting economic development. Ideally, such an alternative would then influence neighboring states.

At the moment, the best location for this kind of effort is Honduras. The April elections restored Honduran faith in the domestic political process and probably halted the precipitate decline in the military's public image. The Carter administration has already indicated through diplomatic channels its hopes that the new Constituent Assembly will not limit election voting rights to assembly members but rather will open political participation to include the general population and the leftist parties excluded from April's voting. The United States has also encouraged the government, the military, and the assembly to work for honest and prompt direct elections for a new president and congress. Recent statements by the military and the major parties in Honduras suggest that this scenario may actually occur.

A hopeful U.S. government has attached requests for a Honduran package to current emergency aid proposals for Nicaragua and El Salvador. Unfortunately, the Honduran proposal is no exception to the rule that Central America aid packages are small, poorly focused, and contingent upon approval by a slow-moving Congress. In the case of the Honduran development package there is no assurance of any significant funding beyond the upcoming fiscal year. Moreover, the proposed assistance does not address such fundamental problems as access to American markets, terms of trade and technology transfer, or guaranteed energy supplies. Once again, U.S. rhetoric seems to outstrip its ability or willingness to commit American resources.

An example of the type of program which could restore American credibility and promote positive development throughout Central America is the current national literacy campaign in Nicaragua. Financed and inspired by Cuba, Nicaragua is endeavoring to eliminate nearly 50 per cent illiteracy in less than a year. Major U.S. assistance would make possible a similar effort in Honduras. A literacy project would mobilize national energies, especially among the youth; support future education programs in health, sanitation, and agriculture; and give both Honduras and the United States a badly needed sense of accomplishment. A literacy campaign in Honduras would also provide opportunities for cooperation with other regional powers in Central American development efforts.

Central America's problems are critical, and the time left for dealing with them in a peaceful, democratic manner is extremely short. Despite the polarization of internal politics and the lack of credibility in U.S. policy, positive elements do exist. Guatemala should soon be more than self-sufficient in petroleum. Honduras and Nicaragua have significant areas of undeveloped land, and Costa Rica, with its democratic traditions and high level of literacy, can draw on valuable human resources. Important support for reform could come from the Roman Catholic Church, whose energies in Central America are already devoted to promoting justice and human development.

Many Central Americans share the sentiments of a Costa Rican congressional leader who stated sadly that "the United States does not really care about Central America." What has been lacking is a definite commitment by the United States to support political and financial alternatives to the violent revolutions of the far left or the brutal repression by the entrenched right. Any verbal commitment by the president and Congress to the future development of Central America must be coupled with significant amounts of long-term economic assistance. In the conclusion of his April 8 address, Bowdler recognized the urgency of responding to the current situation in Central America: "Central America is in a critical period of its history. Our support for peaceful change can increase the likelihood that more democratic and equitable societies will evolve out of the present crisis. Conversely, our failure to be responsive can only help the enemies of freedom."

Unfortunately, if history offers any guide, it is that the United States will probably fail to be responsive. Domestic politics, budget concerns, and preoccupation with big-power politics may well keep the United States from making any serious commitment to Central America. If, after a century and a half of involvement in Central America, the United States can still offer no positive commitment to nonviolent and democratic development in that region, then its hopes for peace and justice in more remote areas are slim indeed.

AUTHORS

JOSE A. CABRANES, a federal judge with the U.S. District Court for Connecticut, was special counsel to the governor of Puerto Rico and administrator of the commonwealth's Washington office while the Popular Democratic Party was in power. He is the author of *Citizenship and the American Empire.*

RICHARD R. FAGEN, professor of political science at Stanford University, is the author of numerous works on comparative politics and Latin America and has been awarded research grants in Mexico, Cuba, and Nicaragua. He most recently co-edited *The Future of Central America: Policy Choices for the U.S. and Mexico* with Olga Pellicer.

RICHARD A. FALK, Albert G. Milbank Professor of International Law and Practice at Princeton University, sits on the editorial boards of *World Politics* and *The American Journal of International Law* and has written numerous books and articles on international law and national policy. His most recent book is *Human Rights and State Sovereignty.*

ROGER W. FONTAINE, senior staff member for the National Security Council, was director of Latin American Studies at the Center for Strategic and International Studies at Georgetown University. He is the author of many books, including *U.S.-Cuban Relations: A New, New Look.*

THOMAS M. FRANCK, professor of law and director of the Center for International Studies at New York University School of Law, was the director of the International Law Program of the Carnegie Endowment for International Peace. His most recent book is *Human Rights in Third World Perspective.*

NORMAN GALL, a contributing editor to *Forbes* magazine, was a senior associate at the Carnegie Endowment for International Peace from 1974 to 1977. During this time he engaged in a major study of Brazil, where he now resides. He has been writing about Latin American issues for various publications since 1961.

GEORGE W. GRAYSON, professor of government at the College of William and Mary, has served five terms in the Virginia House of Delegates. He is a contributing editor to the *Handbook of Latin American Studies* published by the Library of Congress and the author of *The Politics of Mexican Oil.*

MARIANO GRONDONA, professor of political science at the University of Buenos Aires and editor of the Latin American magazine *Vision,* is responsible for "Tiempo Nuevo," a political TV talk show in Argentina. In addition, he has written numerous articles and books on modern Argentina.

LAWRENCE E. HARRISON, visiting scholar at the Center for International Affairs, Harvard University, was with the Agency for International Development (AID) for more than 20 years, serving at AID missions in Costa Rica, the Dominican Republic, and Nicaragua. He is the author of *Underdevelopment Is a State of Mind.*

ROBERT LAPORTE, JR., acting director of the Institute of Public Administration at Pennsylvania State University, has served as a consultant to a number of government agencies. He has lectured and written extensively on Pakistan, India, and South America.

ABRAHAM F. LOWENTHAL, on leave at the Truman Institute of Hebrew University in Jerusalem, is secretary of the Latin American Program at the Woodrow Wilson International Center for Scholars in Washington, D.C. He was a lecturer at Princeton University, a consultant to the Commission on United States-Latin American Relations, and served as director of the April 1983 *Report of the Inter-American Dialogue.* The author of numerous books and articles, Lowenthal most recently co-edited *The Peruvian Experiment Reconsidered* with Cynthia McClintock.

RICHARD MILLETT, visiting professor at the Air War College, Maxwell AFB, Alabama, has written many articles about U.S. and Central American Policy. His most recent book is *The Restless Caribbean.*

JAMES PETRAS, visiting scholar at the Center for Mediterranean Studies in Athens, frequently lectures in South America and Europe and contributes to *Le Monde Diplomatique*. His most recent book is *Class, State, and Power in the Third World.*

DONALD E. SCHULZ, assistant professor of social sciences at the University of Tampa, Florida, has written many articles on Latin American and communist issues. He is currently working on two books, *Revolution and Counterrevolution in Central America and the Caribbean* and *The Cubans, the Soviet Union, and the United States.*

EDWARD WEISBAND, professor of political science and director of the Ph.D. Program in Public Policy Analysis at the State University of New York in Binghamton, is a frequent guest on television and radio programs concerning foreign affairs. He has written many books and articles dealing with national and international politics.

INDEX